Moral Philosophy and De-Colonialism

See also from Bloomsbury:

Black Existentialism and Decolonizing Knowledge by Lewis R. Gordon
The Bloomsbury Research Handbook of Indian Ethics edited by
Shyam Ranganathan

Moral Philosophy and De-Colonialism

The Irrationality of Oppression

Shyam Ranganathan

BLOOMSBURY ACADEMIC

LONDON • NEW YORK • OXFORD • NEW DELHI • SYDNEY

Bloomsbury Publishing Plc, 50 Bedford Square, London, WC1B 3DP, UK
Bloomsbury Publishing Inc, 1359 Broadway, 12th Floor, New York, NY 10018, USA
Bloomsbury Publishing Ireland, 29 Earlsfort Terrace, Dublin 2, D02 AY28, Ireland

BLOOMSBURY, BLOOMSBURY ACADEMIC and the Diana logo are trademarks
of Bloomsbury Publishing Plc

First published in Great Britain 2026

Copyright © Shyam Ranganathan, 2026

Shyam Ranganathan has asserted his right under the Copyright, Designs and
Patents Act, 1988, to be identified as Author of this work.

Cover design by Louise Dugdale
Cover image © Trifonov Evgeniy/iStock

A catalogue record for this book is available from the British Library.

A catalogue record for this book is available from the Library of Congress.

ISBN: HB: 9781350464131
PB: 9781350464148
ePDF: 9781350464155
eBook: 9781350464162

Typeset by Deanta Global Publishing Services, Chennai, India
Printed and bound in Great Britain

For product safety related questions contact productsafety@bloomsbury.com.

To find out more about our authors and books visit www.bloomsbury.com and
sign up for our newsletters.

For Bhūmi, Nīla, and Śrī

Contents

Preface

The one thing that has died for me over the past thirty years, since I began as an undergrad in philosophy, is the idea that the academy is a place for the exploration of ideas. I now know it to be entirely treacherous and also a place with little appetite for that exploration. This lack of curiosity makes it easily manipulated by fascists and dictators, who find in the academy intellectuals who are easily spooked by oppression as they have, for the most part, relied upon it for their careers. This may have been easier for me to see, as my research project, before it matured into an exercise of de-colonialism, was to answer the question of: why does the academy get the study of so much of the history of philosophy wrong, along weird racial lines? My naïve optimism in my colleagues persisted even until I clearly formulated the distinction I lead with now, between interpretation (explanation in terms of propositional attitudes) and explication (explanation by way of reasoned thinking). I recall when I put this distinction down on paper; I felt like it was a breakthrough, as it was a way to get past the muddled thinking and discourse on what good scholarship looks like. And to my great (naïve) surprise, the hostility my work encountered only increased. But it was a mixed response.

My Analytic philosophy colleagues (who are mostly White) found it interesting and often wanted to hear more about my research. I had the same reaction from the rare few in Religious Studies who took a historiographical approach: the implications of my work on the spread of religion were something readily accessible to them. My South Asian Studies colleagues, who are of South Asian descent, tended to be receptive and wanted to know more. My colleagues who are scholar-practitioners of any "religious" tradition tended to be open and curious, regardless of race. My Continental philosophy colleagues tended to be less receptive, more dismissive. My White colleagues who worked in the area of Indian Philosophy who were not scholar-practitioners were largely the most hostile. (This was before I took to openly criticizing their work; they got upset by just being presented with an explicatory approach to scholarship.) On a blog, one such colleague claimed that my work should not be shown to undergraduate students. Others would attempt to block me from participating in panels or talks, or publications, on the basis of confused criticisms that always displayed a lack of understanding of basic considerations of logic. This typically involved confusing whether an argument was reasonable with whether it agreed with their outlook. But this problem is far wider than academics who work on Indian Philosophy. This is not a minority problem but really represents a large swath of tenured academics who confuse being "critical" with whatever they believe. They would fail Logic 101. Among my students, I found a strange, opposite effect. My White students tended to be open and interested in my research. Some of my racialized students were too. But it was usually among my racialized students that I found the most hostility to my research. And if a student were to have a *complete meltdown* in one of my classes, it would never be when I taught Locke, or Descartes, or Plato. I could teach Analytic ethical theory or philosophy of language indefinitely and no one ever gets upset. The meltdown would always happen when I was teaching South Asian moral philosophy—and often they would be racialized students who got upset. I can now see the ways in which these complex responses are a result of what I call White Irrationality (Chapter 4). I think the hostility to my work has to do with how much effort a person is putting into interpreting on the basis of the West to create space for themselves. Those who think this exercise is central to their livelihood (many of my White Indian Philosophy colleagues) or future employment opportunities (many of my racialized students) will find what I have to share infuriating. And yet, teaching the *Yoga Sūtra* in almost any class had *the most* transformative impact on my students. And this transformative impact is never anything I mean to impart.

This book represents decades of thinking about various related topics, and I have many people to thank for keeping me company and being supportive while I engaged in what to others would appear like strange, unrelated research questions in the philosophy of language, ethics, and South Asian Studies. I had a sense of the importance of the overlap of these issues, but it was not always easy to articulate that connection.

It was in my then-York colleague Kristin Andrews' graduate seminar on Animal Minds, maybe twelve years ago, which I sat in on, that these connections started crystallizing. I recall one clarifying conversation when she noted that many of the conversations in the Animal Minds world revolved around whether nonhuman animals had certain propositional attitudes. My reaction was to wonder why anyone would believe that a pig had to have beliefs to think. I was also struck by the structural similarity (identity) of arguments against nonhumans being thinking creatures and South Asians having a tradition of moral philosophy. In every case, the skeptic draws a negative conclusion about the matter on the basis of whatever they believed was essential to the matter—as though it was up to them. In the case of animal minds, the expectations were so onerous even humans wouldn't be able to satisfy them. They involved the expectation that thinking required having representations of other people's thinking, which is not only strange but also an expectation that philosophers of language began moving away from.

By the end of Wittgenstein's work, he rejected his earlier, *Tractatus*, view that language (which he equated with thought, as all *Westerners* do) was underwritten by representational content. If it were, then my understanding others would be a matter of my having representations about others' mental representations. He switched in the *Philosophical Investigations* and suggested that representation is the output of social interaction, not the condition of understanding others. To claim the latter would be to endorse the reality of a private language, which he rejected. Indeed, he and others noted that if we try to interpret others by our expectations, then we are at a loss: every set of observations is consistent with any interpretation we choose—an observation that came to be known as his rule-following paradox. If we go with the latter Wittgenstein, then understanding others is not about having representations of their representations. It is about pragmatic social interaction. If we allow that representation is the output of interaction, not its condition, then we ought to see human and nonhuman thoughtful interaction as no more problematic than human-to-human interaction. Yet Wittgenstein wouldn't allow himself to consistently follow his own reasoning to its anti-speciesist conclusion because of his undefended commitment to treating thought as language. That's just the *Western* tradition for you. Its inconsistencies are always in favor of oppression.

I would like to thank (in no particular order) Colleen Coalter, Aimee Brown, Niamh Rogerson, ~~Baynard Woods~~, Randy Lundy, Maura Finkelstein, Yonatan Yisrael Brafman, Sherry Kao, Anusha Wijeyakumar, Jeffery Long, Christopher Chapple, Christopher Jain Miller, Rita D. Sherma, Paul A. Bramadat, Ethan Mills, Purushottama Bilimoria, Chakravarthi Ram-Prasad, Jyotirmaya Sharma, Raghuramaraju, Joydeep Bagchee, Vishwa Adluri, Michael Giudice, Robert Myers, Claudine Verheggen, Alice MacLachlan, Kristin Andrews, Brian Huss, Jacob Beck, Vanessa Lehan-Streisel, Alicia M. Turner, Raju Das, Ajay Rao, Chandan R. Narayan, Owen Ware, J. Moufawad-Paul, Neil Braganza, Nalini Elisa Ramlakhan, Mich Ciurria, Shelley Lynn Tremain, Philip Wilson, Alice Leal, and my Yoga Philosophy Institute students. Vanessa Lehan-Streisel, a logician, was most helpful in double-checking my brackets and notation in my main standard form arguments. I have an undiagnosed learning disability, I'm sure. I can get by with text-to-speech software, but I miss matters of unvoiced notation. She caught a misplaced bracket. Thanks, Vanessa!

A special thanks is owed to all of the students I have taught over the years, especially the first- and second-year students, and especially the non-philosophy majors.

My family is owed a special thanks for their love and support. I also want to thank anyone who takes the time to read this book.

Toronto, August 2025

p.s. For those who want to access the free course in support of this book, find it under "Free Courses" at: yogaphilosophy.com

Part One

Introduction

1

Colonialism and Philosophical Apartheid

"The Master's Tools Will Never Dismantle the Master's House."
Audre Lorde

1. Introduction: Moral Philosophy versus Colonialism

Philosophy in the simplest terms is the exercise of clear thinking. Everyone has an interest in learning philosophy and being philosophical. All learning requires philosophy because all learning requires clear thinking. Moral philosophy in the simplest terms is clear thinking about morality or ethics (called "dharma" in Sanskrit, and "*tao*" in Chinese), which are words to talk about the *right choice* and the *good outcome*. It is the exercise of thinking clearly about options as such and specific options in particular. This is not a specialized activity. People when they are free, or when they are ridding themselves of oppression, take the time to think about practical options. Indeed, the activist struggle to undo oppression rests on a clear-headed appreciation of choices and outcomes. And yet, not only is moral philosophy treated as an elective or diversion in education systems in a world of oppression, it is recast as the luxury of the few. But this is a sham: we all have an interest in thinking clearly about practical options, and depicting it as something that oppressed people cannot afford to engage in is an important part of maintaining and cementing oppression. An important way that this myth and sham is institutionalized is by the academic erasure of moral philosophy from colonized traditions.

This is a book in moral philosophy about moral philosophy. It is written for anyone interested in ethics on the one hand and oppression and colonialism on the other. If your conclusion is that genocide and oppression are bad or wrong, you are already thinking about oppression and colonization in terms of moral philosophy, for it is in this space that we can draw conclusions of the badness or wrongness of colonialism and oppression. This investigation will not assume any background in these topics, nor any background in the adjacent topics explored, but it will require getting up to speed on many adjacent areas of philosophy in the course of this exploration—and getting up to speed with what it is to engage in moral philosophy. It is not possible to do justice to our topic without thinking more broadly about many issues, such as epistemology (knowledge), the nature of thought, the philosophies of language, translation, religion, race, science, artificial intelligence (AI), and, more generally, the requirements and possibilities of reason. But what will hold this book together is the thesis that colonialism (and oppression), on the one hand, and moral philosophy, on the other, are mutually exclusive activities. Every chapter will explore this incompatibility while we explore the topic through moral philosophy. The observation that colonialism and moral philosophy are mutually exclusive derives from the premises that colonialism (and all oppression) is irrational, while moral philosophy is an exercise of reason. Colonialism consists in imposing a perspective on victims so no other can be contemplated under existential threat. Oppression is the consequent deprivation of the possibility of living under values of one's own choosing—a possibility deprived by the enforcement of a perspective that makes choosing one's values impossible. Under oppression, when we behave in accordance with some value, we do so because choice is deprived to us. Moral philosophy in contrast is a self-directed, open exploration of divergent and contradictory options concerning the right choice and the good outcome. When people engage in moral philosophy they are free to choose the values they wish to live under. If they lack this freedom to choose, then they are not engaging in moral philosophy. In contrasting the options of colonialism and moral philosophy we are allowing ourselves to transparently choose what is important to us, which is what moral philosophy facilitates. When people live under oppression, this freedom to choose the values one lives under is denied. In engaging in moral philosophy, not only are we doing what is rationally required: we are also undermining space for colonization and oppression. Anti-oppressive activism is hence a pure exercise of reason. Agents of oppression are irrational.

We will be butting up against a pervasive myth: colonized peoples are backwards and irrational and they have to be improved, saved, and propped up by the superior colonizing peoples. The opposite is true: there is nothing more Indigenous and anti-colonial than reason and moral philosophy: the Colonizer is an idiot. We will see that the Colonizer is an idiot because they would sooner oppress and destroy those they oppose than allow for the controversy about the right choice and good outcome to play out, publicly, as an exercise of moral philosophy. They are literally scared of research and innovation. Certainly, terms like "idiot" have been used historically as a way to oppress people who are differently abled. But one implication of our investigation is that oppression appropriates critical ideas as a means of rhetorically legitimizing itself. To allow such usage to stand and not reclaim critical terms for the sake of rational criticism is to normalize oppression.

I will treat "reason," "rationality," and "logic" as synonyms going forward. ("Rationalization" in contrast will retain its negative connotation of trying to justify something arbitrary after the fact.) According to the argument I will be pursuing, we are rationally required to engage in de-colonization and to get rid of oppression. Another important implication of the argument I am pursuing is that oppression is literally stupid as it is irrational. Hence, oppressive people are in proportion to their oppressiveness stupid people. And this irrationality and its concomitant stupidity are demonstrable. And we shall go through the motions of spelling out, explicitly, how and why oppression is irrational and thereby stupid. Some might object that this is a cruel way to talk. I counter with the observation that oppression and oppressive people are actually cruel: criticizing oppression and oppressive people for their stupidity is not cruel. No one is actually hurt by this criticism, though the ego of the oppressor will no doubt be bruised.

One reason not to bring up the stupidity of oppression is the worry that it has a negative rhetorical impact on those one wishes to persuade: calling oppressive people stupid will not help you change their minds. But if it is true that oppression is irrational and hence oppressive people are irrational, one is not going to be able to rationally persuade oppressive people of anything. We will have to offer an alternative to their irrationality in our own behavior that the irrational person can also choose, and part of that alternative involves clearly and unambiguously distinguishing rational behavior from the irrational variety. And there is no way to engage in this distinction without being clear how oppression is irrational and hence an epistemic failure. "Stupid" is the colloquial term for "epistemic failure." Oppression is stupid. If you do not like the connotation of "stupid" you can say "epistemic failure," but I'm not sure there is much of a pragmatic difference in these phrases. In contrast, de-colonialism is not stupid, because it is not irrational. And while the oppressor may be inclined to engage in unfounded mudslinging at the De-Colonizer (as though being called *woke* is an insult), they would be mistaken to impugn the intelligence of those who are anti-oppression.

In this act of clearly distinguishing the rational from the irrational, we will have to part ways with worrying about the feelings of oppressive people. Too often, weight is given to the negative reaction of oppressive people over the actual cruelty they exact, as though their mental lives are more important than the bodily impact they have on the oppressed. Or too often, those who are worried about standing up against oppression reduce the oppressor and themselves to a common denominator of people acting on their own values. Then we might wonder, who am I to criticize others for their values? We shall see, the problem with oppression has nothing to do with the values oppressive people endorse: it is rather their choice to be irrational. And this distinguishes them from de-colonial people. Oppressive people make an erroneous metaethical, pre-substantive, pre-evaluative, choice to be irrational. Then any value they endorse will become part of their oppression. They could hence champion a person who articulated a de-colonial philosophy—who went as far as to recommend that we turn the other cheek and who died as a result of colonial violence—and still manage to be genocidal Colonizers.

A third and important implication of the argument I am pursuing is that some traditions are anti-moral-philosophical, and oppressive. They manage to last not because they are enlightened but because they create intergenerational trauma that continually renews the oppressive order. Colonial traditions are hence oppressive and stupid. Their irrationality is not a matter that can be separated from their oppression, because irrationality is the infrastructure of oppression. Indigenous traditions in contrast resist this irrationality.

We can summarize the difference thus:

- Indigenous traditions and people think (reason) and choose.
- Colonial traditions and people confuse thinking with believing (or other emotional states) and choosing with desiring (distinctions we will make clear in this chapter).

Colonial people neither reason nor fully choose across the range of substantive options presented to them. They choose at the abstract, pre-evaluative metaethical, level to be irrational—and that results in behavior that is oppressive.

The *Western* tradition is the world's preeminent colonial tradition. It survives by denying people the freedom to engage in moral philosophy as the basis of social interaction. It is an endless source of intergenerational trauma. It normalizes epistemic failure as though a requirement for public participation. One way it hides its irrationality is by attempting to present logic—reasoning—as something that comes apart from social and other moral consequences. In the *West*, logic and ethics are then depicted as distinct philosophical pursuits that have no intrinsic connection. Yet oppression is just the social side of irrationality: it's not a separate problem but the objective manifestation of not reasoning. Reasoning in turn is the responsible deployment of agency in a world of information. To choose to reason is to make a moral-philosophical choice to be responsible as a processor of data.

The purest contemporary manifestation of the *Western* tradition is the far-right, which is an exemplar of stupidity. It depicts itself as the perennial victim, being cancelled for its beliefs, acting as though it is uniquely denied the substantive choices everyone else has, somehow aggrieved but conveniently removed from any responsibility for the way things are. It is an exemplar of oppression as the far-right lives to impose its option on everyone else. Like all versions of oppression, it has no tolerance for philosophy, which consists of an openness to a diversity of ideas, arguments, and theories, from a diversity of sources. If it entertains what it calls "philosophy," it rather revels in ideology: a one-sided view of things. The far-right is itself a manifestation of authoritarianism (the rejection of political plurality and the centralization of power) and often fascism (which organizes authoritarianism around a cult of personality that suppresses opposition through force). These are dramatic manifestations of colonialism when it happens at home. There are many less dramatic versions of colonialism, like Liberal societies—most all founded on a history of colonization and genocide, most all which have not reconciled with their foundations and with the Indigenous people they wronged. The reason all these versions of colonialism in our world fester is because people greenlight the *Western* tradition as blameless. This amounts to a global case of Stockholm syndrome, where people are disposed to be sympathetic to the origins of their lived oppression. We will have to part ways with this normalization of stupidity.

Philosophy is the foundation of de-colonization as it involves both reason but also a free exploration of options denied to us by oppression. Whereas in Indigenous traditions, such as the South Asian tradition, moral philosophers are praised as teachers, *ācārya*-s, who should be revered, in the *West*, from its ancient times, whether it be the case of Socrates or Jesus, they are treated as threats to the social order who have to be exterminated if they behave de-colonially. Oppressive traditions tolerate moral theorists only insofar as they can articulate the prevailing ethos of oppression. And often this requires giving de-colonial figures like Socrates or Jesus a second posthumous rehabilitation (whether in the later dialogues of Plato or the religion Christianity) that treats them as mouthpieces for the very colonial oppression that led to their executions.

There are some who periodically will make a case for the civilizing force of *Western* colonialism as a source of "*Western* values," which (supposedly) prioritizes human dignity, freedom, and the like. Folks who make that claim are confused in more than one way. Most importantly, they are ahistorical. Go back to the beginning with Plato and Aristotle (who dominate the *Western* tradition), and you will see the two founding theorists of the *Western* tradition working hard to justify oppression in the exact sense of denying the freedom of all to engage in moral philosophy. In their view, only the few have what it takes to do that kind of work: everyone else has to be subordinated and told what to do. Much later, in the modern period, Western moral philosophers start theorizing in terms of autonomy, egalitarianism, and freedom after their states begin ratcheting up their colonial expansion into Indigenous territory. What gets labeled as "Western values" is the appropriation of Indigenous wisdom, while denying it to Indigenous people. We can know that these values are appropriated because they are absent, historically, in the Western tradition and show up just as this tradition begins to deprive these values to the people they are colonizing. In any other case, if we were considering impoverished thugs who suddenly start showing off gems after having attacked and controlled the living space of other people, we would know that these gems were literally stolen: they become enjoyed by the thugs, and the people they were taken from are deprived of them. So, Western Enlightenment values of freedom and egalitarianism are just like these stolen gems. The freedoms that are celebrated are recast as only for Europeans (as though they came up with these ideas themselves), while those they colonized have to contend with less, as though deprivation is their natural lot. Some try to make the case that Western colonization has been a good thing (the "White man's burden" to use Rudyard Kipling's phrase), and evidence of this is the violence and depravity of states formally colonized by Western powers. This is ahistorical. Using these appropriated values to justify colonialism is diabolical. It is the scheme of the mafia shakedown, which deprives victims of freedom and security (via brutality and oppression) and then offers to sell it back at the cost of freedom and security.

Not seeing this mafia shakedown for what it is leads to treating these appropriated values as Western and then it seems, to the ahistorical, wrong to criticize the tradition as it's *prima facie* a tradition of human dignity and equality. And one result of this ahistorical normalization of the crimes of the West is the *ad nauseam* restriction of moral and political theorizing to Western theorists and resources, as though the very tradition that gives us a global history of colonization is also going to be the place to look for anti-oppressive moral and political theory. In this book, we will resist the usual academic version of the mafia shakedown in two ways. First, we will treat the West as an object of study. What is usually the case in a colonized world is to treat it as the platform of inquiry. In this way, the irrationality of oppression is normalized as the foundation of any further inquiry. The normalization of irrationality as the foundation of inquiry is made possible by being inattentive to what irrationality is, and how it functions as the mechanism of oppression. In engaging in a de-colonial exercise of moral philosophy, we will correct this confusion. Secondly, the argument I am rolling out is sourced historically from South Asian moral philosophy. Our topic is hence not only de-colonization but our method is also de-colonial as we will be relying upon Indigenous moral philosophy from a colonized tradition to bring attention to what the colonizing tradition cannot recognize in itself: its foundational irrationality. The reason this has not been done before is that colonialism creates myths about the nonexistence of Indigenous, non-Western moral philosophy. To think about colonialism globally and historically is to understand the origins of these myths. As oppression and colonialism are irrational, diagnosing the origins of bad (stupid, irrational) scholarship is diagnosing the origins of colonization and oppression.

1.1. Colonialism Should Not Be Normalized. Talking About It Should Be

I was born and raised in Canada, a country founded on colonialism. My parents are immigrants from South Asia, a region that was colonized for over a millennium. This is not so strange. Most people around the Earth today are born into countries that were colonized or have ancestors that were colonized, or ancestors that engaged in colonization—or are people actively involved in genocidal colonization today—or are on the receiving end of genocidal colonization today! And while all of us have colonialism in common, not all of our ancestors and not all of us are equally to blame for colonization. There were and are noncolonial people and traditions—Indigenous people—and then there are people engaged in colonialism. Famous moral philosophers that we know of today are not known to center colonialism in their discussions. Magically, the tradition that is uncontroversially acknowledged as having a robust history of moral philosophy—the Western tradition—is the global colonizing tradition. Inversely, traditions described as lacking any history of moral philosophy in the academy by area experts—such as the South Asian tradition—are traditions that have been colonized for over a millennium. The entirely racist idea that Black, Indigenous, People of Color (BIPOC) traditions have no history of clear thinking about right choices and good outcomes—moral philosophy—and that they are correlatively deeply religious and spiritual, concerned with the next world, is exactly the story a colonizing tradition would like to propagate to make colonization seem like a gift to the colonized: the colonized apparently need the Colonizer to tell them how to live because they gave no thought to the issue.

Colonialism and imperialism are often confused or not clearly distinguished, and there is a limited literature on the topic (for a review of the literature, see LaMonica Accessed 2021).

Imperialism is a power structure that allows subordinates. Subordinates in an empire are not without knowledge of alternatives. They know their place and often accept it as a calculated risk. As subordinates know the risks, they may switch feudal allegiance or even vie to be the emperor.

Colonialism, in contrast to imperialism, *denies the existential contemplation* of any perspective except the imposing perspective and thereby undermines agential freedom to self-govern on the basis of an exploration and investigation of novel options. Those who are imposed upon in colonization may either perish (for the colonizing perspective is inimical to the colonized), learn to adopt the imposed perspective as their own (if, that is, permitted), or resist.

Margaret Kohn and Kavita Reddy open their *Stanford Encyclopedia of Philosophy* article on colonialism with the description: "Colonialism is a practice of domination, which involves the subjugation of one people to another" (Kohn Fall 2017 Edition). This is too wide as it blurs the line between a variety of forms of political domination (such as imperialism) and colonialism. More recently, Barbara Arneil has argued that we can distinguish between colonialism and imperialism by looking at how the distinction evolved in the seventeenth century to the middle of the twentieth century European discussions of the topic. Accordingly, colonialism is "animated by an internalized, penetrative, and productive form of power," while imperialism is an external domination by a superior of inferiors (Arneil 2024, 148). I shall argue that when we are interested in a mistake or error, such as colonialism, then looking to the beliefs of those involved is necessary to understand the phenomenon. So looking to European explanations of colonization is insightful. However, we can also simply look at colonialism's impact. What this teaches us is that colonialism, in addition to denying the contemplation of alternatives, results in *agential injury*, which is the injury to the procedural health of the agent—to sort through options and to choose freely. Colonization is hence also a form of *epistemic injury*, depriving victims the capacity to contemplate alternatives. Imperialism need not result in agential injury but colonialism does as colonialism denies agents the possibility of understanding options by imposing only one option.

To flesh out this distinction let us consider the case of schools for children.

Schools especially for minors who are not in a position to consent or opt out are sites of the subjection of one group by another: teachers and administrators literally politically subjugate students. Given our account of imperialism, grade schools with compulsory attendance are imperial. Young students may imagine a life of skipping school but in many jurisdictions, they do not have the option not to go: in such cases attendance is mandatory, under coercion and under the power of parents, teachers, and administrators.

Ideally, education should help students develop their own agency (as opposed to injure it) and hence successful education provides students the tools to research and consider options, and to make responsible choices. Students who learn from this exercise have the skills to learn and problem solve in the face of new information. (Literacy, for instance, is a basic skill to this end.) Forcing students to undergo this training is arguably to their benefit. I say this appreciating full well that most examples of forced education fall considerably short of this ideal as they are often exercises of indoctrination—and that if students choose not to learn, or if they are suffering from other forms of systemic discrimination that already undermine their agency, the exercise of forced education is a disaster as it turns into an exercise of oppression. Yet, aspirationally, at least, education is supposed to help and foster a student's agency to explore epistemic options and make responsible choices. This can and often does occur within varying degrees of imperialism.

The case of Residential Schools, also called Boarding Schools, that Indigenous children the world over were condemned to (A. Smith Accessed 2021) brings to the fore the difference between contexts of political domination, which are not examples of colonialism and those that are. As colonization is the existential imposition of a perspective that prevents the contemplation of alternatives and results in agential injury, and Residential Schools are instruments of colonialism, they are schools in name only. Students are not there to learn: they were kidnapped by the state from their Indigenous families and put there to be on the receiving end of the imposed perspective of those in power. The project is designed to change Indigenous students into cultural examples of the Colonizer. In Canada, that meant that the kidnapped children were to be made English or French speaking—*only*—and turned into some kind of Christian (Indigenous Foundations Accessed Spring 2015). In this case, kidnapped children are punished for speaking their native language or celebrating their culture—and subject to various forms of mental and physical abuse, which are part of agential injury. The aspiration of the Residential School program is not to support the healthy agency of Indigenous children. They are denied the opportunity to explore different life options, including those that are Indigenous. The point is to make them suitable replicas of the Colonizer.

Part of what makes discussing colonialism difficult is that when it is successful in imposing a view we live in an ahistorical landscape defined by colonial narratives. One such colonial narrative is the idea that we exist in a post-colonial epoch. Another such myth has to do with a lack of clarity on the nature of the preeminent colonial force in the world today, which I call the *West*.

When people talk of "the west" they actually mean states and traditions that are European derived. Geographically, the west is large, encompassing BIPOC in Africa and the Americas, and yet, when we talk about the "west" to only mean the European regions, we are erasing people who have been colonized by European powers. So as to not further this, I identify the *West* (the "*W*" that leans on the "est") as a specific colonial tradition with roots in ancient Greek philosophy, which through several iterations (the next being the Romans, followed by others), colonized Europe, the Middle East, and then, in time, the whole globe. It is not the only colonizing tradition with ancient roots, but it is the most global in its impact. As we can distinguish between being *Western* (capital "*W*" that leans on the "est") and geographically western, we can and should treat being *Western* (capital "*W*" that leans on the "est") as a political choice. For those listening to this book, you can assume that by *Western* I am speaking about the capital "*W*" that leans on the "est"—unless I specify that the west (lower case "w") being discussed is geographical. To be *Western* is to treat the *West* as one's frame of explanation of everything. As the *West* is the tradition of White people, to treat it as the explanation of everything is to engage in White Supremacy. To reject this identity is to treat the *West* as something that can itself be studied and critically evaluated for its theories. To reject this identity is to reject treating the *West* as the explanation of everything. This is essential to appreciating how there were and are Indigenous, noncolonial peoples in Europe—such as the Sámi, Nenets, or Inuit of Greenland—that were wiped out or are oppressed by the *West*. Hence, referring to BIPOC will include these peoples from Europe on the receiving end of the *West's* colonization.

1.2. End-State Colonialism

In pursuing this line of inquiry, we will push back against *end-state colonialism* that has taken over the humanities. Colonialism is about the imposition of a perspective on others, and once *Western* colonialism has colonized the whole globe with nowhere else to spread to (in the twentieth century), it starts producing various doctrines of moral skepticism, moral irrealism, moral relativism and criticisms of the pretense of engaging in objective moral research (Mackie 1977; Ayer 1946; Harman 1977). It is as though the echo of the *Western* colonial project that involves imposing its perspective on the whole world comes back to say: all *anyone is doing* is imposing their perspective on others (Gadamer 1996). This is of course a convenient position to forward as it depicts *Western* intellectuals as morally blameless for their role in sustaining *Western* colonialism—blameless because all moral criticism is somehow faulty, baseless (meaningless, always false), relative to community standards (which Western intellectuals meet), or unobjective. If any of this is true, there are no objective grounds for criticizing the injustice of Western colonization.

End-state colonialism also characterizes popular attempts to be sympathetic to the plight of the oppressed. Here, those sympathetic with the plight of the oppressed wrongly conclude that the way to criticize the pretense of any authority is to claim that *everyone* is engaging in some type of relativistic project. On this view, Western colonialism's pretense to being universal and generic is faulty not because it is merely regional, ethnic, and relative to its culture, but because *everyone* is always simply speaking from their own perspective and making sense of the possibilities in terms of their own beliefs. This cuts oppression down to size, but at the expense of losing any moral high ground to criticize oppression. This speaks to a paradox involved in this universalization of subjectivity: it appears that anyone making a claim that we are always just speaking from our perspective and in terms of our own beliefs is either (a) making a claim that transcends the limits of their own subjectivity or (b) just speaking about themselves and their perspective. If the former, they are committed to something that contradicts their relativism. If the latter, it's unclear why anyone else should care. End-state colonialism takes us to this well-known problem of *alethic relativism*. As a strategy for criticizing oppression, it is self-defeating. What this teaches us is that any reliable criticism of oppression cannot give up on objectivity: it must rather provide an objective criticism of oppression otherwise it risks being self-defeating in this way.

Colonization and oppression are actually efforts to deny the exploration of the objectivity of reason.

2. The Irrationality of Interpretation, and the Rationality of Empathy

To understand the argument of this book, we need to review basic, introductory considerations and distinctions that are essential to introductory logic, critical thinking, and introduction to philosophy. In a traditional South Asian context, where Yoga, the philosophy and practice, was valued, these distinctions would have been widely explored, in culturally local ways. What is remarkable about these distinctions is that they are not entirely unknown in the Western tradition: they are just ignored in the advanced high-status philosophy of the West. It's as though the more advanced one is as a student of Western philosophy, the more one transcends logic and enters into a realm of normalized irrationality. The "advanced" work in Western philosophy tries to take up the unfinished business of its original commitment (what I call the "Linguistic Account of Thought"), which is irrational. And as irrationality produces no clarity, Western philosophy will perpetually fall back on its roots and recreate its history of oppression. And it does this by perpetually reapplying ideas from its tradition, sometimes even with the pretense of doing something new. Before we move to look at this basic feature of the West that generates its history of colonialism and oppression, I want to review these basic distinctions essential to logic.

A thought—also known as a proposition—p, has two important qualities. Frege, for instance, defines propositions as the things that can be true or false (Frege 1988, 36). This, as we shall see, is a colonial way to think about thought. A de-colonial approach recognizes that thoughts can also provide inferential support for other thoughts. The thought "it is raining outside," if true, inferentially supports the thought that "water is falling from the sky." A belief is a *propositional attitude*. To believe that p is to have the attitude of endorsing p as true. A belief in contrast to a thought has no inferential properties. It does not follow from my belief that it is raining outside that water is falling from the sky. There are other propositional attitudes, like *desire*, which is about wanting a certain proposition to be true. If I desire to be a tall man, I want the proposition, "I am a tall man," to be true. I will focus on belief when I am talking about propositional attitudes as it's the easiest to mistake for the thoughts that we can reason about. But what I will say about its limitations applies to all propositional attitudes insofar as they are a way to relate to a thought via an emotional state. To make use of a term from the literature, I will call any explanation by way of propositional attitudes an *interpretation*.

Logic is about the ordered processing of thoughts or information—quite independently of the question of whether the information is true or false. There are at least three varieties of logic: deduction, induction, and inference to the best explanation. Logic is the essence of research for when we engage in research we do not know what is true with respect to the question we have before us, but we can nevertheless process the data responsibly and see where it takes us.

In the case of deduction, we judge an argument according to the standard of logical *validity*. Accordingly, if the premises (reasons) are true, the conclusion must be true. This is not the same as claiming that the reasons are true. In some cases, it's unclear what the truth of the propositions would even consist in. The deductive inference rule, Modus Ponens, is:

(1) *If* P, *then* Q.
(2) P.

(*Therefore*) Q.

We know that this argument is always valid given its structure: there is no assignment of truth values to P and Q that ends up with true premises and a false conclusion. But what would it mean for the premises to be true? They are comprised of variables, which are neither true nor false. If an argument is valid, and the premises are true, we call it *sound*. If the argument is not valid, whether or not the premises and conclusion are true, it's *invalid*.

In the case of inductive arguments, we do not judge them by logical validity. Inductive arguments are ampliative: the evidence considered is a sample that (like what we find in polling), under ideal cases, supports a wider generalization. When the sample supports the generalization, we have a *strong* induction. If the sample is reliable or true, and it is a strong induction, we call the induction *cogent*. Even if the sample is reliable or true, if it does not support the generalization, it is called a *weak* induction.

Inference to the best explanation (IBE) concerns adjudicating between competing explanations of an observation. Like induction, the conclusion of such a process is not judged by the standard of logical validity. Unlike induction, or deduction, IBE has before it a conclusion, and the challenge is not to generate it, but rather to identify the *best* explanation for this observation among available alternatives. And because IBE concerns the best available explanation, it may not be the true explanation. Typically, disciplines furnish criteria for adjudicating between competing explanations in cases of IBE, and this ensures that the selection process is not conflated with the beliefs of the reasoners. Hence, it comes as a surprise to logically illiterate people that scientists can revise their account of what is the best explanation of a phenomenon if new information or explanations come to light. And indeed, the revised, better explanations may also not be true. They are just the best given the known alternatives judged by disciplinary considerations.

This cannot be overemphasized in a climate of colonization: good reasoning is something definable *independently* of the truth of the reasons or conclusion. And bad reasoning can be created out of completely true claims and a true conclusion. If the truth of the considerations were determinative of the reasonableness of the various kinds of arguments, then our *beliefs* and other propositional attitudes about what thoughts are true (and even attitudes to only true propositions, what are called "factive states") would be distantly relevant to adjudicating whether something counts as good reasoning. But that is not the case.

(1) The Planet Mars is an Eggplant.
(2) Eggplants are Reptiles.

(*Therefore*) The Planet Mars is a Reptile.

Anyone who understands English and can hence understand these sentences will know they are false. They are hence not believable for speakers of English. And yet, the argument is logically valid: if the premises are true, the conclusion has to be true. Now consider the following:

(1) Biden was the President of the United States in 2023.
(2) The Sun rises in the East.

(*Therefore*) Shyam Ranganathan is the author of this book.

Everything I say in this argument is true. And I would further suggest that most people would believe these claims as they are obviously true. Yet, this second argument is logical nonsense: it is not logically valid.

Given these simple considerations, a very common way of framing the project of reason is revealed to be mistaken. Hume, not the first to say it and not the last either, claims that "Reason is the discovery of truth or falsehood" (*Treatise* III.1.1.). If that is what reason is, we should be satisfied by the observation that the first argument is comprised of falsehood, and the second of the truth. Similarly, if reason is merely the search for the truth—an idea that seems to go back to Plato's description of the activity of reason, *logos*—we ought to be satisfied in discovering the second argument. This is not what reason shows us. If reason is the same as, or a species of, logical thinking, then what reason actually reveals is that the first argument is reasonable, and the second is not. And what reason shows us is that the second argument would be unreasonable whether or not the premises and conclusion are true. Whatever the truth or falsity of the premises and conclusion of the second argument, it would not be reasonable as the premises do not support the conclusion.

These considerations, namely comparing the reasonableness of the first argument with false premises and a false conclusion, and the unreasonableness of the second argument with believed premises and a believed conclusion shows that interpretation (explanation in terms of propositional attitudes like belief) is a *formal logical fallacy*.

It is common to identify some fallacies as informal, and others as formal. A formal fallacy is some way of thinking that violates logical validity and thereby leads us to draw conclusions that do not follow from the premises. Interpretation is a formal logical fallacy because if one attempted to understand an argument in terms of one's own propositional attitudes like belief, or if one restricted one's arguments to them, it would be a complete accident if one were to correctly identify an argument as being valid, for the validity of an argument has nothing to do with its conformity to your propositional attitudes—even if you only had attitudes to the true propositions. Moreover, interpretation would lead one to incorrectly identify logically invalid arguments (like the second one here) as good arguments because they are comprised of propositions one believes (or you endorse because they are true) and to reject valid arguments because they are comprised of propositions one does not believe (or you reject because they are false).

In the case of known formal logical fallacies (such as *Denying the Antecedent—If* P *then* Q, *not* P, *Therefore not* Q), we know that these inference forms depart from logical validity: there are assignments of truth values to P and Q that lead to true premises and a false conclusion in these cases. The only thing going for formal logical fallacies is that someone believes them. Interpretation, then, accounts for the general formal error of mistaking an argument with premises one believes for a good argument, but also for the specific error of specific forms of formal fallacies.

Informal fallacies do not violate validity, but yet they represent defects in reasoning. And here too interpretation rears its head again as the culprit. For instance, *to beg the question* is to repeat the same thought *p* as the reason and the conclusion of an argument. Question begging arguments are *always* logically valid because if the premise *p* is true, the repeated conclusion *p* has to be true. And yet, to beg the question fails at an important task of reasoning. It doesn't really provide a reason for a conclusion as both are the same claim. So, it is an informal fallacy. In actual cases of question begging arguments, we find that people are inclined to repeat reason for conclusion because they believe the repeated claim. And as belief is a nonrational state, repeating the belief as both reason and conclusion is a way to mimic reasoning while failing at it.

An *ad hominem* argument is also an informal fallacy. It involves dismissing what someone says on the basis of irrelevant considerations that one *believes* are relevant—typically, this involves an objection to the person or what they are doing or have done. In this case, the person guilty of an *ad hominem* argument believes something is relevant to dismissing what someone has to say, when beliefs in general are not relevant to assessing reasons. And I think this generalizes.

In cases where someone is engaged in a mistake in reasoning, formal or informal, they are misled by their propositional attitudes. These attitudes take center stage and obstruct the activity of thinking. We are so transfixed by our emotional attachment to thoughts when we interpret that we fail at actually engaging with reasons or in providing reasons.

Interpretation is a psychological problem too.

Interpretation is the mechanism of Narcissism. The American Psychiatric Association's *DSM-5*, in its chapter "Personality Disorders," defines Narcissism as a "pattern of grandiosity, need for admiration, and lack of empathy." The interpreter treats their propositional attitudes as the only available explanation for anything. This is not true but that is how they proceed. In reality, they have elevated their own perspective to a universal standard—itself an act of grandiosity—and insofar as they can only understand in terms of their propositional attitudes, they will lack empathy for anyone who is not valued by their outlook. They will need to have their opinions continually affirmed and never criticized because of their need for admiration, and this need is generated by this conflation of themselves as agents with the propositions they are connected to via their attitudes. In Yoga, this conflation is called egotism, or *asmitā*. The result of this conflation is an intellectual fragility—and tone sensitivity. Interpreters will hear malice in any criticism because they cannot tolerate dissent as they have emotionally identified with the propositions being controverted. And hence they project this intolerance on to those who would criticize them as they feel they are not being tolerated because their propositional attitudes are not affirmed.

The interpreter will also be *ahistorical*. Any psychological state, consisting of a set of propositional attitudes, has a prehistory that gives rise to those states. South Asian moral philosophers knew this, and hence largely discredited psychological states as epistemically probative and often emphasized some activity or practice (a yoga, or discipline) to sort out states of knowledge from states of ignorance that were constrained by the past. The interpreter treats the end result of a historical process—their propositional attitudes—as their explanation of all topics, and hence has no awareness of its conditions.

Interpreters will lack empathy as they have no *functional* capacity to empathize. Insofar as they explain in terms of their propositional attitudes, they are unable to understand anyone else's point of view. Colonial oppression such as what was done to Indigenous children in Residential Schools is distinguished as an interaction where those in power lack all empathy. This is a result of interpretation, where the school administrators *impose* their perspective (their propositional attitudes) on the Indigenous children they kidnapped. This amounts to the only option that these colonized children have to conform to, resist or perish under.

Explanation in terms of propositional attitudes is largely prejudicial: it is to engage in *judgment in advance of the facts* (Gadamer 1996, 270). It is bias as a method of explanation.

Interpretation is an essential element in *conspiracy theorizing*. The conspiracy theorist uses a particular set of beliefs, desires, and other propositional attitudes to explain anything that deviates from their expectations as a purposeful plot to undermine them. One could not manufacture such a theory without propositional attitudes.

In contrast, the person who reasons, who can evaluate perspectives on the basis of reasons that provide inferential support for conclusions they may not agree with, can empathize with a diversity of perspectives because they can understand others' perspective, *without having to agree.* This shows that empathy is actually a rational capacity, not an emotional capacity. Irrational people—interpreters—cannot be empathetic. That is part of why they are oppressive. Their emotional states get in the way of understanding other points of view.

As a method of research, in addition to being irrational, interpretation is the method of *confirmation bias.* Confirmation bias is the tendency to search out explanations that conform to one's views. Interpretation, explanation in terms of one's propositional attitudes, is hence straightforwardly an exercise of confirmation bias: it uses one's own view as the criterion of what counts as an explanation.

The previous faults of interpretation serve to show how interpreters are inclined to *blame the messenger.* Reasonable people would be able to consider counterevidence and criticism as data that one could reason about. But in the case of the interpreter, they functionally do not reason about what they do not agree with, experience alarm at having to consider what they do not believe (owing to their narcissism), and then perceive whoever brings such matters to their attention as at fault for their psychological pain.

These observations show how and why interpreters who generate oppression are usually confessing when they offer criticism. Because they confuse thinking with *their* propositional attitudes, they are really, always, just talking about themselves. So, when they deliver a criticism, it's about them too. Hence, when they blame the messenger, here too, we can learn something about them being at fault from what they say. This renders interpreters *dud* interlocutors. It sounds like they are engaging in a conversation with others. But they are just talking about themselves. And given their narcissism and fragility, they will seek out the company of others who share their propositional attitudes. In this case, everyone is still talking about themselves, but everyone's narcissism is indulged. For interpreters, this is a good time.

It will do the interpreter no service to point out that there are different forms of reasoning, such as induction and IBE—in addition to deduction—with the hope that somehow interpretation finds a home there. They are out of luck as all reasoning is about *inferential support,* and not truth. If reason was about truth, we would have to prefer candidate reasons that were true even if they lack logical connections. Correlatively, we would have to reject reasoning that displayed logical connection because they were (considered) false. But these are reasonable.

- The rational failure of interpretation and its oppressive effects are the same problem, namely employing one's attitudes toward propositions as explanations.

This is a driving point of the argument in this book. One doesn't get to be oppressive but accidentally rational. One cannot be rational while being oppressive insofar as oppression is generated by deference to propositional attitudes, like belief or desire, and that deference is irrational as it interferes with reasoning. The idea that one can be evil and also cold, calculating, and rational in one's execution of oppression is a myth. To the extent that one is oppressive, to that extent one is irrational.

Yet, interpretation is likely the default approach of Western academic authors, and it is acclaimed by leading twentieth-century Analytic and Continental philosophers as our only choice. In this tradition, *no one* seems to notice that interpretation is textbook irrational *and* that it is a moral failure of oppression. That says a lot about the Western tradition. And perhaps, given the history of colonization and racialization, it would have to take a Brown, Indigenous, philosopher to point out how ridiculous interpretation is, for leading Western philosophers do the opposite: they acclaim it.

W.V.O. Quine (1960, 59), early Donald Davidson (2001, 101; 1986, 316), Martin Heidegger (2010), Hans-Georg Gadamer (1990, 1996)—all stress the importance of interpretation—often employing the term itself (Quine, Davidson) or an analog such as "hermeneutics" (Gadamer) or "Auslegung" (Heidegger) that are readily paraphrased or translated as "interpretation." It continues in the widely influential idea that reflection is about arriving at an equilibrium of considered judgments (Rawls 1971, 18). Sometimes, in Western critical thinking textbooks, it is described as a *coherence strategy*: the expectation that new information can only be accepted if it coheres with considered beliefs. The Western attachment to interpretation can be found in its ordinary assumptions that knowledge itself is some type of special propositional attitude, like a justified true belief, or a factive state (an attitude to a true proposition). I do not know of any prominent Western theory of knowledge that does not frame knowledge in terms of propositional attitudes. If knowledge is always constituted by propositional attitudes, then all knowledgeable explanations are interpretations, which are irrational.

The case of W.V.O. Quine is very telling. Quine was a logician and knew well enough that propositional attitudes like beliefs, also called *intentional contexts* in the literature, are rational duds. He demonstrated as much in his classic "Quantifiers and Propositional Attitudes" (Quine 1956; see also Kaplan 1968; Kripke 1988). In intentional contexts, the content insofar as there is any is mediated via the psychology of the person creating the psychological context. Hence, beliefs are creatures of psychology and not creatures of logic. And yet, when it comes time for him to account for how we can make sense of foreigners, he claims we have to interpret them in terms of what we take to be true, which is to use our beliefs to understand others (Quine 1960, 59 fn2). This sets off a long tradition of people endorsing Quine's strategy of interpreting others as the *principle of charity*, which has been proposed as essential to the study of philosophy and BIPOC philosophy (for example, Adamson 2017). Some rework this into the idea that to understand someone else's argument is to understand it in its strongest form. That's no less narcissistic, for it requires that we, in understanding others, treat them as saying what we would prefer. The idea that interpreting others in accordance with one's own beliefs is a kind of beneficence is as warped as thinking that beating someone is a sign of love. It's entirely remarkable that the cruel absurdity of this measure isn't noted by its proponents. But that's a result of confusing reasoning with believing, which is inexcusable but ordinary in the Western tradition.

Given what we have already reviewed, we have the information we need to appreciate why interpretation as a method will not allow self-correction. First, because it is an exercise of irrationality, interpreters are disposed not to engage in self-correcting behavior. Self-correction requires the capacity to draw inference from assumptions, consider their implications, and then revise in light of those projections. This is a kind of Modus Tollens (*If* P *then* Q, *not* Q—because that would be bad—*Therefore, reject* P) that reasonable people can engage in. Interpretation is not reasonable. Secondly, given the narcissism of interpretation, interpreters will be psychologically *fragile* and unable to contemplate their own corruption. Their emotional life is dominated by a need to have their outlook affirmed, and hence, they will not be inclined to take a critical look at employing interpretation as an explanation.

As we shall explore in subsequent chapters, the interpretive thrust of any colonizing human tradition is bound up with what I call the *Linguistic Account of Thought* (LAT). This was universally rejected in ancient India, controversial in ancient China, but acclaimed with no critical alternative or even discussion in the Western tradition. In the West, it goes back to the ancient Greek notion of *logos*—one word for reason (the processing of thoughts) and speech (for an account of the centrality of this notion to this tradition, see Derrida 1998). With this model, thinking and speaking are collapsed: what we mean when we speak are our thoughts. This confuses thoughts with propositional attitudes like beliefs in at least three ways. First, what we typically say in speech is what we believe. This is celebrated in Alfred Tarski's famous disquotational schema: to assert p is equivalent to the metalinguistic claim that "p is true," which is the full articulation of a belief. As what we typically say is what we believe, this model of thought confuses thought and belief as a matter of practice. Secondly, what our words mean is not an unexplained accident. Words encode cultural beliefs of formative generations—beliefs about syntax (word order) and pragmatics (effective usage) but also semantics (meaning). Languages hence come to embody a culture's outlook, and so confusing thought with language confuses thought with the dominant beliefs of a culture. Third, in confusing thought with linguistic meaning, LAT confuses thought with linguistic representation. And then, knowledge is portrayed as a matter of having the right attitude to linguistic representations that it treats as thought. This is an interpretive endeavor.

And, given this foundation in language as a model for understanding that results in normalizing interpretation, LAT produces many characteristic features of the resulting colonialism. As language is a human matter, this model generates a politics of anthropocentrism: prioritizing the human. As language underwrites and is supported by communal expectations, it leads to a politics of communitarianism: defining the agent in terms of communal expectations. The resulting anthropocentrism and communitarianism problematizes agents of all species outside of one's community, and depicts them as things to be brought within one's social fold in order to relate to them ethically: colonialism. Imposing one's outlook on others, which is colonization, is a way to cope with the parochial limitations of LAT.

In appreciating the role of LAT in oppressive traditions, we are not committed to the claim that they do not have different words for beliefs (*doxa*) and reasons (*logos*). The problem is not that they are incapable of drawing such a distinction. Rather, their model of what counts as a reason blurs the line between thoughts and propositional attitudes. So while in theory, oppressive traditions like the *West* can distinguish between thinking and believing, in practice they do not. In theory they ought to think. But when it is time to explain *any* reason (thoughts in arguments), they talk about their beliefs. As we shall see, when *Westerners* talk about other traditions (especially critically), they just talk about themselves and their beliefs. When they are boasting, they are taking credit for something they stole.

Insofar as colonialism is the imposition of a perspective on victims, interpretation, which is the essence of irrationality, is the method of colonization for interpreters impose their perspective—their propositional attitudes—on others as they try to make sense of the world according to their own standards. Before closing this preliminary account of irrationality, consider this example of how irrationality and oppression go hand in hand.

I was on a scholarly listserv, Indology (archives are online), when a relatively junior, South Asian (philosopher), scholar was making a general point about gender discrimination in our interdisciplinary field of Indology and cited an article that brought up accusations of sexual impropriety against a senior White (male) Indologist as an example (April 16, 2019). The conversation followed the resignation of a female scholar from the listserv committee who accused the committee of sexism. The listserv's governing committee member on duty (a senior non-philosopher, White male) speaking for the committee claimed that this left him "no choice" but to remove the South Asian scholar from the list, who dared bring up issues of moral relevance to our field (April 17, 2019). Specifically, the South Asian colleague was found to have made *ad hominem* arguments for referencing an article that brought up accusations of sexual impropriety against a senior (White) scholar in a wider discussion about sexism in our field. He was banned. Very few colleagues stuck up for him. Those who did not, and the listserv on the whole, owe him an apology. I quit the list—this was not the first time I had observed senior or other White colleagues piling on South Asian colleagues or scholar-practitioners of South Asian traditions in this area. What I said prior to quitting (April 19, 2019), and will repeat again, is that an *ad hominem* argument is not a criticism that someone did something abhorrent. It is also not a moral criticism of someone's character, which is a legitimate topic of criticism in moral philosophy. Nor is it the criticism that a certain posture is an epistemic failure—which is to say, colloquially, stupid. It is a specific rhetorical move aimed at dismissing what someone says on the basis of something not directly relevant, such as their character, their standing, their epistemic failure, or even an actual moral failing. Criticizing the Western tradition for being morally depraved or stupid is not an *ad hominem* argument. Saying that we should ignore what the Western tradition has to say because it is colonial or stupid is an *ad hominem* argument. In fact, if we are serious about offering a moral or epistemic criticism of the West we should take special care to scrutinize its claims and assumptions, which is to head in the opposite direction of an *ad hominem* argument. The more we are involved in the activity of criticizing commitments and assumptions of a figure or tradition, the less we are anywhere near delivering an *ad hominem* argument.

What this academic listserv *did* to the junior scholar was *actually an example* of an *ad hominem* argument: they decided the junior South Asian scholar had nothing to contribute to the conversation because of some perceived moral transgression—of raising a moral criticism of another participant. This was not only an oppressive move. It also exemplifies a feature of oppression: oppressors' criticisms of others are typically confessions brought on by their own fragility. And this fragility is an aversion to considering options that one does not endorse, which is always raised by moral-philosophical issues. If Indology was a place that was friendly to moral philosophy and philosophers, the South Asian colleague would not be silenced for bringing up concerns about sexism in this interdiscipline. It is instead an exercise of oppression.

What is notable about this example, which we can generalize, is the ways in which not being reasonable, in this case, the listserv leadership engaging in an *ad hominem argument*, constitutes an act of oppression, and moreover, it is couched in a rhetorical appeal to the very rational failure (the *ad hominem argument*) that it is guilty of. And the oppressive failure and its rhetorical appeal come to the same thing: imposing one's propositional attitudes. Irrational people hence often exemplify exactly what they complain about. In being irrational they project what they do not like about themselves and their history onto others. We shall also see, as we progress, that interpreters correlatively claim credit for what is not their innovation. Their accusations are confessions. When they take credit for something, it's stolen. They get everything backwards.

3. Objectivity of Reason: Explication

In the previous section I reviewed the connection between colonization (the imposition of a perspective that people must conform to, resist, or perish under) and irrationality. Both arise from engaging in interpretation, which is to use one's propositional attitudes—one's perspective, one's outlook—as one's explanation. Colonizers interpret when they explain the colonized by the Colonizers' perspective. The Colonizer's perspective is the only option they tolerate, and the colonized are then forced to conform to the perspective, resist the outlook or perish under the outlook. Irrational people fail at reasoning when they interpret, for interpretation is the essence of irrationality. Whereas interpretation constitutes the rejection and departure from logic (*not* L), call *explication* the employment of logic (L) as a method of explanation. As an exercise of logic, it makes empathy possible as it allows us to transcend our perspective and understand others' reasons. "Explication" is a term of art, and has been used by others (Carnap 1950, 3). The methodology I call *explication* is called thus because it is about rendering reasons and conclusions *explicit*. And what holds the exercise together is the responsible ordering of information so that some information functions as reasons, and others as the conclusion. We succeed at this task when we establish a relationship of inferential support, which is not the same as whether we believe the information or whether the information is true. Insofar as any discipline is a reasoned exploration of contrary perspectives, which gets us away from assessing everything in terms of our outlook, explication is essential for moral philosophy.

In Subsection 3.1, Main Argument, I am going to spell out in detail the arguments of this book. People with interpretive tendencies will find this tiresome. But what is worth noting about an argument is that it is not a perspective. A perspective is a world view constituted by propositional attitudes, such as beliefs and desires. A successful deductive argument is an arrangement of propositions for a conclusion that exemplifies the logical virtue of validity. To state the arguments of this book explicitly and in logically valid form is to engage in de-colonization, insofar as de-colonization requires moving away from the irrationality of interpretation that is the mechanism of colonization and oppression. I will also take the time to explain why we should acknowledge the valid arguments of this book as being comprised of true premises and true conclusions, which makes them sound. And the explanation revolves around the requirements of reasoning, not propositional attitudes.

In Subsection 3.2, The Objectivity of Moral Philosophy, the Moral Requirement to Reason, I will move to a discussion of the objectivity of reasoning, how pursuing this objectivity allowed me to de-colonize the study of moral philosophy and how the exercise of explication allows us to deflate the dangers of a perspective, by rendering explicit reasons that it is committed to. In both cases, I will be rendering explicit guiding ideas from Yoga, which is a unique ethical option to South Asia, which is depicted by the Western academy as lacking all moral philosophy. In case it's not obvious by what I have said, to take time to meticulously articulate these arguments about moral philosophy from the South Asian tradition is an act of Indigenous resistance to the oppressive irrationality of colonization. If you are impatient with this, you have acclimatized to oppression.

3.1. Main Argument

The background argument that this book relies on starts out the *Yoga Sūtra* (YS I.2–4), the foundational text of the philosophy, Yoga. There it appears as a disjunctive syllogism (an argument of the form, P *or* Q, *not* Q, *Therefore* P), albeit in compressed *sūtra* form.

Call this basic argument from the *Yoga Sūtra*, *Argument 1*.

(1) *Either* we should choose explication (L), *or* we should choose interpretation (*not* L).
(2) We should *not* choose interpretation (as it renders understanding reasoning impossible) (*not* (*not* L)).

(*Therefore*) We ought to choose explication (L).

The same options function in a contrary syllogism about an *error theory* (an account of how things go wrong). Call it *Argument 2*.

(1) *Either* we should choose explication as an *error theory* (L as an error theory), *or* we should choose interpretation as an *error theory* (*not* L as an error theory).
(2) We should *not* choose explication as an error theory (for it explains how to reason correctly) (*not* (L as an error theory)).

(*Therefore*) We should choose interpretation as our error theory (*not* L as an error theory).

In our investigation here, these two disjunctive syllogisms will play an important role in accounting for the options. They inform the following main argument of this book. Each chapter will be an exploration of this argument. Call this main argument, *Argument 3*.

(1) *If* one is engaged in moral philosophy (M), *then* one is explicating a diversity of perspectives on THE RIGHT OR THE GOOD (L).
(2) *If* one is engaged in colonialism (C), *then* one is interpreting—imposing a perspective as explanation—which violates basic considerations of logic (*not* L).

(*Therefore*) Colonialism and moral philosophy are incompatible, inimical, endeavors *not* (C *and* M)—put another way, one has to reject either colonialism or moral philosophy (*not* C or *not* M).

One can prove this argument indirectly by assuming both colonialism and moral philosophy. That leads to a contradiction of engaging in not logic (interpretation) and engaging in logic (explication). Hence, we have to conclude that we cannot do both, colonialism and moral philosophy. Another way to say this (by De Morgan's Law) is that either we have to reject colonialism or we have to reject moral philosophy. We can know that moral philosophy is a de-colonial exercise, given this conclusion, because the conclusion presents colonialism and moral philosophy as *incompatible*. If we engage in moral philosophy we are erasing room for colonization.

Arguments 1 through 3 are logically valid. A logically *valid* argument is a deductive argument where *if* the premises are true, the conclusion has to be true. Valid arguments exemplify the logical virtue of *inferential support*: the premises in these cases support the conclusion. Moreover, a valid argument with true premises (and hence a true conclusion) is called a *sound* argument. Are they sound? How would we figure out if the premises are true and if the conclusion is true?

There are many theories of truth from so-called deflationary accounts, which reduce the truth to the mere saying of a claim, to robust metaphysical theories where truth has to do with the way things are (Glanzberg 2023). A challenge for explicators is to account for truth in a way that whatever is true is not reducible to what one believes. And the easiest way to produce such an account of truth is to identify the true as what doesn't involve interpretation— the rejection of logic. The truth would then be what we cannot deny without abandoning the explicatory project and falling into some interpretation. What logically follows from such true claims would also be true for the same consideration. If we arrive at something false on explicatory grounds, we would have to reject it, and whatever premise got us there as false too. The criterion of validity, that *an argument is valid (if the premises are true, the conclusion has to be true)*, would be true as it avoids interpretation and to deny it would be to abandon the explicatory project. Empirical claims about the world would be true insofar as they can be the conclusion of a logic-driven exercise of research that begins with the available evidence, *and* we couldn't reject these conclusions without also abandoning the entire explicatory project that allowed us to test and explore these conclusions. Empirical science is a lot of work: it takes a lot of work to get to this point. In many empirical cases, we may have explicatory grounds to doubt that we have all the relevant evidence (for we may not have access to that) and so our conclusions in these cases are to this extent not essential to the explicatory project, and to this extent we lack grounds for treating them as true.

The false, in contrast, represents an interpretation, a departure from reasoning, and speaks more to the attitudes and expectations of anyone who would endorse it, than the way things are or could be.

We can reason about both, the true and the false. Consider the argument:

(1) P and *not* P,

(*Therefore*) P.

The argument is valid (if the premise is true, the conclusion has to be true); however, the first premise cannot be true as it is a contradiction, and a contradiction cannot be true because it violates the logical requirement that a conjunction is composed of two conjuncts that are both true—if P is true, *not* P can't be true, and vice versa. It represents an interpretive confusion that both could be the case at the same time.

We know that arguments 1 through 3 are valid: if their premises are true, the conclusions have to be true. A sound argument is a valid argument with true premises, which leads to a true conclusion. To determine that they are sound we need to apply our explicatory account of truth to adjudicate each claim. If the claims are all true, then these valid arguments are also sound.

Argument 1. The conclusion, that *we ought to choose explication*, we have to count as true if truth is about the absence of interpretive confusion. But that means that the second premise, that *we ought to reject interpretation*, is also true. The first premise explicates the methodological options, so it too is true as it renders explicit explication as an option we can choose. To deny this is to engage in interpretation.

Argument 2. This argument inverts the first argument consistently. If it is true that *we should choose explication* so as to facilitate a transparent appreciation of truth, characterized by a lack of interpretation, then if we want to understand error, we need to endorse the opposite methodology: interpretation. That shows that the conclusion is true. This also provides us reason to affirm the second premise as true—*We should not choose explication as an error theory.* The first premise presents the explicated options with respect to error theories. We cannot deny it without falling into an interpretation. So it too is true.

Argument 3 (Main Argument). We can prove the conclusion of Argument 3, that moral philosophy and colonialism are incompatible, by assuming its negation. So if we were to really make a go of it, rejecting this conclusion means that we would have to engage in moral philosophy while experiencing, or undergoing, colonization. What would that look like? How could we think about options of THE RIGHT OR THE GOOD while we are being kidnapped, brutalized, forced into labor, or facing genocide? Under the best of times, it's hard to do moral philosophy as one has to contend with one's own prejudices and assumptions that get in the way of thinking clearly about the right choice and the good outcome. Imagine trying to do this while having to contend with the existential imposition of colonization. This is so hard that colonized people often give in and accept colonization. Similarly, on the opposite end, if we were imposing our perspective and way on others via colonization, how would we ourselves have the mental space to think about moral-philosophical options? That imposition of a perspective is an interpretive project, and that methodology is not consistent with the explicatory skills we need to explore moral-philosophical options. So when we take a peek at this *negation* of the conclusion of Argument 3, we see that it involves a contradiction as it entails two incompatible options of doing moral philosophy while engaging in colonization. So we have to affirm the unnegated conclusion as true, otherwise we are in the realm of irrationality.

We could similarly deny Premise 2, that colonialism involves interpretation. If it doesn't, then colonialism would be consistent with engaging with explication. But that would require an exploration of options independently of our perspective, and to think that way, we would no longer tolerate a mono-outlook that constitutes colonization. And then, we would no longer engage in colonization, though we may continue to *believe* we are. This would be a state of interpretive confusion (of believing that we are engaged in colonization when we are not) and so it's false: we have to rather affirm Premise 2 as true.

Similarly, we could deny Premise 1 that moral philosophy involves explication. But then, if we tried to do moral philosophy, we would engage in interpreting, and instead of exploring moral theory, we would simply be exploring our various propositional attitudes as though that is appropriate. This is the normativization of interpretation, which is not true on explicatory grounds. Hence, we have to reject the rejection of Premise 1. We have to count it as true.

From these considerations, we can formulate a further coda argument that is valid, but also sound as it is comprised of premises we have shown to be true.

(1) *If* one is engaged in colonialism (C), *then* one is interpreting— imposing a perspective as explanation—which violates basic considerations of logic (*not* L).
(2) We must reject interpretation (*not* (*not* L)).

(*Therefore*), we must reject Colonialism (*not* C).

The first premise is from Argument 3, which is sound (so we know the first premise here is true). This argument adds a second premise, from Argument 1, which is also sound (so we know the second premise here is true). And by the logically valid rule of Modus Tollens (*If* P *then* Q, *not* Q, *Therefore not* P), we get to the conclusion, so we know the conclusion must be true given the truth of the premises of this valid argument. This argument shows that we have a *rational obligation to reject colonialism*. It is also sound. That means that we have a factual imperative to reject colonialism, on purely rational grounds.

3.2. The Objectivity of Moral Philosophy, the Moral Requirement to Reason

When I brought my explicatory approach to translating the *Yoga Sūtra* (Patañjali 2008), I translated its opening lines thus: "Yoga is the control of the (moral) character of thought. Then the seer can abide in its essence (YS I.2-3)" (Patañjali 2008). The *sūtra* text format is a very challenging way of writing as words are chosen for their polysemy, and the goal is to cram as many ideas in a sentence as possible. In time, I also came to appreciate that another way to render these sentences is that "Yoga is the responsible ordering of mental content (propositions) to a conclusion; then the epistemic agent can abide in its essence." And while not inconsistent with my earlier published translation, this way of rendering it brings to the fore a central insight: *reasoning*, explicating mental content to a conclusion, protects autonomy. It protects autonomy for it protects us from being limited in our capacity to understand by our attitudes to thoughts. As we are tied to propositional content via attitude, our autonomy from such thoughts is thereby hindered. When we limit ourselves to our propositional attitudes, we interpret and thereby self-colonize: we limit ourselves to just one outlook that we must conform to, resist, or perish under. I noted earlier in this chapter that there are three forms of reason (deduction, induction, and IBE); there could be and are likely many more. But as forms of reasoning, what they have in common is that they are the responsible approach to data, and the result is agential autonomy. Agential autonomy consists in the very least of being free of oppression, and that means that when agents are autonomous, they are not oppressing themselves with propositional attitudes. This situates knowers in an objective world, not outside of it. Their autonomy is not about being unresponsive to information or others—it's about relating to information responsibly in ways that do not lead to colonization. This is also a state of epistemic objectivity as the knower in this case is not conflating themselves with their propositional attitudes, which are biases.

In the South Asian tradition, the objective was modeled both as something public and as something we can disagree about as we observe the objective from differing perspectives. One famous South Asian model of objectivity is the Jain Parable of the Blind Men. Each man feels some part of an elephant, but only knows their impression given the aspect of the elephant they are grasping. If they speak truthfully, they describe what they are experiencing from their vantage. One could say: I feel something like a tree, while feeling the leg. This allows them to render explicit the data of their part of the elephant and they could even come to switch spots while appreciating that they are continuing to study the same thing. In tracking objectivity, none of our elephant feelers have to identify with their vantage—they can move and record changes in experiences. But if they speak falsely, they *identify with their perspective* (*asmitā*) and confuse their propositional attitudes with what they are interacting with. So falsely, the man feeling the leg declares he is feeling a tree. The man feeling the ear concludes he is feeling a giant leaf. In this case, there is no possibility of further research: when the one observer moves having concluded that they were feeling a tree, when they come to the trunk and believe it is a snake, they have lost the objectivity of the data and are assessing it in terms of their propositional attitudes. The difference, which we will come back to: when our blind gropers of an elephant are doing research, they are tracking the *thing* they are feeling (*de re*). When they switch to propositional attitudes, it's now a claim they are attached to (*de dicto*).

Similarly Viṣṇu, a procedural ideal of South Asian moral philosophy, holds a conch on display, while also depicting himself as a disk formed by systematic self-triangulation. To know oneself via self-triangulation is to situate oneself in a public space that can be observed from differing vantages. The conch that he displays, in contrast, represents objectivity—it is a perfectly asymmetric object, and our observations of it will be aspect dependent, and what we say about it will depend upon what aspect of the conch we are viewing. And yet, the conch as an object transcends our vantage.

Arguments are objective in two ways. First, arguments, like conches and elephants, are asymmetrical, consisting of reasons and conclusions, and they relate to each other asymmetrically. Reasons support conclusions, not the other way around. Secondly, even after we converge on the validity of an argument, for instance, we can disagree about whether the premises or conclusions are true—just as the blind men converging on an elephant can disagree about the facts they are perceiving. What this entails is that we can work with logic to relate to each other in a public space, without having to expect each other to conform to anyone's perspective. In revealing the objective in the realm of thoughts and data, reason undermines oppression, as oppression comes about by expecting others to conform to our perspective in order for them to be understood. Moral philosophy as an exercise of considering incompatible, objective, moral theoretical options is anti-colonial: it relies upon logic to elucidate its various objective arguments, unseating interpretation, which results in colonialism, or the imposition of perspective that someone has to contend with. The exploration of a diversity of objective options undermines a state where we can only contemplate the one option of the oppressor.

There are three steps to what I call explication. Engaging with any of the steps counts as explication. In general, and applicable to all avenues of research, the first step employs deduction to identify substantive options in a debate, the second inductive step arrives at a generality about the disagreement across the first-order options, and the third step determines the best explanation of the disagreement. The best account is the best because it *explains what is objective,* the topic of the controversy. The best account helps us understand how the first-order differing accounts of the objective are true, to the extent that they can play a role in the explicatory project. They have a contribution to make to our appreciation of the thing that requires explanation—the object. These three steps would be what our blind men would have to engage in to determine that they are feeling an elephant, for instance, and the way to fail this exercise is to fall back on propositional attitudes. They would have to render explicit the data from their different vantages, generalize about it, and then come to the best explanation of this generalization that explains the data recorded from differing perspectives.

In philosophy, in the first step, one uses logical validity to derive from a perspective a theory that entails its various controversial claims about a topic *t*. This is the first step of making reasons for a conclusion *explicit.* Once you have explicated various dissenting theories on a topic *t*, the second step generalizes the concept of *T* as what the competing theories of *t* are disagreeing about. And finally, we would select out of the available options the option that best explains the disagreement—which will be one of the first-order options. Explication hence involves all three basic forms of reason: deduction, induction, and IBE.

Here's the more technical specification of this first step as it applies to philosophy:

> To explicate a perspective *P*—formally called a "philosophy"—about topic *t*, is to:
>
> Discern the reasons of *P* that constitute *P*, which entail *P*'s use of "*t*", and to arrive at a systematization of *P*'s reasons that entails the uses of "*t*." The systematization of *P*'s reasons that entails *P*'s t-claims is *P*'s theory of *t*. The reasons of *P* may be what P explicitly says, or what is entailed by *P*.

The main point of the first step is to discern options that have something to say about something controversial. This is the crucial step as it *deflates* the irrational component of a perspective by extracting the propositions that are believed, or desired, as part of the perspective. It liberates them from being the content of attitudes and allows them to be understood in terms of their implications for objectivity. Then there is the second step:

Compare theories of t: what they converge on while they disagree is the concept *T*.

Once we have the inductive generalization of the first-order disagreement, the concept of dissent, the best account allows us to understand what the disagreement is about.

Being explicit about explication was a research breakthrough in the study of South Asian moral philosophy. There is a term, "dharma," that is ubiquitous in the South Asian literature that is *prima facie* the term South Asians use to discuss ethical matters. Why didn't others see this? The problem is that it was interpreted by Western commentators in accordance with Western beliefs. They would hence correlate uses of "dharma" with their substantive beliefs, and the result was less understanding not more clarity. Commentators claimed, "DHARMA is a concept difficult to define because it disowns or transcends distinctions that seem essential to us (Lingat 1973, 3), that it is used in a "bewildering variety of ways" (Larson 1972, 146) and that "It stands for nature, intrinsic [ontological] quality, civil and moral law, justice, virtue, merit, duty and morality" to name a few (Rangaswami Aiyangar 1952, 63). In the Indian Constitution, it is also the term that has been conscripted to stand for religion in its self-description as a secular state: *dharmanirapeksa rājya*—"it is a state with no dharma" (India; Government of 1950). In each case, the interpreter would use their doxastic outlook as a frame to correlate uses of "dharma." When "dharma" was used to discuss what the interpreter would call nature, or intrinsic quality, it would be pegged as having, in that context, the meaning of nature or intrinsic quality. The narcissism of Indologists who interpreted South Asian philosophy leads to this myth that "dharma" has many meanings. No one seemed to notice that the proliferation of meanings violated Ockham's Razor, and was gratuitous, depending upon the substantive convictions of the Indologist (for a survey of such claims, see Ranganathan 2017, 52–5). The narcissism of interpretation prevents this insight. But it also leads to the erasure of South Asian moral philosophy, to the point that most people who think they know something about either ethics or Indian philosophy would not have much to say about classical Indian moral philosophy. They will tend to assume it does not exist.

I was the first to formulate explication explicitly as this project that gets us to the topic of dissent, and the first to apply it to the study of South Asian philosophy. And the result is that by using deduction to derive from competing perspectives on dharma their theories of dharma, that entail all their uses of the term "dharma," and then comparing this pool of first-order theories, we can generalize the topic of dissent: THE RIGHT OR THE GOOD. The concept of DHARMA is the concept of THE RIGHT OR THE GOOD. Explication involves no violation of Ockham's Razor. No reliance on my beliefs: I got this conclusion using just logic and the backdrop data of a philosophical disagreement. The resulting concept is the same concept one arrives at by explicating theories of ethics in the Western tradition or theories of the *tao* in the Chinese tradition. Explicating philosophy hence showed that philosophers in these three traditions were all contributing to moral philosophy via their disagreements about THE RIGHT OR THE GOOD. This concept, like all concepts we arrive at via explication, is objective: it is what we can disagree about. It also thereby serves to locate competing theories of ethics as different accounts of THE RIGHT OR THE GOOD.

This research method can be applied to any philosophical topic. If we explicate epistemology, we would find that the basic concept of dissent is the TRUE OR THE JUSTIFIED. Western theories tend to prioritize truth over justification, while approaches usually depicted as mystical in BIPOC traditions are often positions, like Yoga, that prioritize justification over truth (Ranganathan 2018b). Metaphysics explicated reveals that the basic concept of dissent is the NECESSARY OR CONTINGENT. Theories in this debate hence take different approaches to the priority of the necessary or the contingent and take different positions on what fulfills these requirements.

Ethics explicated, *and* dharma explicated, leads to important *discoveries*. Whereas we can learn nothing if we explain by way of our beliefs, for anything we will accept is what we already believe, when we explicate, taking the investigation to the level of objectivity (dissent), reveals things we didn't know.

First, I found, all *basic* ethical theories can be divided into a list that on the one hand contains *teleological* theories (which prioritize the good or the end) and *procedural* theories (theories that prioritize action, choices). Second, these theories are mirror opposites of each other. Third, if we set these possibilities out, there is a fourth ethical theory unavailable in the Western tradition that is the mirror opposite of Virtue Ethics. This is Yoga.

- *Virtue Ethics*: The Good (character, constitution) conditions or produces the Right (choice, action). (Vaiśeṣika, Madhva's Dvaita Vedānta, Jainism)
- *Consequentialism*: The Good (end) justifies the Right (choice, action). (Nyāya, Kāśmīra Śaivism, Cārvāka, Buddhism)
- *Deontology*: The Right (procedure) justifies the Good (actions, called duties, or omissions, called rights). (*Bhagavad Gītā*'s Karma Yoga, Pūrva Mīmāṃsā)

- *Bhakti/Yoga*: The Right (devotion to the procedural ideal, Īśvara, Sovereignty) conditions or produces the Good. (*Yoga Sūtra*, *Upaniṣad*, *Bhagavad Gītā*'s notion of Bhakti Yoga).

Included here are names of South Asian examples of these theories. It would be difficult to find Yoga in an ancient tradition of colonization for Yoga is the practice of devotion to Īśvara—Sovereignty—and the perfection of this practice, the good, is one's autonomy (*kaivalya*). Colonialism in contrast emphasizes subservience to authority, and a loss of autonomy to the colonizing project. In common interpretive accounts of South Asian philosophy, Yoga is depicted as a version of Theism (a mistake I once made) where Īśvara is the theistic God. However, Theism is a version of Virtue Ethics that claims that the paradigm virtuous agent is God, and God's preferences and choices are dispositive of the things to be done. Īśvara in contrast is not Good (as is usually said of the Theist's God) but Right. The theist's God as all Good is a teleological ideal. Īśvara as all Right is a procedural ideal. In being devoted to Īśvara we take on the challenge of being independent ourselves. Specifically, this involves practicing the two component traits of Sovereignty: unconservatism (not being stuck with past choices) or *tapas*, and self-governance (the self-determination of values and choices) or *svādhyāya*. While absent from the Western canon, it is a classical and ancient source of contemporary progressive politics, which emphasizes nonviolent direct action, and an anti-oppressive politics that deprivileges natural attributes (like race, sex, gender, or species) as a criterion of moral standing. Persons on this account come in all sorts of shapes and forms and their commonality is an interest in their own Sovereignty.

Contrary to the view in the literature that South Asia has no history of moral philosophy, explicating its philosophy shows that not only was the topic of ethics or morality—dharma—ubiquitously discussed in philosophy, it was *the most basic philosophical topic of concern*: party lines were mostly drawn on the basis of one's theory of dharma. Moreover, the spread of moral-philosophical theories in South Asia is wider than that of the West, containing a fourth basic ethical theory. This explicatory approach made possible my edited volume, the *Bloomsbury Research Handbook of Indian Ethics*, where I encouraged authors to pursue an explicatory approach showcasing the wide diversity of Indian moral philosophy. It also renders explicit that the disappearance of South Asian moral philosophy from view is no accident. It is by design: it comes about by *choosing* to interpret on the basis of the Western tradition.

We have enough on the table to respond to a certain feminist criticism about reason. Lorrain Code writes that formal notions of reasoning, like validity, not to mention objectivity, "have been modeled on and generate models for White male achievement" and result in exclusion, "that derive, ironically, from reason's claims to formal purity and universality" (Code 2013, 74). We do not need to deny Code's observations that the rhetoric surrounding validity, objectivity, or reasoning has been employed in oppression. But we also do not need to agree that this rhetoric actually tracks anything objective. Just as oppressive traditions do not practice justice, oppressive traditions do not practice reasoning, are not objective, and ignore validity. To jettison the ideal of formal reason because it is misused by oppressive traditions is like jettisoning the ideal of justice because oppressive traditions misuse the concept of *JUSTICE*. Fortunately for us, reason and objectivity are not the Master's Tools. They destroy the Master's House.

We also have enough to respond to a certain diminutizing view of philosophy that depicts it as failing to reach the rigor of the empirical sciences. The reason the empirical sciences are worth taking seriously—and the reason that any discipline is worth taking seriously—is that they provide a principled way to distinguish reasons for conclusions from beliefs and assumptions. Scientific testing facilitates this: if an empirical hypothesis is confirmed by the evidence, there is reason to take it seriously and if it is falsified by the evidence, there is reason to reject it, quite independently of how we feel about the hypothesis. What makes science worth taking seriously is not that it permits testing (there are ways to engage in testing that are exercises of bias, which is what interpretation is). Rather, the reason to take it seriously is that scientific testing is a species of explicatory reasoning. Explicatory reasoning allows us to distinguish between reasons and propositional attitudes. Philosophy, too, is an explicatory endeavor and hence as rigorous and objective as empirical science. Like the sciences, philosophy provides a way to test and assess our beliefs (say, about what dharma or ethics is about), as it distinguishes them from explicated reasons. (The main difference is that in the empirical sciences, it is empirical evidence that decides what counts as a reason. In philosophy, people determine what counts as a reason by the exercise of their agency. Ultimately, all reasoning is philosophical as we are always choosing our reasons even when we defer to the empirical evidence. Oppressive traditions confuse this with people choosing their beliefs or propositional attitudes.) The only reason this is missed is that *Western* philosophers lead with their beliefs and assumptions as their explanations while often betraying a cringeworthy envy of the empirical sciences. The only reason that philosophy fails in comparison to the sciences is the *West* and its interpretive proclivity. And this is another way to note that this embarrassment of how philosophy is talked about and conducted in the *West* is a manifestation of oppression. It's framed stupidly on purpose, as an exercise of interpretation that relies upon propositional attitudes, to entrench colonization.

As I complete this passage, my email notifies me of another university philosophy department's closure. The idea that philosophy is expendable is the collateral damage that comes from rendering it an exercise of colonization. In a Western world, philosophy as an exercise of irrationality is redundant.

4. Erasing the Indigenous

As an influential example of interpretation on the basis of the *West* that brings to the fore its connection with LAT, consider this pronouncement by a famous Indologist, who, from 1977 to 1991, was the Spalding Professor of Eastern Religion and Ethics at Oxford:

> Professional philosophers of India over the last two thousand years have been consistently concerned with the problems of logic and epistemology, metaphysics and soteriology, and sometimes they have made very important contributions to the global heritage of philosophy. But, except some cursory comments and some insightful observations, the professional philosophers of India have very seldom discussed what *we call* [emphasis added] "moral philosophy" today. It is true that the *Dharmaśāstra* [Brahmanical, ritual purity] texts were there to supplement the Hindu discussion of ethics; classification of virtues and vices, and enumeration of duties related to the social status of the individual. But morality was never discussed as such in these texts. (Matilal 1989, 5)

Here Bimal Matilal, born in India and of South Asian descent, shows that he is able to fit into this ubiquitous exercise of White Supremacy as he has acquired a White Eurocentric identity, from where he could talk about how South Asians don't talk about what "we" call moral philosophy. Here, he is relying heavily on the kinds of things he would say about ethics by way of his affiliation group—people who speak English. This is the linguistic aspect of the explanation. But it's also an interpretation insofar as it is an explanation of Indian ethics (or the lack thereof) on the basis of what he believes ethics is about which comes to the same thing as what he is willing to say about ethics. And notice in this conflation, what Matilal allows himself to think about the topic of ethics is constrained by his beliefs and linguistic practice, which amounts to the same thing. When I bring this up, and point out how

Matilal's pronouncement is so telling of Indology and the study of South Asian philosophy, I have been rebuffed by people who do a little bit of work on South Asian ethics. There are more than a few people who work on the ethics of this or that specific figure or tradition in South Asia. But globally, nothing has changed since Matilal made these pronouncements over thirty years ago.

When I wrote my MA South Asian Studies thesis in the 1990s that became my first book, *Ethics and the History of Indian Philosophy* (2007), there had not been a monograph on the topic in decades. And, no such monograph on this topic has been published since the publication of my first book. My edited volume, the *Bloomsbury Research Handbook of Indian Ethics* (2017), an anthology on classical Indian moral philosophy, has not been superseded to date of writing this. Purushottama Bilimoria's several anthologies on Indian Ethics, which often explore contemporary Indian ethical thinking, including his most recent one which I wrote the foreword for—*The Routledge Companion to Indian Ethics* (2025)—are important contributions. Bilimoria deserves recognition for keeping this topic alive. But otherwise it is a very small club. In the academy, what is normalized is the erasure of BIPOC moral philosophy. Explication requires that we look at the issue of classical South Asian moral philosophy, like all areas of philosophy, in big picture via logic: only then do we see the various options and how they fit into the debate. No one else does this but me, to date, because in modern times no one else explicated the options before me. To explicate is to be explicit about choosing explication over interpretation. And before I formulated it, it was not an option that was articulated in the literature of modern scholarship. (I am careful not to claim that I invented the explication-interpretation distinction as it comes from the Yoga tradition.) Recall, the leading figures of Analytic and Continental Philosophy recommend the opposite: to interpret. To explicate is to depart from the winds of Western colonization.

In time, I came to see that this institutionalization of White Supremacy and the erasure of BIPOC moral philosophy by interpreting on the basis of the West is part of a larger pattern in the academy, which I call *Philosophical Apartheid*. This, in turn, reflects the power structure of a colonized world.

Apartheid in South Africa was a regulatory system organized around White Supremacy, where BIPOC were relegated to a lesser level, kept separately from folks of Western descent, and moreover, policed by folks of Western descent. In the literature, *Philosophical Apartheid* serves to keep the philosophical activity of the majority of the world, outside of an area populated by European and European-derived contributions that are depicted as high-status scholarship, while also depicting the excluded content as primitive and not worthy of participating in the Western arena as it fails by these Western standards. This was, and is, apparent in four ways.

- (1) While European and European-derived philosophy was and is studied by professional philosophers with doctoral degrees in philosophy, many, if not the vast majority, of authors writing on South Asian philosophy in the West have their highest degrees in other disciplines or interdisciplines, whether Religious Studies, the study of languages, or the Social Sciences.

Having a PhD in Sanskrit does not disqualify one from writing on South Asian philosophy. It also does not qualify one to write on South Asian philosophy, anymore than a PhD in English qualifies one to be a Russell or Quine scholar, though they both wrote in English. We wouldn't dream of treating someone who is an expert in German as a Frege scholar, unless they were also a philosopher of mathematics or language. But when it's philosophy written by Brown people, the idea that you actually need to have scholarly and professional expertise in philosophy and the specific philosophical topic that the Brown philosopher wrote on goes out the window: why bother when it's just Brown people whose intellectual work you are writing on? In the West the professional disparity results in a literature on South Asian philosophy written by people lacking professional competence in philosophy. But it is also systematically racist. If one were to actually do philosophical work on a BIPOC tradition, like South Asian moral philosophy, and send it out to any Western publication, it will most likely be peer-reviewed by people with no professional training in philosophy but who do have some knowledge on the BIPOC tradition, such as South Asia, because of work on the relevant language, like Sanskrit, or Religious Studies. It would be like a theoretical physicist who does advanced work on the topic having her work peer-reviewed by someone who hates physics, and didn't spend much time studying it, ever—but only because the theoretical physics was based on ideas from Brown people: the White people physics gets peer-reviewed by physicists with expertise on the topic. The experience of sending out work on South Asian moral philosophy for peer review is this ridiculous and this frustrating. You can hence do good work, but its publishability is only as likely as it accords with the professional incompetence of the peer reviewer selected by that publication. One might generalize this problem across disciplines: the publishability of good research is always limited by the least competent colleagues in a field tasked with review. But in the case of philosophy, there is a *structural* obstacle that is a result of the racist disvalue of the professional and rigorous study of BIPOC philosophy. This ensures that most of what is written and published on the topic is stupid. It ensures that what is written and published on the topic reflects racist expectations about the topic.

Now, surely, one might respond, there are some professional philosophers, with degrees in philosophy or with jobs in geographically western philosophy departments, who are also South Asianists, who would provide some balance to this professional disparity. There are many philosophers in South Asia, and the global South, who are excluded from this exercise. But with respect to those who are included, because of their *Western* pedigree and their employment in geographically western academic institutions, insofar as they have been successful by *Western* academic standards, their work has passed peer review by non-philosophers uninterested in South Asian moral philosophy. And so the few 'philosophers' in this area tend not to correct the problem but participate in it. At least half of this small group are part of the problem. This book was not, for instance, spared this problem. When a South Asianist philosopher reviewed the final draft for this book, their lack of interest in ethics and their ignorance on the topic posed an obstacle. Exactly what is a virtue in this book, that it focuses on moral philosophy, on the basis of the South Asian tradition, as a way to understand colonization—exactly what was pitched in the book proposal, exactly what I signed a contract to write about with the publisher—became a problem that the reviewer thought had to be corrected by *rewriting the whole book* to get rid of all the ethics (never mind that the book has 'moral philosophy' in the title). Their review typified the failures of interpretation (to be discussed in Chapter 4).

- (2) While academic journals that describe subdisciplines (like *Ethics*, or *Journal of Moral Philosophy*) are typically populated by publications on philosophy derived from the European tradition, philosophy from outside is discussed in journals with ethnic titles, like *The Journal of Indian Philosophy* or *The Journal of Chinese Philosophy*.

European-derived philosophy is hence treated as unethnic and universally relevant to topics like Ethics or Political Philosophy, while BIPOC philosophy is frequently qualified by ethnic or geographic origins, and *not in discussions of* Ethics or Political Philosophy. This ghettoization of "ethnic," BIPOC—not White—philosophy also serves to create publications that claim to be on philosophy but are not. In the *Journal of Indian Philosophy*, for instance, one will frequently find papers on philology, or linguistics. Such titles include "How Many Sounds Are in Pāli?," "Defining the Other: An Intellectual History of Sanskrit Lexicons and Grammars of Persian," and recently "On the Notion of *anabhihite* in the Cāndra Grammar." And this functions to represent South Asian philosophy as not philosophy but something else, which also serves to justify the subsidiary role that BIPOC philosophy has in Philosophical Apartheid. The political function of such ethnic philosophy journals that are not really on philosophy and marginalize BIPOC ethics is to confirm all the stereotypes about BIPOC philosophy, such as that BIPOC intellectuals are somehow just uninterested in practical questions of moral philosophy and moreover that their intellectual output isn't even philosophy.

- (3) Philosophers from the Global South, including South Asia, are not represented in high-ranking journals of philosophy.

This is too easily explained by financial disparities. Philosophers in the Global South typically do not have access to expensive journals published in the geographic west in Western states, and hence cannot interact with them. But, *even if they had financial access*, for reasons of Western interpretation, they will be shut out for they lack the Western doxastic commitments to be accepted by these publications that peer review by interpreting on the basis of the West.

With this spread of discrimination and the offloading of the study of BIPOC philosophy to scholars who are neither trained, competent, nor interested in philosophy, and the correlative marginalization of philosophers from the Global South, BIPOC moral philosophy that could challenge Western colonialism is discussed nowhere prominently or in the spaces one would expect to find it—in journals dedicated to moral philosophy or journals dedicated to BIPOC philosophy.

One main outcome of Philosophical Apartheid is the segregation of moral philosophy. Within the academy, BIPOC philosophers, albeit relegated to the conservancy of non-philosophers, are acknowledged as having made contributions to various fields of philosophy *except* moral philosophy—as Matilal observed. And this conclusion is drawn by using the West as the standard of what counts as moral philosophy. This renders moral philosophy *the most* White Supremacist subfield of philosophy. The Western tradition is the only one acknowledged as having a robust history of thinking about ethics. What holds this together? The short answer—interpretation on the basis of the Western tradition, which is no different than Western colonialism as colonization depends upon interpretation and in this case the power structure of interpretation points West.

If we expect to interpret all philosophy according to the Western tradition, then we might be able to badly interpret many areas of BIPOC philosophy. But Western doxastic resources will not be able to explain values that are outside of the West's tradition and call into question its authority to interpret everything. In part, this explains why there is a common expectation that one doesn't have to be a philosopher to study BIPOC traditions—against the backdrop of *Western* interpretation one doesn't expect to find anything that isn't already in the *West's* tradition. This reduces the study of BIPOC philosophy to the exercise of discerning whether BIPOC say things that White people say, as though their intellectual contribution can only be measured against the standard of the *West*.

Crack open the *Journal of Indian Philosophy* for instance and one will find articles on metaphysics, epistemology, and logic, but not ethics—except for an exceedingly rare contribution. Philosophical Apartheid is expressed in moral philosophy being treated as the primary domain of *Western* philosophers. Confucius, at the very start of the Chinese tradition, is acknowledged in a *Western* world as having made contributions to ethics, but Confucius also sounds a lot like Aristotle. His emphasis on the doctrine of the mean and the importance of the elevated person who can provide moral guidance for everyone else in a stratified society is also what Aristotle argues. Taoism, China's competing source of philosophical thinking, which denies the primacy of the human and prioritizes the cosmic norm of the *Way*, is typically treated as religious mysticism. In Philosophical Apartheid, non-*Western* philosophers can be acknowledged as making contributions to ethics when they did what "we" call ethics (to echo Matilal).

It is possible to read these complaints about the academy and assume that Philosophical Apartheid is just an academic problem. However, the academy is just a reflection of the world we live in, and these dynamics of oppression that created a tiered and racialized academy are a reflection of the politics of a tiered and colonized world. What the academy serves to do, thus, is reify and provide legitimacy to a world structured by *Western* colonization and White Supremacy. To identify this as a structural problem of the academy is to identify a structural problem of the world we live in. To identify the bungling of the study of BIPOC moral philosophy via interpretation on the basis of the *West* is to identify the architecture of colonization the world over. It reflects our actual lived power structures around the globe. As moral philosophy is de-colonial freedom (as we noted at the start of this chapter), the restriction of moral philosophy to the *Western* tradition, and the systemic bungling and ethnic ghettoization of BIPOC philosophy, reflects the idea that freedom is really only for the *West* (White people) and not for BIPOC traditions and peoples.

The fourth important component of Philosophical Apartheid brings this to the fore:

- (4) By interpreting BIPOC traditions on the basis of the *West*, from Roman times, the *West* has created a category of marginalization that serves to protect the *West's* colonialism from criticism, and at times provide it support and cover. This is the category of RELIGION.

Modern, Western, Anthropology began in the 1600s with a deep commitment to scientific racism that attempted to track and study racial differences, with racialized people being classified as primitive. We've come a long way from this because of the general appreciation that racial categories were created by colonization and are not a result of rigorous scientific research. There is enough information in the world of Religious Studies to show that religion is very much like race: a creation of colonization. And hence we ought to give up studying religious differences or religious traits as though we are studying something that isn't, like race, a complete creation of colonialism. And yet, most participants in Religious Studies, and virtually all philosophers of religion, do not treat the topic of religion historiographically (as a matter of how the history of colonized peoples is discussed) but as though the idea of religion tracks something real, precolonial, and not constructed out of oppression.

Western interpretation normalizes this outcome of colonialism as a way to understand colonized people as though they never had moral philosophy and were always worried about religious and spiritual matters. This serves to make Philosophical Apartheid seem like nothing constructed by colonialism, and simply a reflection of the noninterest colonized peoples show to moral philosophy. Then it would seem appropriate to send non-philosophers to study these traditions because, really, what importance do they have to research in moral philosophy anyways. By historicizing BIPOC thought, and treating it primarily as a matter of ethnographic study, the normative challenge to the *West* is closed off (Adluri and Bagchee 2014).

The cumulative effect of Philosophical Apartheid is to erase the Indigenous and replace what should be an exploration of moral philosophy with the ethnography of White people. Hence discussions of ethics and moral philosophy are, in the academy, restricted to Western (White) sources. It is a politics aimed at making reason socially impossible. But it is also a politics of ensuring that *actual* moral philosophy, as an exercise of reason (that departs from the oppression of interpretation), is not politically possible. All of this is another way to say that Philosophical Apartheid is colonialism, which is a result of interpretation on the basis of the *West*.

De-colonialism rejects the idea that we can know without having an impact on what we know. Sending a particle out to determine the place of another particle alters its activity at the quantum level. Interpretation is like this method of interference as though a method of knowing. Explication, which makes moral philosophy possible, is a macroscopic organizational effort—it has an impact of preserving options in a controversy. One way or another, we have an impact on what we attempt to understand. Explication—moral philosophy, or logic—destroys irrationality and preserves options. Interpretation—colonization and oppression—destroys options and maintains irrationality.

5. Learning Moral Philosophy from the Colonized

While the chapters ahead will have many critical things to say about the West, these are really criticisms of the West insofar as it is a tradition of interpretation based on LAT. In our world, it is distinguished for acclaiming LAT. And its excellences are, sadly, not its excellences but colonially appropriated excellences. Conversely, to the extent that we can learn anything about freedom—the public practice of moral philosophy—we will have to look to Indigenous traditions. Colonizers make a mess of learning from Indigenous people as they try to interpret them. We can instead explicate our way to an Indigenous approach to life.

The next three chapters concern Metaethics. As Geoffrey Sayer-McChord notes, "Metaethics is the attempt to understand the metaphysical, epistemological, semantic, and psychological, presuppositions and commitments of moral thought, talk, and practice" (Sayre-McCord Spring 2023 Edition). Irrationality and its consequent oppression constitute metaphysical, epistemic, semantic, and psychological presuppositions that get in the way of doing moral philosophy. Without clearly identifying this obstruction to moral philosophy, we cannot engage in a reason-based, de-colonial activity.

In Chapter 2, Moral Semantics, Genocide, and Indigeneity, I begin contrasting an interpretive model of thought, LAT, with an explicatory and Indigenous model of thought I call Linguistic Externalism (LE). Not only is LAT a key ingredient in genocide, when we compare the three ancient traditions of philosophy—the Western, Chinese, and Indian—we see that only the West begins assuming and not controverting LAT. This explains how it grows into a global colonizing tradition, which often turns into a project of *eliminative colonialism*. Indigenous traditions based on LE in contrast, such as the Indian tradition, are moral-philosophical in orientation and avoid the oppression of colonizing traditions. LAT, as a model that conflates thinking with language, leads to modeling thought as uniquely human but also bounded by the communal limits of one's language. In contrast to the colonial we can understand the Indigenous, LE-based, paradigm as open to a diversity of agents across biologies and species, equitable in its thinking about agents, and inclusive in the way they think about moral issues. The Indigenous typically acknowledge the Earth as a person, to whom we owe moral consideration. LE allows us to appreciate that the Wind is an agent, or that ecosystems or rivers are persons, and to understand our moral lives as relating to a universe that is social. LAT makes it impossible to translate what other humans who speak very different languages say as it confuses one's own perspective with the thinkable. It is a uniquely dysfunctional model of thought that underwrites the *Western* tradition where it is assumed and in which no alternative is considered. This cements the essential and persistent irrationality of the *West*. The only way to transcend this irrationality is to explicate it as an option that we are free not to choose.

Chapter 3, Religion: Two Millennia of the White Supremacist Erasure of Moral Philosophy, picks up on the observation that as a uniquely LAT-based tradition, the *West* manufactures the idea of religion as part of its ancient rollout of *exploitative colonialism*. Accordingly, the *Western*, no matter what, is secular, and the BIPOC, no matter what the content, is religious or spiritual. The same position can on this bifurcation be secular or religious depending upon its racial origin. Call this Secularism$_2$. This contrasts with genuine, Indigenous Secularism, which consists in the free, unconstrained exploration of moral philosophy as we find in ancient South Asia— rebranded as "Hinduism" by *Western* colonization. Call this Secularism$_1$. To get Secularism$_2$ off of the ground we interpret against the backdrop of the *West*. To get Secularism$_1$ off the ground, we explicate the disagreements of philosophy. The political function of the creation of religion is to normalize the irrational, *Western* interpretation of ethics as constrained to the anthropocentric and communitarian, while rendering explicatory, rational, de-colonial, anti-oppressive moral philosophizing from BIPOC traditions as inarticulable—because it is on the one hand religious and not permitted in secular spaces, and because the de-colonial is defined out of language as spiritual, or mystical. For the unconstrained, reason-based exploration of moral philosophy we have to look to Indigenous traditions.

Chapter 4, Gatekeeping, Peer Review, and the Normalization of Appropriative Stupidity, picks up with Chapter 2's finding (that the *West* is the preeminent irrational, interpretive, colonizing tradition) and Chapter 3's observation (that it creates a two-millennia history of White Supremacy). Here, the focus is on how oppression and colonization are maintained as an everyday feature of life. This accounts for how all oppression functions in our world. Oppression in our world—speciesism, sexism, racism, transphobia, homophobia, ableism, economic oppression . . . is a function of interpreting on the basis of the *West*, and then the oppressed is anyone and anything that has to conform to, resist, or perish under believed priorities of the *Western* tradition. This shows that:

- Oppression is not definable by a hatred or intolerance of a specific group, such as Black people, or nonhuman animals.
- Oppression is a function of valuing an interpretive paradigm, against which everything else suffers in proportion to their deviation.

This chapter connects how this historical process of *Western* interpretation that structures a world of *Western* colonization also dominates the academy: peer review in the academy and ordinary exercises of gatekeeping function according to the same interpretive dynamics. It connects the logical criticism of the interpretive paradigm with its oppressive outcomes. It also explains how *Western* thinkers begin talking about equality and freedom in the modern period when their societies were engaged in genocidal colonialism: the very practice of interpretation that creates colonization is shown to be appropriative, creating a mediocracy. Its appropriative function is a function of its epistemic failures, undermining the transparency of the interpreters' agency and activity as thieves. Interpreters take other people's intellectual labor as they are being oppressed, and represent it as their own opinion. I call this process the *colonial-exchange,* which is the colonial appropriation of Indigenous intellectual labor while the colonized tradition is saddled with the pathologies of the Colonizer. In the process, Indigenous people now colonized understand themselves via the outlook of the Colonizer. Inversely, we will see that science and all research depend upon an Indigenous, explicatory frame, and that interpretation creates oppressive models of knowledge, founded on irrationality. All innovation is Indigenous.

Each of these chapters in the course of our exploration of Metaethics shows how irrationality gets in the way of doing moral philosophy and how Indigenous traditions in contrast are our only source of how to be reasonable. The violence of colonialism explains how reason-based people are oppressed, from the outside.

Chapters 5 and 6 switch the focus to Normative Ethics, which is the part of moral philosophy where we investigate theories of THE RIGHT OR THE GOOD. Here too we will investigate the incompatibility of oppression and engaging in moral philosophy. In Chapter 5, Conventional Morality: Good Character, Good Outcomes, Good Rules, we examine what the Indigenous South Asian tradition has to say about how people voluntarily accommodate themselves to oppression. This has to do with a depreciation of the importance of Normative Ethics and a naïve endorsement of teleological (Consequentialist) thinking. In Chapter 6, Devotion to the Ideal of the Right:

Three Levels of De-Colonization, I review what the de-colonial, Indigenous moral theory of Yoga has to tell us about resisting oppression so that we can exercise moral philosophy as a public practice. Normative ethics according to Yoga is the public practice of moral philosophy. Its metaethics leads us to choose explication, and its applied ethics has to do with remediating a world that is averse to this freedom.

The penultimate chapter moves to Applied Ethics, which is a problems-based approach to moral questions. In Chapter 7, Applied Ethics and the De-Colonial Politics of Moral Philosophy, I explore the main normative theories from Plato to Mill in the Western tradition and note that they are designed to *normalize* oppression as the price of bureaucratically approved activity. The "problems" that fall outside of this narrow anthropocentric or communitarian focus are what it identifies as applied ethical problems. By prioritizing moral philosophy as opposed to oppression, the main unavoidable applied ethical problem is the politics of de-colonization. Here I consider residual objections.

In Chapter 8, Research and Activism, I conclude.

Insofar as anyone would care to object to the arguments and explication I unfold, they would have to reject explication and thereby forward some interpretation as an objection. But in order to mount an objection, one has to be able to disagree. And the interpreter—Colonizer, oppressor—cannot disagree, for they frame everything in terms of their point of view. Anecdotally, I have observed that interpreters faced with my work usually just have meltdowns, not reasoned responses. De-Colonizers, who are interested in moral philosophy and its explicatory infrastructure, can clearly demarcate the differing projects of interpretation (colonialism and oppression) in contrast to moral philosophy (explication, de-colonization). We, De-Colonizers, can do that as we use logic, which does not require that we conflate the intelligibility of a proposal with our view of things. We De-Colonizers can hence mount objections to oppression, colonization (interpretation), because we can disagree. But this political room for disagreement is the political room of de-colonization, to not be constrained by the interpreter's emotional incapacity to allow for us to live in ways that they disagree with.

Unlike an interpretive approach (that only considers what is believed by the interpreter), an explicatory approach is not scared of dissent (even at the meta-explanatory level, where we contrast interpretation and explication)—it is a case about the possibilities of dissent.

- Interpreters (Colonizers, oppressors) are contemptible not because they disagree with us (the explicator, the moral philosopher, the De-Colonizer) but because they will not permit the disagreement.

What the interpreter (Colonizer, oppressor) is likely to do, because they cannot actually understand an argument, and in an attempt to mimic reasoned discussion, is appoint themselves as fact-checkers, assessing each claim explored in this book against the backdrop of their beliefs. If they find something said that conflicts with their opinion, they will conclude that the argument and subsequent dialectic are mistaken (often with delusions that they have identified logical problems with the argument). And this only shows that Colonizers, oppressors—interpreters—do not know what an argument is and how to assess it. Arguments are not assessed in terms of their conformity to or deviation from someone's beliefs. They are about inferential support. Having established that an argument supports its conclusion, we can move on to the question of truth (whether the premises and conclusion are true). But if we are to avoid falling back into irrationality, we have to have a way of determining truth that is not reducible to our beliefs or our way of looking at things. The only reason that the opponent to the project of de-colonization will fail to see this is that they have made hay with Western colonization, and to do without interpretation that they would have to abandon to follow the argument is, for them, terrifying. That's like a thug having to contend with being unarmed and vulnerable. The upside of what follows is that we all have an interest in being done with oppression. We all have a rational obligation to de-colonize. And if, as argued, irrationality causes epistemic and social problems, we have rational grounds to be optimistic—a doctrine we could describe as *rational optimism* (*śraddhā*, YS I.20).

Part Two

Metaethics

2

Moral Semantics, Genocide, and Indigeneity

... And what of the sixty million dead in the Americas in the first hundred years after contact? But that's too abstract. Just statistics. And you'll be accused of confusing, of conflating ... Do not speak of it. Do not try to make a link. Connect nothing. ... Fortunately, most of those who might read this will not recognize it as a poem.

Randy Lundy, "A Note on the Use of the
Term Genocide" from *Something For the Dark*

1. Introduction

In a world of interpretation, we have propositional attitudes about what Indigenous people are like and what Colonizers are like and we use these propositional attitudes to interpret the world. That is the problem: we typically use the very exercise of oppression—interpretation—that generates colonization to understand the colonized. If we explicate, we look rather to the different ways that Colonizers and Indigenous people have to approach questions, and to model possibilities. To explicate is to render explicit the differing approaches to thinking.

This chapter sets up a sustained criticism of the Western tradition that will be the focus of the rest of this section on Metaethics, and will return when we look at the applied ethical challenges we have today. What makes the Western tradition problematic is that it is based on LAT, and LAT, on an explicatory account, is a maximally, always, *false* theory of thought. It is false as it introduces interpretive confusion into all matters. It's a toxic idea, which, if taken seriously, undermines people's capacity to reason, and turns them into bullies. It is always false as it encodes a conflation of thinking and believing that renders all explanation by way of thought an interpretation. On the flip side, it creates a psychology of fragility that depicts the LAT-based thinker as under threat from diversity. It creates a psychology of victimhood, and the behavior of oppression.

Whereas LAT, the Linguistic Account of Thought, the interpretive model of thought, characterizes the paradigm of the Colonizer, what I call LE, Linguistic Externalism, an explicatory approach to thought, characterizes the Indigenous. Whereas LAT conflates thinking with a culturally encoded linguistic vantage, LE shows thought to be an exercise of diversity, equity, and inclusion. Colonizers can be Native; they can't be Indigenous. The idea that we cannot choose to be Indigenous is colonialism. As colonialism is irrational, we have a rational obligation to learn how to be Indigenous.

The genocide of Jews by Nazis, Palestinians by Zionists, and every other example we can find, including the typically ignored, near-extinction-level-genocide of Indigenous people in the Americas—which killed nineteen out of twenty Indigenous people—all require LAT. So too does the total subjugation of the nonhuman world. Those accused of genocide, Colonizers, will always defend their actions by way of a narrative they believe. Against the backdrop of an appreciation of the colonial and oppressive nature of interpretation, those narratives are not exculpatory: they are practically confessions. What the Colonizer will not allow is everyone affected to engage in open philosophical conversation about who belongs, who has rights, who gets to decide where they want to live. Colonization is an effort to cut this conversation short by imposing the Colonizer's perspective on everyone so there are no choices to be made. And as a contribution to the debate, the interpreter has lost track of objectivity: for instead of describing how things seem from where they are, and allowing everyone to track the objectivity of the topic—the philosophical controversy—they engage in propositional attitudes. And since they know they will lose the debate, they have to kill and oppress those who would dissent to save themselves the embarrassment of being demonstrably stupid. They are still demonstrably stupid. It's just that they've marginalized or killed those who would point that out.

In the next section I review my own research in Translation Studies that led me to identify LE as a distinct alternative, and to also observe that LAT is never questioned and always assumed in the *Western* tradition. It is because of LAT that in the *West* there is no distinction drawn between the philosophy of language and the philosophy of thinking. LAT is a disaster as a model of thought when it comes to translation: it cannot explain how translation is possible in cases when we need translation—cases of linguistic difference.

In the third section, beginning with a famous thought experiment concerning translation that assumes LAT, I consider how the conditions of genocide are created by LAT and undermined by LE. LAT is a key ingredient in *eliminative colonization,* genocide, sometimes non-transparently called *settler colonialism.*

In the fourth section, I review the unfolding of the three ancient traditions of philosophy, the Western, Chinese, and Indian, relative to their different starting points with LAT. Only the West acclaims LAT and grows into a global colonizing tradition. In China, LAT was entertained and criticized, leading to a complex but colonial history. Only the ancient Indian tradition rejects LAT, and operates according to LE. Whereas LAT leads to a politics of anthropocentrism, communitarianism, and colonization, LE accounts for the Indigenous approach to moral thinking as situating every agent within a cosmic ecology of agency, which frequently identifies the Earth and nonhuman animals as people. Given that the oppressive irrationality of LAT leads to anthropocentrism and communitarianism—not to mention, genocide—and the de-colonial, explicatory, rationality of LE leads to acknowledging a wide diversity of agents, we can know that it is irrational to deny the agency and moral standing of the nonhuman, such as the Earth. Indigeneity in the wide sense is rational. These considerations show that it is not possible to be anti-oppression and de-colonial but only with respect to humans, or a narrow subset of humans. Moreover, appeals to the shared humanity or human equality as a response to genocide, sexism, or ableism are symptoms of the LAT-based foundations of such oppression, not their solution.

In the fifth section, I conclude.

2. Thinking Is DEI

Translation is an underrated moral-philosophical topic, which, like logic, is treated as a separate matter in the West. Yet, we live in a small world, and if we can't understand each other because of linguistic and cultural differences, we're in practical trouble. I thought for instance that if we could just clearly translate South Asian discussions of the term "dharma" as "ethics" because "dharma" was the most obvious correlate to the English term "ethics," we would see that South Asians were *always*, ubiquitously, discussing moral philosophy. That was what I tried to defend in my first book, *Ethics and the History of Indian Philosophy.* I had not yet repudiated LAT for I didn't really understand it either. That was a mistake, for in not appreciating LAT my own thinking about why and how "ethics" and "dharma" are intertranslatable was confused.

LAT claims that the content of a word or sentence is its linguistic meaning and so translation is about switching up expressions across languages on the basis of sameness of linguistic meaning. Thinking about translation in terms of sameness of meaning of words dooms the exercise: so even if "dharma" means the same as "ethics" there would be problems for translation.

Languages are constrained by the meaning of their units (semantics), rules for combination of the units (syntax), and their social or practical implications (pragmatics). These are all very specific to languages. A word-for-word exchange on the basis of any one of these considerations is fraught with problems as languages are very different. Moreover, syntactic differences between languages make a word-for-word translation on the basis of sameness of meaning impossible (for an examination of these challenges, standard but failing solutions in the literature, and the solution I recommend, see Ranganathan 2018a). As I started thinking about what I learned from historical linguistics *and* important contributions to the philosophy of language, the evidence showed that what words mean is an outcome of linguistic use. Even if we define a word into existence by fiat, or we use it to name something that we do not fully understand until we can discover its properties later (Kripke 1980), that's a new meaning of a word created by our usage. Hoping for sameness of meaning as the ground for translation across language is tantamount to hoping for a sameness of history across languages, which is impossible—if languages had the same history they would be the same language.

Let us assume the orthodox account of literal meaning. Accordingly, the literal meaning of an expression is its basic or systematic role in a language—the meaning that if we knew would help us understand derivative uses, whether ironic, dramatic, or metaphorical (Davidson 1996b; Salmon 2005). According to this orthodox view, there is no such thing as metaphorical or ironic meaning. There is only literal meaning, and then various deviant uses. But, an implication of this view rarely noted is that if use changes enough, so that the basic use changes, so too will literal meaning change (cf. Evans 1996). One factor that changes the use of words is moral and political choice. In some versions of English, "marriage" might literally mean a union between a man and a woman, only, but that is because of the politics of formative generations that used "marriage" in deference to heteronormativity so that this usage becomes basic. What "marriage" means, for instance, is not self-caused, but an outcome of intergenerational politics. Similarly the literal meaning of "ethics" or "dharma" in a specific linguistic community will come to be exactly what their dominant theory of ethics or dharma is, for this theory allows us to appreciate what is basic to the linguistic usage. *Linguistic meaning is a political fossil. It encodes the beliefs of a formative generation.*

To treat what our words and sentences mean as the content of what we can think, and then what we could translate, is to treat the politics that gave rise to those meanings as *beyond* debate. LAT is hence *deeply conservative*. It cannot ever allow us to consider possibilities that go against the beliefs that gives rise to a certain way of framing an issue because this way of framing an issue becomes the meaning of what we say, which is then treated as what we are allowed to think about the issue.

As I started to dive into Translation Studies and how education in Translation Studies works, a second important conclusion of this research dawned on me. What philosophers call "translation," the exchange of expressions with other expressions, is actually closer to what is known as "simultaneous interpretation": we see this when someone signs along with speaker so that sign readers can follow along. In contrast, actual translators don't translate languages (such as ancient Greek into English) or spontaneous speech acts. They translate texts, such as Plato's *Republic,* which are artifacts comprised by an author with semiotic resources, *and* the considerations that guide translation are discipline or genre relative. Translation is then much more like the process of replicating a painting or a sculpture but in a different medium and with different materials. This is a macroscopic project and the accuracy of the result is assessed macroscopically: not by the concordance of the respective mediums. LAT makes it seem as though translation is about pairing up words across the original or source language and the language of translation or target language. That would be like attempting to reconstruct a sculpture made of pebbles into a sculpture made of elbow macaroni by paring a pebble in the original and the macaroni in the reproduction: it won't work as they have different sizes and properties. However, macroscopically, the reproduction using pasta for a sculpture originally made of rocks can be accurate, judged by the considerations that lead us to identify macroscopic, salient features in the original. And in the case of translation, each discipline or genre is a type of text (a *text-type*) defined by essential features that specifies these macroscopic saliences. What all of this entailed is that the kind of meaning that we save in translation, which transcends language and culture, is *discipline relative*. This justifies why if one learns how to be a translator by undertaking a degree in Translation Studies, one doesn't learn how to translate languages, but rather one specializes in kinds of translation (such as legal or scientific translation).

Given the disciplinarity of translation, words with different meanings can be an exact translation if they serve the same genre-specific purpose. In English, "The Good is the Form of the forms," and "The Good is the Idea of the ideas" are equivalent when treated as translations of Plato, even though "form" and "idea" have different linguistic meanings in English. They play rather the same text-type theoretic role to articulate Plato's notion of universals. In philosophy in particular, I came to realize that terms that I call "key philosophical terms," like "good," "right," "knowledge," "reality," "dharma," and "morality," play essential roles in being *textual* devices in philosophy. They allow an author to articulate in the text their theory that is a contribution to a debate on the topic the term is used for—independently of what their linguistic meaning may be in various dialects. We know this not by interpreting these terms by our beliefs but explicating philosophy where these terms are what contrasting theories are dissenting on. Literature has plot and character as text-type features. Philosophy has key philosophical terms and argument as essential text-type features. So whereas "dharma" may not have the same meaning across dialects, it can play the same philosophical role to articulate theories of THE RIGHT OR THE GOOD. As I was working out the details of this approach to translation and semantics in my PhD dissertation, I called it *text-type semantics.* Accordingly the meanings of concepts of inquiry are themselves creatures of those disciplined inquiries, and to get to the bottom of those meanings we have to see what role they are playing in the relevant disciplinary inquiry.

I decided to translate Patañjali's *Yoga Sūtra* from Sanskrit as I was working out the details of text-type semantics. What unfolded before me as I translated the *Yoga Sūtra* according to text-type considerations was literally an account of thinking as something that was dependent upon disciplinary organization (YS I.2–4), which was what I had independently come to via thinking about translation. Not every South Asian philosophical text expressed this theory, but it spoke to certain general features of the tradition. I realized that text-type semantics I was arriving at was *very* South Asian—very Indigenous—and entails a model of thought I came to call *Linguistic Externalism* (LE).

Among LAT-based philosophers, a controversy rages. Some like Frege hold that there are two aspects to a thought or a concept: its intension (its definition or how the meaning appears to us, what Frege called "Sinn" translated as "sense" in English) and its extension (what it is about, what Frege called "Bedeutung" translated as "reference" in English). An example that motivates this distinction is the claims "the evening star is bright" and "the morning star is bright." EVENING STAR and MORNING STAR are two concepts for the same thing: the planet Venus. According to Intensionalists like Frege, the intension of these concepts and the resulting propositions are different *modes of presentation* of the same thing. In the case of the concepts EVENING STAR and MORNING STAR, they refer to the same thing (Venus). In the case of a thought like "the Morning Star is on the horizon," the extension is always its truth value (whether it is true or false) but it is a different proposition from "the Evening Star is on the horizon," which it shares a truth value with, as it has a different intension. Extensionalists such as Millians deny that there is any intensional aspect to a thought: a thought is really just what it is about.

According to what I call LE, a thought's intension (its definition) is the *discipline-specific* use of a semiotic resource (a sentence, emoji, bark, chirp) and the extension (what the definition is about) is the set of devices with the common use. Accordingly, a thought is not reducible to the literal meaning of a sentence, but rather the use we make of it in disciplinary investigations.

For instance, according to LE, "The Good is the Form of the forms" and "The Good is the Idea of the ideas" are semantically different sentences that share a common philosophical use, so they are hence both in the extension of the same proposition about The Good and universals in Plato's thought. For this reason, they are literal translations of each other, relative to the discipline of philosophy (though if assessed by linguistic standards would be treated as nonliteral translations). Thinking in LE is an exercise of *deflating* the representational importance of language in favor of disciplinary use. Moreover, on LE, thinking is not a matter of linguistic competence. It isn't about being human. We do not even need to intend a disciplinary use when we speak, for those considerations are literally *external* to our linguistic practice. Hence, a cat's meow, or a dog's pleading stare at you as they stand over their empty bowl, can be the extensional equivalent of the English sentence "I'm hungry" given certain disciplinary considerations. According to LE, thought is radically unspeciesist and not anthropocentric. The thinker—person, agent—is just whatever is responsible for a contribution to thought's extension.

Knowledge, on this very South Asia model, consists in disciplinarity that would help us determine the extension of a thought. The Sanskrit word for that disciplinarity is "yoga." For modeling thought, what this entails is that our semantic representations, in language or other systems, only convey thought when their representational capacities are deflated according to disciplinary considerations (cf. *Yoga Sūtra* I.42–6). In very Indian terms, the resulting understanding transcends conventional truths about the meaning of our words (*saṁvṛti* or *vyāvahārika satya*) that encode a shared perspective (shared propositional attitudes), and relates to ultimate facts (*paramārtha satya*). These ultimate facts are explicatory facts: what we cannot deny without switching back into the world of propositional attitudes. In the latter case, we relate directly to how things really are, not how we represent them. LE explains how we succeed in translation in practice (Ranganathan 2018a, 2011, 2007). When translators succeed, they pair up translation units (the smallest unit translated as a whole) on the basis of genre or disciplinary considerations.

Another important difference between LAT and LE that has to do with the contrast between interpretation and explication is that LAT makes it seem as though we have to *ascribe* to others beliefs, desires, and other propositional attitudes to understand them. Why? Because to count someone else as thinking on LAT, we have to ascribe to them an appreciation of the meanings that inscribe these attitudes. This is sometimes called a *theory of mind*: the idea that we have to have a theory about other people's minds to understand them. As an interpretive exercise, it is irrational and oppressive—as though it is up to us to decide what others are thinking, and not for them to express it themselves. According to LE, we explicate perspectives, and these are themselves public features of the world, not hidden. The universe is already meaningful. The contribution that anything makes to a thought is its disciplinary use, and the thing responsible for that semantic presentation that shares a disciplinary use with other semantic artifacts—the Earth, the Sun, rivers, mountains—just is the person *thinking*.

Finally, whereas LAT conflates thought with meaning, which then creates pressure for social consensus to form around linguistic meaning, LE treats thought as an exercise of dissent. The extension of a thought according to LE is a collection of semantically inconsistent representations that share a disciplinary use. To think in LAT is to adopt the shared subjectivity of a linguistic vantage. To think in LE is to adopt the objectivity of debate as the essence of thinking.

LAT is an interpretive model of thought because it identifies thought not only in terms of how it represents things (in language) that already encodes a culture's propositional attitudes, but what we have to believe in order to participate in a language's representational practices. We cannot use language subversively to think, given LAT, for that would be to transcend the perspective that is the content of thought on a LAT-based account. But for LE, thought is not captured in a perspective or propositional attitude but in ways in which a divergence of contradictory representations, with differing truth values, that people have differing attitudes toward, from differing perspectives, can play the same role in thought given some criterion that allows us to distinguish the common disciplinary use, from the propositional attitudes encoded in extensional elements of a thought. Explication allows us to distinguish thoughts from propositional attitudes. *LE is hence explicatory*: it treats thought as something that is defined as independent of propositional attitudes that constitute the extension of thought. Anything can contribute to this: the mood or behavior of an ecosystem, a mountain, the stars. And if agency has to do with being thoughtful, the universe is populated with a diversity of agents whose thoughtfulness—their semantic behavior—is the universe.

In the previous chapter I noted that all serious research is explicatory as all serious research helps us distinguish between reasons and propositional attitudes. In philosophy, especially in the Analytic tradition, there is a tendency to want to treat important questions as settled by the empirical sciences. However, in this same tradition, assuming LAT, the result is that the empirical sciences do not help us distinguish between reasons and propositional attitudes for the linguistic evidence of what our words mean (which are taken to be the content of reasons, or thoughts, by LAT) is constructed out of propositional attitudes. Empirical evidence here is not evidence of what is independent of propositional attitudes (as we find in the natural sciences) but of political perspective. The question of which model of thought we should choose is philosophical, and it has to do with what model would be responsible for us to endorse. The question comes down to: which model will help us reason. LAT will not as it conflates thought with propositional attitudes. LE does not engage in this conflation.

What does "dharma" mean? The right answer is that there probably isn't just one linguistic meaning of "dharma" nor is there just one linguistic meaning of "ethics." But if we explicate, we will see that all uses of the terms are answerable to the core concept of THE RIGHT OR THE GOOD. So "dharma" and "ethics" are intertranslatable not because they share a linguistic meaning but because in philosophy they serve the same function in thought, to articulate theories of THE RIGHT OR THE GOOD.

Already given what we have reviewed in this section, we can observe how politically different LAT and LE are. The far-right in the United States and Canada have taken to criticizing DEI, and have a stated preference for the politics of formative generations. One couldn't get this off of the ground without LAT, for LAT makes it seem as a matter of thought that DEI initiatives are violations of what is acceptable to think and announce, which is structured by the political choices of formative generations. LE in contrast is an ecological approach to thought. Thought is such that our beliefs about who is thinking are immaterial: a thought just is the common disciplinary use of semantic expression. And hence thought is inclusive of a diversity of agential expression, and it treats all of these on par, with equity. LAT-based thinkers like Wittgenstein claim we can't have a private language as we need a shared language to account for its significance. For LE, there is no possible *private thought*. Thinking is a receptivity to diversity and every thinker contributes to the objectivity of thought by living meaningfully. The actual facts—true thoughts—we discover via research are just those we already ecologically participate in, minus the confusion of interpretation.

3. LAT, Colonialism, and Oppression

In this section, I want to focus on LAT and its moral and political implications. The Western world we are forced to live in is a world of LAT.

3.1. Moral Twin Earth

In a very famous thought experiment, Hilary Putnam posed the scenario where, in addition to Earth, we know of a Twin Earth. On both planets, people speak a mutually intelligible language that sounds like our English. However, on Earth, the chemical structure of what is called "water" is H_2O, and on Twin Earth it is XYZ. The question posed by Putnam is whether we could treat "water" on Earth and Twin Earth as intertranslatable. He concludes we couldn't insofar as the meanings of these two words were different, and the meaning simply was the chemical they named in their respective worlds (Putnam 1975).

This naturalistic approach to semantics was taken up by some philosophers wanting to provide a naturalistic (empirical scientific) account of the meaning of ethical terms (Boyd 1988). On the naturalistic account, the natural properties that moral terms name just is the meaning of these terms. Terence Horgan and Mark Timmons repurpose Putnam's scenario as Moral Twin Earth (Horgan and Timmons 1991). On Earth and Moral Twin Earth, people speak an identical-sounding language to our English that is pragmatically indistinguishable. However, the natural properties of the two worlds are different. While Earth moral vocabulary is responsive and appears to refer to natural properties that encourage a Consequentialist ethical theory, Twin Moral Earthlings use moral vocabulary that is responsive to different natural properties that encourage a Deontological moral discourse.

The question posed by Timmons and Horgan is whether people across these worlds can be understood as having a conversation about ethics with each other. If we assumed a semantic externalist position, where the meanings of moral terms are the natural properties they name, then we would have to conclude that Earthlings and Twin Moral Earthlings are not having a cross-world discourse on morals.

It is also worth adding that if we adopt the perspective dictated by our moral vocabulary—and LAT—we couldn't acknowledge that Moral Twin Earthlings were engaged in their own moral discourse, for we would use our semantics as a frame to evaluate their discourse and their discourse would fail to be ethical by our standards. And yet the way the scenario *is described* (perhaps question-beggingly) both communities are engaging in moral discourse: one in a Consequentialist conversation, and the other in a Deontological conversation. This description and the unargued assumption of LAT, along with the further assumption that the moral semantics on both worlds is externalist creates a contradiction. Timmons and Horgan suggest it can be resolved by assuming that the proper account of moral semantics on both worlds is *internalist*—its meaning has to do with the mental outlook of the speakers: then even though on both planets they are speaking about different properties, the moral vocabulary will have the same internalist meaning. Then when on both planets people say "hitting your neighbor is not good," they would be articulating the same sentential meaning and then according to LAT the same proposition. Hence, they could jointly consider this proposition in cross-world conversation.

The pressure to choose an internalist semantics across these two worlds to facilitate moral discourse translation is created by LAT—something not acknowledged by Horgan and Timmons or apparently any of their peer reviewers. LAT is so basic to *Western* modeling that no one even notices it. What makes a thinker *Western* in part is their unquestioning assumption of LAT. And if colonization and genocide are outcomes of this model of thought (as we shall see), it too will seem to disappear as it's so basic to the *West*. If we assume, for the sake of argument, LE instead, we would allow linguists to determine the semantics of the respective languages. If it turns out that the semantics of the respective languages is best explained by a semantic externalism, where the moral vocabulary are referring to differing natural properties in their respective worlds, and hence what "ethical" linguistically means on each planet is different, we could still see that the sentence of the form "hitting your neighbor is unethical" in both languages are part of the extension of the same philosophical proposition insofar as they share a philosophical use to express a philosophical proposition about THE RIGHT OR THE GOOD, namely that HITTING YOUR NEIGHBOR IS NEITHER RIGHT NOR GOOD. So on LE's account, the respective communities would be engaging in a cross-world conversation about ethics when they use their linguistically particular moral semantics to talk about hitting one's neighbor.

So if the goal is to try to account for what would allow cross-linguistic conversations about ethics, LE will work in contexts where the moral semantics of respective communities are different, whereas LAT will fail. And that was the purpose of the Moral Twin Earth thought experiment: to determine how we could account for cross-linguistic moral discourse. LAT rigs the outcome so that the only way such a conversation is possible is if there is *no* moral diversity across communities. Colonialism is about the imposition of a perspective. The expectation that there has to be just one common moral semantics—a common perspective about ethics that is semantically encoded—that could facilitate cross-cultural discussions on ethics assumes colonization as a backdrop. When *Western* moral semanticists want to know what the "right" moral semantics is, they are asking the question: what is the account I want to impose, or I hope has been imposed, on everyone.

3.2. Planet Ethics

Planet Ethics is an ancient place, where an original linguistic community split up into various descendant communities, which in conjunction with local challenges and selective pressures evolved their own cultural and national identities. In time, owing to the political choices of formative generations that influenced linguistic usage, the national moral identity of each descendant culture was encoded in the respective languages. Moral semantics in each case was the moral and political identity of the respective culture: "ethical" simply meant whatever the national moral identity says it means. Moreover, in general, everyone on Planet Ethics appreciates this history. There is no skepticism about what "ethical" means anywhere.

In Nation Plato, ruled by a philosopher king, moral vocabulary tracks the knowledge and insight of those elevated enough to appreciate what our words mean, and to prescribe everyone's proper place in society. In Nation Kant, "ethical" and "morality" mean what passes Kant's test of the Categorical Imperative. In Nation Positive Utilitarianism, "ethics" or "morality" is about maximizing happiness. In Nation Negative Utilitarianism, "ethics" or "morality" concerns the minimization of suffering. In Nation Aristotle, ethics is what one needs to know to get along in one's community, inculcated by a proper upbringing. In Nation Non-Analytic Naturalism, ethics has to do with human thriving. In Nation Expressivism, ethics is about expressing one's mind. Next to them is Nation Emotivism, an older nation from which Nation Expressivism grew out of and separated from. In Nation Emotivism, moral terms express our emotions: "Hitler is evil" means "Hitler boo" here. Next door, there are two differing nations that share in the spirit of relativism. One is Nation Individual Speaker Relativism (Metaethical Subjectivism): here ethical terms are quasi-indexical—they allow the speaker to input their own values, and the output is a claim that is true of them. Two speakers with differing motivational input can differ about whether x is good, and both speak truly, so long as they accurately describe their motivational states (Dreier 1990, 7). In Nation Societal Speaker Relativism (Metaethical Moral Relativism), "ethical" and related moral terms input the wider society's motivations and values. Members of this society speak truly if they produce a claim that accurately describes and responds to the groups' motivational structure.

If we assume LE, then speakers across Planet Ethics can use their native sentence of the form "hitting your neighbor is unethical" to translate sentences from other languages, for they are treated as extensional equivalents of the same proposition: a philosophical claim about hitting your neighbor being neither right nor good. Moreover, speakers can use their own native vocabulary to philosophically criticize their nation's linguistically encoded moral theory. In other words, assuming LE, cultural diversity in the form of radically distinct moral semantics poses no obstacle to moral-philosophical research or conversation on Planet Ethics. If we assume LAT, in contrast, we will find grief and pain.

3.3. Moral Perspective Essentialism and Genocide

If we assume LAT, then several problematic outcomes ensue. There are two forms of LAT which amount to no difference here. According to one version, *linguistic internalism*, people in different languages can express the same proposition so long as they have an equivalent sentential meaning (as we find assumed by Putnam and Horgan and Timmons). According to another, *linguistic particularism*, no cross-linguistic similitude in proposition, is possible as linguistic meaning is always particular to a language (cf. Wittgenstein 1958 I §241; cf., McDowell 1998b, 61–3; 1998a, 128; Derrida 1981; Gadamer 1996, 1990). On Planet Ethics, given the vast cultural diversity, the result is the same regardless of which version of LAT we endorse: no speaker of any language can translate their sentence about the ethical into any other language as these will always be semantically dissimilar.

Moreover, whether the claim "it is unethical to hit your neighbour" is true or not will be constrained by the culture's moral semantics. If the sentence expresses something true given its culture's moral semantics, it is *analytically* true, which is to say, true by definition. So then no one in their respective culture could criticize or deny the governing moral assumptions of their nation without contradicting themselves. This will be most apparent in the case of theoretical claims. In Nation Kant, to deny the sentence "the ethical is what passes the Categorical Imperative" is to deny something analytically true. This means that affirming the values encoded in one's language— believing the values—given LAT, is *necessary*, just to speak meaningfully. Correlatively, it means that we cannot disbelieve or deny this claim without veering in to the meaningless. But it is also because of LAT *sufficient* to engage in moral discourse. So LAT leads to treating the moral semantics of one's language—the political fossils of formative generations whose choices lead to the crystallization of one's nation's moral semantics—*as necessary and sufficient* for moral discourse. In effect, LAT leads to the *essentialization* of the encoded moral perspective of one's language—whatever that is. Call this *moral perspective essentialism.*

Here, we see how belief and thought are fused by LAT: it conflates thought with linguistic meaning—"the ethical is what passes the Categorical Imperative" in the language of Nation Kant—and thereby the belief we have to endorse just to speak in ways that are in conformity with the semantics of the language. Failing to do so is not only contradictory but meaningless as it fails to respect what is basic to the semantics of the thought. This pressure to confuse a linguistically encoded belief with a thought against LAT will occur anytime deviating from a sentence involves some violation of semantic requirements, and this will always be answerable to the politics of the use that gave rise to the literal meaning of the components of the sentence. So, for instance, being anti-trans is, against LAT, as easy as conforming to the semantics of pronouns if in one's language that is supposed to track sex. On LAT, all explanation by way of thought then becomes explanation by way of linguistically encoded belief: interpretation.

While it may be hard for us to imagine this outcome in every case on Planet Ethics, the point about moral perspective essentialism is invariant across moral semantics. That is because the pressure that LAT generates to conflate national moral identity and moral semantics and to further define the governing values as analytically true is not a function of the values encoded in the semantics—nor even the seemingly vacuous, internalist, forms of moral semantics—but the inflated importance it gets via LAT. So even in Nation Emotivism, where "ethical" means "yay," the sentence "The ethical is what one says yay about" is analytically true, and to deny it is to say something linguistically contradictory. But just as in Nation Kant, we would here have to conclude that our language is both necessary and sufficient for moral discourse. We would have to draw the same conclusion no matter what language we speak. Moral perspective essentialism and the problems that ensue are hence structural features of LAT: not substantive entailments of a culture's values. If violence follows from attempting to conform one's behavior to LAT, then this violence may actually contradict the values that one's language ethically encodes. That is because that violence that follows is generated metaethically, not substantively. Nation Christianity that values turning the other cheek would also be led to violence by LAT.

As LAT essentializes the values encoded in one's language, on Planet Ethics, this entails that every other culture (aside from one's own) will be an essential moral failure; a failure to engage in what is essential to moral thinking and practice—namely, one's language. The linguistic outsider's group identity will be neither necessary nor sufficient to engage in moral discourse given your language. In contrast, if we assumed LE, for instance, everyone would be able to appreciate that all participants of all the various nations on Planet Ethics are able to engage in what is necessary and sufficient for moral thinking and practice. Moral thinking necessitates an appreciation of a moral proposition as the common philosophical use of a diversity of semiotic resources. Moral practice as conformity to what is morally essential on an LE account is indistinguishable from moral-philosophical inquiry, and so insofar as people are able to think moral-philosophical propositions (propositions defined by their common moral-philosophical use), they can engage in the essentials of moral practice. Moreover, as everyone is able to contemplate the *same* moral proposition (one defined by a common moral-philosophical use) with their national sentences of the form, "it is unethical to hit one's neighbour" everyone is free to take opposing views as to its truth—and citizens can thereby criticize and dissent from their nation's founding values. No substantive perspective is conflated with the thinkable given LE. But in the case of LAT on Planet Ethics, we must believe what is linguistically encoded in the language's moral semantics or we are thinking in contradictions.

If colonialism is the reduction of options to only one package that can be contemplated, then LAT generates colonialism via moral perspective essentialism.

- LAT generates colonialism because it conflates the thinkable on an issue with the one view that is encoded linguistically, which is then imposed on everyone as part of the exercise of thinking.

This one view in actual cases of ordinary languages refers back to the politics of formative generations and dominant political forces that lead to such literal meanings. Colonization begins domestically before it is exported. LAT-based colonial communities colonize themselves by not allowing the contemplation of moral theoretic options and by rendering the criticism of linguistically encoded values *absurd*. But it also extends to others.

To judge linguistic aliens as lacking the essential moral perspective to properly situate moral activity (namely, one's language) is to judge others as not being able to act in accordance with what is morally necessary as they lack one's language. In accordance with one's values, moral perspective essentialism entails that one has to treat others as though they cannot and should not be allowed to live their own lives as they see fit as they cannot do what is morally necessary. Of course, this is violent. To treat others, living life according to their own moral theoretic choices, as though they cannot be allowed to do so is to impede their lives as agents. And insofar as this interference in others' lives is a function of their group identity (problematized as a deviation from one's own morally essential identity) the violence that ensues is group directed. This looks like:

a) Killing members of the group;
b) Causing serious bodily or mental harm to members of the group;
c) Deliberately inflicting on the group conditions of life calculated to bring about its physical destruction in whole or in part;
d) Imposing measures intended to prevent births within the group;
e) Forcibly transferring children of the group to another group.

As a matter of international law, these are acts of genocide, which are framed as "acts committed with intent to destroy, in whole or in part, a national, ethnical, racial or religious group, as such" (UN 1948). In short, genocide is the act of disrupting a group. Of course, anyone can *choose* not to treat others as though they cannot and should not live life on their own terms. But the conditions of LAT generate something else represented by this: the *genocide dialectic*. It consists in two linked arguments.

(1) If someone respects what is necessary and sufficient for moral practice, then they are part of our language-based moral practice.
(2) Group X is not part of our language-based moral practice.

(*Therefore*), Group X does not respect what is necessary and sufficient for moral practice.

The first premise is an expansion of LAT and its moral perspective essentialism that claims that one's own language-based moral practice is necessary and sufficient for moral activity. So it would of course follow that those who are outside fail morally by these standards. This is the first step. Then, we can add a deontic entailment of moral practice:

• Our, or any, moral practice disallows (prohibits, prevents, interferes with) what is not consistent with it.

A moral practice is a practice based on some theory of *the Right or the Good*, and such a practice distinguishes between the permitted and the prohibited. What is prohibited is contrary to the practice. It is an entailment of the possibility of a moral practice that it has to disallow what is not consistent with it. If a moral practice did not disallow what is not consistent with it, there wouldn't be any moral practice left to speak of. Combining the conclusion of the previous argument with this deontic entailment, we get the second step:

(3)　Group X does not respect what is necessary and sufficient for moral practice.
(4)　Our, or any, moral practice disallows what is not consistent with it.

(*Therefore*), Group X has to be disallowed by our moral practice (i.e., genocide).

The second and last step in the genocide dialectic links up what is essentially an elaboration of LAT, with the deontic entailment that a moral practice has to disallow (prohibit, prevent, interfere with) what is not consistent with it. What this shows is that we can know genocidal intent, as an entailment of LAT and this deontic entailment of moral practice, anytime a group is operating with a shared ethnolinguistic identity as the foundation of their politics. This would be disallowed by LE for LE will not allow us to generate the moral perspective essentialism that is required for the first premise of this dialectic. This shows the origins of conspiracy theorizing in LAT: accordingly, everyone who does not share our normative identity is a threat, but also a threat our normative practice cannot permit to exist. It is worth noting, as before, that linguistic internalism and linguistic particularism are two different versions of LAT that could have differing outcomes in some contexts. In the case of linguistic internalism, there can be two languages (theoretically) that share the same semantics and, to that extent, the genocidal implications of LAT will not be triggered against an external group who are perceived as sharing the same practice. Linguistic particularism will always lead to these genocidal implications. Linguistic internalism will lead to the same genocidal outcomes when every language encodes (or is perceived to encode) a unique moral semantics. And given this is a function of a language's particular history, and the values of formative generations, linguistic internalism will typically lead to the same outcomes as linguistic particularism.

(There is another important way to understand the pathology of colonization. As we shall see in Chapter 4, colonization, via interpretation, is an appropriative exercise. The terror of the oppressed is thereby appropriated by the Colonizer as their self-understanding: the Colonizer acts as though they are the ones in existential peril as they appropriate this legitimate fear of their oppressed group. Genocide is one outcome of this paranoia.)

I began writing this book shortly after October 7, 2023, and the unfolding events in Gaza have haunted me as I worked on this manuscript. Part of the fog around the issue is created by the very conditions that give rise to genocide: LAT. Countries with a history of LAT-based colonization (such as Canada or Germany) will be sympathetic to other societies doing the same.

And this has made talking about what is unfolding in Palestine forbidden: many who spoke out earlier suffered professionally (like the formerly tenured Jewish professor of anthropology, Maura Finkelstein, who was fired for her advocacy for Palestine). Social media algorithms were also tweaked to ensure that such talk was suppressed. People took to misspelling "gen0s1de" to pass the automatic filters. As the genocide becomes increasingly obvious, it is becoming easier to talk about it, but because it simply becomes part of the interpretive nightmare we are living. Increased conversation around the event is a sign that it is approaching completion.

Not all Jews are Zionists (Jewish Nationalists) and not all Zionists are Jews. Zionists, of course, want to speak for all Jews. Contemporary Zionists object to characterizing Israel and its actions in terms of colonization, ethnic cleansing, or genocide. However, Zionists up until the 1960s characterized their project as one of colonialism, but they stopped once de-colonization became politically favored (R. Khalidi 2022, 4, 13). As of 2024, the International Court of Justice found that there is evidence of Israel committing genocide against Palestinians in Gaza—sufficient for prosecution under international law. Moreover, in 2024, the ICJ also found that Israel's settlements in occupied territories of Palestine violate international law. By the end of 2024, Amnesty International and Human Rights Watch concluded that Israel is guilty of genocide in Gaza. (Of late, as I finish this book, the Israeli rights groups B'Tselem and Physicians for Human Rights Israel are coming out with the same conclusion. As I read the proofs for this book, in September 2025, a UN report concludes the same.) Now, as I complete this manuscript for publication, Israel, along with the United States, is planning mass ethnic cleansing, and the goal appears to be a landgrab, which was rather naked from the start of the genocide. A right for Israel to defend itself is widely cited as justification for its assault on Palestinians—and oddly itself, a piece of rhetoric that we find around genocide. But a state has no right of self-defense against occupied territories: it rather has obligations of care (United Nations 2017). Critics who charge Israel with genocide and settler colonialism have these decisions on their side. Those who care have also watched this genocide unfold on social media. But apart from these decisions and evidence, we can know that genocide is an entailment of Israeli politics because of it being an entailment of LAT. Israel is a state built on a Hebrew, ethnolinguistic identity, which allows Jews anywhere in the world a right of return, but does not allow Palestinians expelled from their homes in the formation of Israel—an event called the *Nakba* or *Catastrophe* in Arabic—to return. Israeli culture is hence not a multicultural, multilingual, LE-based political landscape where people can use any language to think as an act of debate and dissent. It is formed around a consensus about the Jewish character of Israel, aided by Hebrew's role as the national language, to inscribe the Zionist character of the state as undeniable. For that, one needs LAT that furnishes the moral perspective essentialism that both delivers consensus but also justification for the occupation and genocide of Palestinians. Once LAT is adopted by Israelis as the infrastructure of consensus, it blocks an appreciation of history as all interpretation blocks history—as interpreters try to understand history in terms of their present beliefs. Moreover, given a LAT facilitation of an ethnolinguistic Jewish state, the resulting culture will see itself as speaking for all Jews, whose interests are thereby conflated with that of Israel in its LAT-based incarnation. From here, we get the fallacy that criticizing Israel is anti-Semitic.

Until Zionism, Jews for millennia had resisted the full implications of LAT—allowing themselves to think with different linguistic frames as we find in LE, in the local, (often native), language, and in Hebrew. The idea that one needs a specific language to function in, such as Hebrew, is an implication of LAT and as *Western* as it gets, and a departure from a more traditional Jewish resistance to the *West's* LAT-based colonization—which many Jews continue today.

Canada's treatment of Indigenous people exemplifies the genocide dialectic: Indigenous peoples were treated as incompatible with what is morally required by Canadian, LAT-based (English or French, Christian) society, and so they were treated as though they as a group had to be destroyed, by remaking them into replicas of Colonizers. This was violent.

The forced sterilization of Indigenous women and the forced placement of Indigenous children in Residential Schools with the associated serious mental and physical harm (in Canada and elsewhere) are literal examples of genocide. The detracting view notes that genocidal activity is not sufficient for the crime: we need a genocidal intent of targeting of a group in part or whole, and this is stereotypically claimed to be difficult to establish. It is noted that legal systems often draw distinctions between different levels of culpability of the same wrong act, given the mental state of the perpetrator. In many legal systems, this underwrites differences in the crime of murder and manslaughter (Ch. 5, Schabas 2009). It then seems like an excuse that administrators of Residential Schools believed they were doing Indigenous kids a good turn. This seems like evidence that they lacked the criminal intent, required for the crime of genocide. So while "the prevailing interpretation assumes that genocide is a crime of specific or special intent, involving a perpetrator who specifically targets victims on the basis of their group identity with a deliberate desire to inflict destruction upon the group itself" (Alexander 1999, 2264)—an interpretation written into the UN document itself—it seems very easy to evade such intent by framing one's actions of genocide in terms of beliefs to the contrary.

In a *Westernized* world, it is ordinary to frame the issue of the intention in terms of the beliefs of the perpetrator (as everything given LAT and its generation of interpretation leads to this). That is a *de dicto* state as it is an attitude toward a claim. An intention to do something is a pro-attitude toward an action. It is a *de re* state, or an intention toward a specific thing, namely an action (for a discussion of different views on intention in the literature, see Setiya 2022 (Winter)). The genocide dialectic above shows how a commitment to LAT and a basic deontic entailment of having a moral practice results in a genocidal intention toward outside groups (the conclusion of the genocide dialectic). This is a *de re* intention: an intention to do something. Given that LAT generates moral perspective essentialism, and an interpretive approach to thought, those engaging in genocide will be inclined to frame their actions as required by *their* essentialized moral expectations. In other words, they will be inclined to provide an *interpretive cover* to their malfeasance that always exonerates them. And indeed, denial is a rather frequent accompaniment to the history of genocide, both during and after (Charny 2003). This generalizes in crimes against humanity: perpetrators rarely transparently confess to the act of genocide. Hence, according to the Nazis, they were not being evil to Jews: they were protecting Germans from Jews (Bytwerk 2005). According to Israel (at the time of writing this), they are not committing genocide of Palestinians: they are protecting Jews against the threat posed by Hamas. Interpreters believe their beliefs of self-defense are evidence of their innocence. But as interpretation is really a colonial and oppressive mode of explanation, we can know that these attempts to justify and couch genocidal action in terms of entirely believed accounts of the innocence of the perpetrator is practically a confession of guilt. When Nazis claim they were just defending Germans from Jews, explicators hear a confession for the Holocaust. Innocent people do not need their beliefs as a defense. Their innocence is a matter of allowing all to participate in a public practice of explication. And if they have to punch a Nazi, or kill them, the reason to do that is to return public space to one safe for everyone to participate in explication. When bullies act, they do so to enshrine their interpretation. When the innocent kill oppressors, they do so to restore explication as a public practice. All political violence is not the same. LAT and interpretation make it seem as though everyone is just fighting for their point of view. Explication is an alternate motive for violence.

No doubt Zionists will protest that the issue is very complicated and that their side has a legitimate claim. Explicatorily, we can begin by assessing when this controversy of who belongs in Palestine began; it began with Zionists deciding that they, not Palestinians, have a rightful claim to the space eventually called Israel. And then, we can jump to the end, since we have established differing sides and the controversy: what's the best account of the controversy? It can't be the Zionist side for they won't allow the debate insofar as their project is about ethnically cleansing, occupying, and now starving and bombing participants. The softer side of this is the censorship exerted on social media and legacy media to not report on the genocide, and to call it a war, or a conflict, as though occupied peoples can be counted as waging war. Whatever the faults of those who fight for Palestinians they have not rendered the debate impossible. Theirs would be the better explanation of the debate—and the possibilities of the disagreement. It would involve acknowledging that Palestinians were in what was to become Israel, that they disagreed with their displacement and the formation of the Israeli state that excluded them. It would not erase the Israeli side, but provide the context of the dissent. And certainly, there would be several versions of this other, anti-Zionist side worth considering.

The *mens rea* or criminal intention of genocide is an entailment of how others are to be treated, given the moral essentialism of LAT. The *actus reus* or criminal act of genocide is the interruption of a people's existence. In general, we can consider a philosophical question about what *mens rea* comprises. One option is to frame it as a *de dicto* affair, such that people who engage in a prohibited act, like genocide, have a belief that they are engaging in the crime and they intend to do it. The alternative is to consider the *mens rea* in terms of an intention to engage in the prohibited action. This is captured by Anthony Duff's analysis in his *Criminal Attempts* that an intent to commit a criminal offence "is an intention such that the person would necessarily commit an offence in carrying it out" (Duff 1997, ch. 13). This would be a noninterpretive—hence rational—*de re*, approach. Correlatively, the expectation that the forbidden intention to commit any crime is a belief is to frame the intention irrationally—as a matter of propositional attitudes. On this ground alone, it is unreasonable to expect that genociders have beliefs that they are engaging in genocide that are their forbidden intentions.

Given LAT and the *de re* intention to commit genocide on the basis of the genocide dialectic, genocide is ubiquitous—or at least, genocidal intent is. Far from being an unusual event, it occurs anytime one group *treats* another group as a threat by virtue of their group identity. Groups engaging in genocide by way of moral perspective essentialism need not themselves be an obviously recognizable cultural group. Against LAT, businesses that develop their own norms and thereby their own corporate dialect whose business brings them in conflict with Indigenous peoples, who are thereby an obstacle to their group's linguistically encoded interests, also have a genocidal intent toward the Indigenous group. The rapid reduction in the population of Indigenous people in North America by way of European colonization was also genocidal. One story, often repeated, was that the population collapse was brought on by the unintentional introduction of germs that Indigenous peoples were not immune to. But as Edwards and Kelton note, Colonizers bear responsibility for creating "conditions that made natives vulnerable to infection, increased mortality, and hindered population recovery" that "intersected with direct forms of violence to depopulate the Americas." Given available information, the precolonial Turtle Island population may have been as high as 112 million, and within a few generations, it dwindled to 5 percent of that (Edwards and Kelton 2020, 54–5). Europeans who imagined the Americas as theirs would thereby view Indigenous people as the outside threat to their LAT encoded plans.

According to the argument I have been pursuing, the issue of genocide is occluded by expecting interpreters to confess beliefs that they are engaging in genocide. Rather, interpretation based on LAT creates the only intention that matters—an intention to engage in the *act* of genocide, namely to interfere with and disrupt a group because their group identity is perceived as a threat to one's own LAT identity. To what extent people based on LAT carry out genocide is a choice. There are reasons for people, even with genocidal intent, to constrain themselves and their project of *eliminative colonialism*. They might decide, as a matter of history, to view other groups as cultural variants of the same moral practice via linguistic internalism. They might choose to do so partially and restrain themselves in other ways, by switching to a project of *exploitative colonialism*, either because there is value to be extracted and gained by enslaving or subjecting a colonized people to colonial rule— or because the Colonizers are outnumbered. This was indeed how the first iteration of Western colonization that expanded over the globe (as we shall review next chapter) constrained itself. But genocidal talk and intent can be found in the ubiquitous depiction of foreigners as a threat to the moral fabric of a LAT-based society.

If we identify genocidal, *de re*, intent as flowing from the LAT-based self-certification of the essential virtues, then many cases of war are cases of genocide. This occurs when the aggressor frames themselves in terms of an essential moral perspective and the victim group as lacking those traits. The Russian war on Ukraine shows these traits. Ukrainians are depicted in Putin's Russia as Nazis, while Russia is essentialized as the defeater of actual Nazis (Nielsen 2022). The Cold War and proxy wars of the US and the USSR also betray this feature of colonial justification for genocide. For the US, belligerence against Communists was justified by their failure to respect the US's way of life, and *vice versa*. Many unfolding mass atrocity events in Africa today, such as in Sudan, show signs of genocide where ethnolinguistic groups on the whole are harmed and treated as a threat to the aggressor's interests.

An obvious historical example of a genocide that is usually just called a massacre is the 1937 Rape of Nanjing, often called the Nanjing Massacre in which the Japanese army killed men, and subjected women and children to sexual assault prior to killing them. An estimated 200,000 died as a result of this campaign. The reasons for not calling this a genocide have everything to do with the idea that the prohibited intention that defines a genocide has to be framed in terms of beliefs that participants have about what they are doing. If we acknowledge the prohibited intention as an intention to do violence against a group, then this was a genocide. This was straightforwardly *eliminative colonialism*. Put against the backdrop of the markers of aggressor and victims, the Japanese and the Chinese, which are linguistic distinguished identities, along with the ethnolinguistic chauvinism of the Imperial Japan at the time, we can see this falling into the familiar pattern. And so too many other examples, such as the genocide of Tamils in Sri Lanka, or the Rohingya in Myanmar.

Political speech in advance of or during a genocide often but not always betrays LAT as a driver insofar as genocidal speech often involves "dehumanizing" the target. Against the backdrop of LAT what is essential to moral practice is some language, and nonhumans (called "animals" in LAT-based societies, as though humans are not animals) are maximally outside of the scope of the essential moral perspective insofar as nonhuman animals do not speak languages. So to call a human an "animal" or some specific animal against the backdrop of LAT is considered derogatory: commentators tend not to appreciate that this depiction of humans as some kind of nonhuman animal (Tirrell 2012) is only derogatory against the backdrop of anthropocentrism. It is often noted that this kind of "dehumanizing" speech is common in genocide: in the Armenian Genocide, Armenians were called "dangerous microbes," Nazis called Jews "Untermenschen" or "subhuman," and in the Rwandan Genocide, Hutus called the targeted Tutsis "vermin" (Donohue 2019). The Israeli Defense Minister Yoav Gallant, in spelling out genocidal action against Gaza (the withholding of food and fuel to Gaza) called Gazans "human animals" (Fabian 2023 (October 9)). But such "othering" speech is really only treacherous given LAT for LAT depicts inclusion in the in group linguistic practice as essential to being spared genocide, for only those in one's linguistic practice (given LAT) are within the scope of the morally essential. The need to *include* to spare people genocide is a need generated by a genocidal approach to outsiders.

LAT, and its *moral perspective essentialism*, creates the phenomenon of selective moral sympathy (for the ingroup) and then depicts those who are outside as deserving no moral consideration, and scorn insofar as they do not conform to the ingroup's ethnolinguistic values. This makes it easier for many of us in relative freedom to sympathize with people at a rave who are abducted than for people living under occupation and periodic assault for decades. It makes it easier for humans to sympathize with other humans than with nonhuman animals born into the terror of factory farming.

In other words, genocide given LAT is not a function of "dehumanization." It is a function of a model of thought—LAT—that entails that the nonhuman as nonlanguage users are maximally out of the scope of the morally essential, as though putting cattle in cattle cars headed to slaughter is acceptable, but putting humans in the same position is not. If we rejected LAT, and its anthropocentrism, dehumanization would entail no violence or mistreatment.

Not every genocide is signaled by dehumanizing talk. Christian clergy in Canada officiating over the genocide of Indigenous people in Residential Schools that consisted of the various harms outlined by the 1948 UN convention openly treated the occasion as an opportunity to evangelize. In this case, Indigenous people were depicted not as maximally out of the scope of the morally essential (like nonhuman animals) but contingently so, given their cultural distance, which could be remedied in theory through forced enculturalization and forced linguistic conversion. And yet, this project of genocide consisting in bodily and mental harm and an explicit plan of reducing the Indigenous population by making them part of the settler population required treating them as though they were maximally outside the scope of what is morally essential. Destroying the group was an instrument to integrating them in Eurocentric Christian culture. Calling this "cultural genocide" ignores all the ways in which it fits standard cases of genocide. It also ignores all the ways in which standard cases of genocide are also examples of cultural genocide. The distinction between actual genocide and cultural genocide is a nonsense distinction as LAT, which confuses cultural values with thinking, and problematizes external groups, slated for genocide, on the basis of their cultural difference, treats the motive for cultural genocide as the motive for genocide, and hence, the resulting actions amount to the same offence.

Interpreters fail to see the genocidal outcome of LAT in part because they cannot understand logic and entailment—though there is plenty of historical evidence of the genocidal actions of LAT-based traditions. But also when they assume LAT and contemplate diversity, they *imagine* something else. They might imagine that the considerations we have discussed about LAT on Planet Ethics entail a moral relativism, where moral questions are raised and answered relative to cultural expectations. In abiding by moral relativism, one does not impose one's moral expectations on others, understanding that they are local and defined by a society's values. However, that's a different Planet:

Planet Moral Relativism. There, every culture has the same moral semantics: Societal Speaker Relativism. Accordingly, "ethical" and related moral terms input the wider society's motivations and values. And in every case, ethical claims would be true insofar as they represent these culturally relative values. But on Planet Ethics, only one culture is defined by this semantics. But Planet Moral Relativism only seems to not lead to moral perspective essentialism for there is no other moral semantics that form the basis of national identity available on this planet. Everyone seems to share the essential moral perspective—Societal Speaker Relativism. But that is only because this planet lacks moral diversity. And indeed, that lack of moral diversity might be an *outcome* of a genocidal campaign by a Nation Societal Speaker Relativism. A lonely Nation Kant on an otherwise Speaker Relativism Planet would also be marked for extermination by the Moral Relativist's moral perspective essentialism if everyone adopted LAT.

LAT for its part cannot generate moral relativism for it treats every context-based, linguistically encoded moral semantics *as the content of thought* on the topic. That's why, it creates moral perspective essentialism, and the resulting genocide.

4. Three Histories, Two Possibilities

The central argument of this book contains the conditional:

(1) *If* one is engaged in colonialism, *then* one is interpreting—imposing a perspective as explanation—which violates basic considerations of logic.

In this chapter, I have made a case for this premise insofar as I have explained colonization as a function of LAT, and interpretation as a function of LAT. So the backbone of colonization would ensure that participants are interpreting. I argued that we can see that this is true, in the explicatory sense of truth, for when we deny it, we arrive at the inexplicable scenario where people are entirely free to explore values and contrary options free from constraints of propositional attitudes, while somehow being colonized, which was incongruous. At some point, colonization would interfere with one's exploration of values, but somehow, in denying the premise, we would have to reimagine colonization as not interfering with options. That is a contradiction that we would have to reject on explicatory grounds.

But we also have human history to help make this point. LAT as an interpretive foundation is a feature of colonizing traditions, but not, at the start, of non-colonizing traditions. They are incompatible starting points and LAT only characterizes the colonial starting point. The tradition that becomes a global colonizing tradition acclaims LAT. The one that lacks it altogether, the South Asian tradition, becomes colonized by the West.

4.1. Starting Points

The Western tradition begins with the ancient Greek commitment to LAT in its classical idea of *logos*—words, logic. Logos encodes LAT for *logos* conflates explanation with speech. Call this the *spoken language* version of LAT: propositional content is the meaning we speak in our language.

China's ancient commitment to LAT can be found in Confucius' doctrine of the Rectification of Names, as found in the *Analects* (XIII, 3, 4–7). Accordingly, "If names be not correct, language is not in accordance with the truth of things. If language be not in accordance with the truth of things, affairs cannot be carried on to success" (Legge translation). To use language correctly is for it to be used in accordance with the facts—true thoughts—it expresses. That's a version of LAT. In contrast, Taoists, such as Lao Tzu, criticized LAT for confusing human artifacts such as language with knowledge of the Way, which insofar as it is true is something beyond contrivance. And to this extent, Lao Tzu and Taoists encouraged a receptivity to what is beyond linguistic practice.

How are these two formative views reconciled? In the ingenious formation of Chinese as an *orthographic language*, that is, the written system for various non-mutually intelligible spoken languages, such as Cantonese and Mandarin. The written system then represents a frame for the regulation of spoken languages that are written in Chinese. This permits both the Confucian emphasis with LAT in the national language of Chinese—the written language—and a Taoist gaze to what is beyond spoken linguistic practice. Call this the Orthographic version of LAT. Insofar as this is a form of LAT and we expect LAT to give rise to colonization, the Orthographic version of LAT will also yield this result. However, as it accommodates a certain criticism of the spoken version of LAT, the colonization that emanates from this uniquely Chinese model of thought will have a different character from the colonization that follows from the spoken version of LAT: it will be bound and connected by written Chinese as an ethnocolonial identity.

India in contrast at its very start lacked LAT. One sign of this is the absence of any concern for truth by definition; analyticity (cf. Siderits 1991, 65). But if we assume LAT, then certain claims are true by definition. Nothing could be true merely by definition in LE: tautologies and what look like definitional claims would have to be flushed out in terms of the use of defined items in inquiry. Some traditions made a big deal of meaning being eternal (Śabara on *Mīmāṁsā Sūtra* I.i.12-19). Yet, no one seems to have held the position that linguistic meaning constitutes the content of knowledge, or *jñāna*. Recall that explication itself as a practice gets us to distinguish between the literal meaning of what is said and the disciplinary function of claims, which is LE. Hence, if a tradition is explicatory, then LE models how they thought about thought, as LE protects this distinction. South Asia was an explicatory tradition. Indians, unlike their Western counterparts, were not confused by the diversity of uses of "dharma" in their tradition. They were able to understand their own theory of dharma in contrast to others' which is made possible by explication, and LE. This was captured in their distinction (not unlike Taoism) between conventional truths (like linguistic meaning) and ultimate truth. This allows thinkers to treat every social convention, even about dharma, as true merely by convention, and for everyone to engage in a philosophical disagreement about what is ultimately true about dharma. That's explication and LE. Finally as a non-LAT, LE-based tradition, we should expect that not only does South Asia not give rise to a colonizing tradition, it also begins with prominent rejections of anthropocentrism as LE entails the rejection of anthropocentrism, which we will examine in greater detail in Chapter 5. But explicated, indeed, the South Asian tradition does not begin on an anthropocentric or communitarian note, and is famous for tolerating intellectuals who exist on the margins of human society who gain this role of independent intellectual by abandoning communitarian roles (*śramaṇa*-s).

With respect to LAT, things do change in time and entirely after the end of the Indigenous tradition. After British colonization, South Asians adopt LAT and begin to formulate nationalist languages based on religious identities. And hence, the same language, Hindustani, gets reinvented as a Muslim language of Urdu (written in an Arabic script) and the "Hindu" language "Hindi" (written in the South Asian Devanagari script) (C.R. King 1994). And this serves as the further foundation for Islamic and Hindu nationalism in South Asia.

4.2. Outcomes

The outcomes of the political histories of the three traditions turn out to track with their commitment or lack thereof to LAT.

The *West* has turned out to be the global colonizing tradition. There are several indications. The fact that we can talk about the *lingua franca*, which is now English, is evidence of its wide colonial reach. As well, Secularism₂ is the oldest version of *Western* colonialism as it defines the secular as the *Western* intellectual tradition and anything initially BIPOC as religious, to be limited and removed from public secular space. This is the default model of secularism the world over. To appreciate its ubiquity we need only reflect on how India and China, the state heirs of the Indian and Chinese traditions of philosophy, *buy and accept* Secularism₂ as part of their understanding of their own traditions. They have hence to this extent been colonized by the *West*. This is written into the Indian Constitution as it defines its Indigenous history of moral philosophy—dharma—as religion and further defines the state of India as a country with "no dharma"—dharmanirapekṣa rājya (India; Government of 1950). China too has adopted Secularism₂, which comes along with Marxism, as its official position that Xi Jinping calls "socialism with Chinese characteristics" (2022).

The Chinese tradition based on the written version of LAT that contains within a moderating or internally critical approach to the linguistic version of LAT presents a restrained form of colonialism. Unlike the *West*, China has not taken over lands far and wide. It rather focuses on the territory it considers Chinese. But within that space, non-Chinese linguistic minorities, who don't use the written form of Chinese, experience the outcomes of colonization.

Uyghurs, a Muslim group, of the Xinjiang Uygur Autonomous Region, speak a Turkic language, and they write the Uyghur language in a Perso-Arabic script. Tibetans, a predominantly Buddhist group of the Tibetan Autonomous Region, have their own Indic-derived segmental script. And it turns out that both populations are being subjected to Residential Schools and re-education projects by China (Feng 2022; UN 2023)—and the reports out of the UN with respect to the Uyghurs have been dire (UN 2022). Both groups do not participate in Chinese (written) linguistic identity and that is enough given the Orthographic version of LAT to treat these groups as moral deviants, and to conceptualize the solution of this deviation as forced education in Chinese values, language, and culture.

The Indian tradition is starkly different from the *Western* and Chinese traditions in two ways. First, it never got around to being a colonizing tradition as we find in the *West*, or in China. Historically, South Asia was a place of philosophical diversity structured by explication and so in ancient times there was no practice of conflating political power and outlook that is essential to colonization. So whereas Socrates is killed for raising questions about how to raise kids and what values (gods) we should worship, that charge would have made no sense in classical South Asia, where that was the philosophical question. Things changed in time as India slowly veered to a *Westernized* existence as *Western Colonizers* started trickling in by the end of the first millennia. But the India of colonization is not Indigenous to India and requires the influence of colonial intruders to understand.

Secondly, South Asian moral philosophy is so profoundly different from the LAT-based focus on anthropocentrism and communitarianism, which conceives of the problem of social coordination among humans in a specific community as the basic moral challenge (we shall examining this further in Chapters 5 and 7). As an LE tradition, moral problems for South Asians were (precolonially) the challenges of agential freedom in a universe of agents, where everyone has to contend with coercion or limits to agency. Moral philosophy in ancient South Asia is cosmic, not communal.

4.3. Discussion: Jews and LAT

Jews are a very important group to keep track of when thinking about these three ancient (*Western*, Indian, and Chinese) traditions. They are among the oldest surviving identity groups that both predates the *West* and grew in the shadow of its colonization. In the *West* too, as noted, they appeared to resist LAT by allowing for nonrelated linguistic identities. But, moreover, Jews appear in all three of these traditions. The Jewish experience, this overview shows, has much more to do with LAT than being Jewish.

The considerations explored in the comparison of the three traditions show why anti-Semitism couldn't get off the ground in China or India—and it has to do with LAT. In China, so long as Jews use their local language and write it with the Orthographic Chinese, they are fulfilling the expectations of Chinese nationalism. Everyone has some spoken language affiliation that is not the same as the Orthographic language: Jews would have two (Hebrew also). So it came to pass that Jews were successful by Chinese standards in China though eventually through their integration into Chinese culture their distinctive identity dissipated (Leslie 2000). And this generalized: China had an important tradition of cosmopolitanism made possible by the same flexibility of the written Chinese identity (Xiang 2023). Recently in a more *Westernized* Chinese context, there is a new and previously unobserved anti-Semitism emerging through a paradoxical Philosemitism, which combines a valuation of Jews along with anti-Semitic tropes (Ainslie 2021).

In general, India was a place of refuge for groups fleeing persecution elsewhere, and hence received Zoroastrians and Christians, for instance, without incident. It is widely known that Jews who were in India—the

Bene Israel—for almost 2000 years, did not experience anti-Semitism (Weil 2023; Indian Jewish "return" to Israel in contrast was characterized by racial discrimination, see Kuikman 2014). In the LE-based tradition of India, there was no way to problematize Jews by way of an affiliation with Hebrew as outsiders, because LE does not entail or support communitarian identity that could be used as a wedge to problematize Jews as outsiders.

Given the *West's* specific commitment to the *spoken language version* of LAT, Jews appear problematic in ways that other minorities will not in the European *West*. Many other minorities will appear as people to be standardized by the colonizing linguistic expectations: Jews appear resistant to this standardization as they will adopt the spoken, local, linguistic expectations of where they live while maintaining an ancestral linguistic affiliation to Hebrew. The latter will on the basis of spoken LAT be seen as grounds for a dual loyalty, an anti-Jewish trope. And whereas other *Westerners* might have theoretical affiliations of Latin or Greek (both central to the *West*) in addition to their native language, Hebrew is non-*Western* and was not part of the infrastructure of colonial expectations in Europe centered on the *West*. Finns, Estonians, and Hungarians, speakers of Uralic languages (not Indo-European, not related to Greek and Latin) in *Westernized* Europe, are colonially standardized by Christianization, which renders Greek and Latin as ancestral identity languages for Christian speakers of Uralic languages as these are classical languages of Christianity, and the *West*. But the Sámi, also speakers of a Uralic language, who for much of their history were not Christianized, were on the receiving end of colonial oppression because of this linguistic divergence from the *Western* identity norm. Jews with a Hebrew ancestral identity are in a *Western* world beyond the pale everywhere they existed. As a diasporic group, this discrimination would be repeated in all *Western* contexts. Europe, taken over by the *West*, as a spoken language LAT tradition problematizes Jews, who are in contrast unproblematized in the LE Indian traditions, and, before its *Westernization*, unproblematized in the Chinese Orthographic LAT tradition. Insofar as Jews had a different experience in the Islamic Middle East as People of the Book, Islamic intellectual life being within the *Western* (spoken LAT) tradition (Islamic thinkers were part and parcel of *Western* medieval philosophy discourse), that would have to do with linguistic similarities of Arabic and Hebrew and the willingness of Arabic-speaking Muslim rulers to view Jews as linguistically related to them—which was not a constant in that history. Superficially all of this looks like it's about religion. Really it's about the genocidal implications of moral semantics and linguistic identity under LAT. We know this because if we keep all these elements the same, but swap out (the spoken version of) LAT for LE, we would not be able to reconstruct anti-Jewish (or anti-Sámi) racism in these same contexts. There would be no grounds for the moral perspective essentialism that problematizes them.

Tracking this history is important for it shows the ways in which the problems that persecuted groups experience are a result of LAT. But also attempts by some of their descendants to rectify their experience of oppression by relying upon ethnolinguistic identity—furnished by LAT—(such as Zionism, or the Hindu Right), is not a continuation of a precolonial tradition but a continuation of the colonizing tradition. It is a way to fail to honor our colonized ancestors by siding with their tormentors. If all of us are not aware that the origin of the colonial abuse we experience is because of LAT and interpretation, it's very easy to take on both LAT and interpretation as though it furnishes a solution. And then, the persecuted become the perpetrators.

4.4. Indigeneity versus Nativism

Indigeneity as a concept was coined in contradistinction to colonization. It functions in some cases as a legal designation, and as for law is concerned, we would have to look at specific jurisdictions to fill out the details of specific conceptions of the Indigenous (cf. Steeves 2018). But our concern with Indigeneity is moral and political. We are pursuing an analysis of the contrast between colonialism and its contrary that permits moral philosophy. Indigeneity naturally occupies the space of the opposite of colonialism. But there are at least two ways we could cash out Indigeneity.

If colonization is generated by LAT resulting in anthropocentrism and communitarianism, the Indigenous rejects its anthropocentrism and communitarianism and thereby LAT. The Indigenous in contrast is explicated as organizing around LE that does not conflate cultural representations with thought. Rejecting LAT and embracing LE allows the Indigenous to have a wider ecological understanding of social relationships, which in many cases includes acknowledging nonhuman animals and the Earth as persons that we have obligations toward. In adopting LE, Indigenous people can allow in unproblematic ways that all agents of diverse species and biological varieties think as their semantic behavior is the content of a proposition—defined by a disciplinary purpose. As observed in a metanalysis of "120 academic publications and the reported experiences of 80 Indigenous-led organizations across 35 countries to identify de-colonized ways of reorienting terrestrial ecosystem valuations" a key distinguishing factor of Indigenous approaches to ecology involves "cultivating moral relationships and responsibilities between human and more-than-human worlds" (Urzedo and Robinson

2023, 5). It is worth noting that this way of framing the Indigenous in terms of a connection between the human and more-than-human world bears the impact of colonialism that separates the two. The South Asian tradition is radically Indigenous as it does not begin with a premise of a human and nonhuman world that requires relating: humans are understood to be a kind of living being—*jīva*—in a universe of radical agential diversity. The moral considerations that scope over the cosmos (*Ṛta*, then dharma) are not specific to human communities but underwrite normative interaction as such. Many of the Indigenous peoples of North and South America, Australia, Africa, and Europe are Indigenous insofar as they share their appreciation of their agency as something that situates them not, primarily, in a human community, but in a universe of agents of diverse species and perspectives. Accordingly the key feature of Indigeneity is the rejection or abandonment of the idea that there is a shared (human and communal) perspective that constitutes knowledge and understanding. The *Western* tradition is not Indigenous given its commitment to LAT and its consequent anthropocentrism and communitarianism. The Chinese tradition has Indigenous expressions in Taoism that criticize both communitarian and anthropocentric approaches to normativity and virtue, but certainly Confucius begins a decidedly non-Indigenous, LAT-based program resulting in Chinese expressions of colonialism.

The alternate approach to the contrast between the Colonizer and the Indigenous is interpretive, and is based on widely held beliefs that the Indigenous are the (a) incumbent population—the native—which (b) the Colonizer oppresses (Alfred and Corntassel 2005). This is the natural way to think about Indigeneity if we prioritize *settler colonialism* in our modeling of colonialism. Settler colonialism is the project motivated to replace native populations to wrest control over their land or resources. Patrick Wolfe, a pioneering scholar of settler colonialism, also notes that the settler is typically motivated to leave their own homeland to escape some problem, often persecution, and that the project of settler colonialism is seen as the solution (Wolfe 2006). This is the form of colonization that is salient in North and South America, Australia, New Zealand, and Israel (cf. Pappe 2007). I would add to Wolfe's analysis that the goal of settler colonialism is not to merely eliminate the native: it is to replace the native. It is hence better known as *eliminative* or *replacement colonialism*: by erasing the native, the replacement Colonizer claims to be native to the land themselves. Thinking about Indigeneity in terms of nativity is straight out of the Colonizer's playbook.

Aside from being irrational, there are two further problems with the interpretive approach to defining the Indigenous.

First, it makes it seem as though incumbent populations cannot engage in colonization as an imposition of perspective. The French were incumbents in New France when the British wrested colonial control. The French in this case were colonized by the British (such as the Acadians of Nova Scotia), but the French were Colonizers themselves, and some, such as the Acadians, expelled. Relatedly, conflating the incumbent with the Indigenous leads to treating immigrants and migrants as Colonizers. Immigrants and migrants often wish to be given a chance to fit in to their adopted home, which is the opposite of the Colonizer's project. In contrast, some of the most genocidal regimes such as Nazi Germany are native to their locale and it was in deference to that claim of nativity that they carried out their genocide. They used their LAT-inspired Indo-European "Germanic" incumbent identity— along with the obnoxious colonial appropriation of Sanskrit terms like "Aryan" and "Swastika"—*they couldn't even frame their own racist narrative without stealing from BIPOC*—to generate genocidal intentions and actions against Jews, Roma, LGBTQ, disabled people, and many other groups. If LAT generates colonization, Nazi Germany is a straightforward example of colonization, which always begins at home first. As Aimé Césaire pointed out in 1955 in his *Discourse on Colonialism*, Europeans categorize the Nazi program as non-colonial and thereby an event of a much more weighty importance than how Europeans have treated BIPOC (which they regarded as colonial), because it was a crime by White people against White people (Césaire 2000, 36–7).

Moreover, if mere geographic nativity is incompatible with a native population being Colonizers, then colonialism is xenophobically reimagined as the foreigner in our midst, in contrast to the native. Worse, this move to treat nativity as a defeating condition of colonization obscures what is bad about colonialism, as though it is merely a matter of what isn't native.

Commentators have pointed out, what the Nazis did in Europe, though they were native to Europe, was simply what Europeans, and Germans, had done to BIPOC people elsewhere: namely, genocide, and the acquisition of the wealth of the colonized (Erichsen and Olusoga 2010). Having a clearer view to genocidal actions of European powers in Africa sets the Nazi program within a longer history of European genocidal activity, which renders the Holocaust not the first, nor the last European genocide, and not one with the most victims (cf. Hochschild 2019)—and of course, if we include the European genocide in the Americas (resulting in the death of around 100 million Indigenous people), then the Holocaust (with around six million Jews killed plus the millions of other non-Jews killed by the Nazis) is a relatively small genocide. To deny that the Nazis were Colonizers because they were primarily focused on their native Europe makes the domesticity of their victims a defeater of their colonial criminality. As an analogy, we might consider the case of sexual assault. In Canada, prior to Bill C-127 was made law in 1983, like many jurisdictions, husbands could not be guilty of raping their wives. Why? It was as though the mere domesticity of the victim made the crime impossible. This is false for a necessary and sufficient account of what makes sexual assault wrong in standard cases (unwanted sexual contact) says nothing about the relationship between victim and aggressor. Similarly, we can provide a necessary and sufficient account of colonialism (an imposition of a perspective that victims have to contend with) that would apply to Nazi oppression in Germany against Germans.

The second problem with conflating incumbency with Indigeneity is that it identifies the Indigenous in terms of its being on the receiving end of colonization, as opposed to understanding it autonomously. That means that the harms inflicted on the colonized by the Colonizer are then treated as essential to the identity of the colonized. This is perverse. This is like defining women in terms of the misogyny they are on the receiving end of. This has the effect of normalizing oppression as part of the identity of the oppressed. We will examine this phenomenon in subsequent chapters, especially Chapters 3, 5, and 6. But if Indigenous cultures are not anthropocentric or communitarian, and they thereby do not understand their place in the world in terms of property rights of land but relationship to the Earth (which is often said to own Indigenous people, and not the other way around), who is treated as an agent, within a wider universe of agents, Indigeneity as defined by oppression will not define these Indigenous moral values as important to Indigenous identity. It will rather look to how the Indigenous are treated by the colonizing encounter to elucidate Indigenous identity. In the case of settler colonization, the Indigenous is treated as lacking property rights in land, and having a language and culture that need to be replaced. And this leads to defining the Indigenous in terms of their property rights in their land, and the anthropocentric and communitarian value of their language and culture. No doubt, Indigenous peoples deserve to be made whole by returning what was deprived of them by colonization, including their language, culture, and relationship to the land. But that's a different matter from defining the Indigenous in terms of what was taken from them. Defining the Indigenous by what was deprived to them by colonization is to employ the LAT-based, Colonizer's anthropocentrism and communitarianism responsible for the harm inflicted on the Indigenous as essential to Indigenous identity. This is an explanation of how colonization succeeds, not how to understand those impacted by colonization.

This generalizes to the problem of trauma-based identity. Before someone's bike they used to get to work was stolen, they spent no time defining themselves in terms of their bike: it was just a means to an end. After it is stolen and they then have to spend a lot of time searching for the stolen bike or replacing it with funds they do not have, their life has been defined by the crime they suffered. In that state, one might come to understand oneself in terms of one's attachment to one's bike, its immense importance to earning a living, and the need one has to get it back, but that would be an identity created by the theft, not something that our victim would have landed on in the absence of the theft.

The explicatory approach to the Indigenous and the Colonizer in contrast accounts for these two paradigms independently as bound up with different models of thought. The Indigenous is not defined by the abuse they suffer or by cultural tropes that freeze them in a mythical past, but rather the philosophical sophistication they have to offer a world of de-colonization. That is bound up with LE: it explains the logic of an Indigenous existence. The Colonizer's LAT-based paradigm explains why they engage in their genocidal exercises and why they cannot comprehend moral disagreement.

This distinction between the Indigenous and the Colonial explains why (entails that) Indigenous people, who maintain their Indigeneity—their connection to their Indigenous tradition—do not dream of revenge or counter colonization as a response to colonization. For them justice is a return to the Indigenous and the devaluation of the Colonial. That means that persons formerly part of a colonial project are welcome to participate in an Indigenous world as people who have to learn to live de-colonially. That would be good for everyone. Colonizers driven by moral perspective essentialism are obsessed with revenge as part of the requirement to rid the world of what does not respect the morally essential, on their view.

These considerations provide some clarity to questions about who is Indigenous to Palestine, which involves moving away from incumbency as the criterion of Indigeneity. Perhaps the Jews were Indigenous in Palestine (ancient Judaism apparently opting for a non-anthropocentric and non-communitarian modeling of ethics in the *Book of Genesis*, 1.29-30, with a God prescribed vegan diet for all creatures). In contrast, there is that strange matter of God telling Jews to occupy the land of the Canaanites (which became Israel), and the biblical depiction of the Canaanites in the *Book of Joshua* as peoples to be resisted and destroyed (Doak 2020 ch. 2), which is genocidal. If this is history, Jewish history apparently begins with Jews engaging in eliminative colonialism: that would have created nativity but not Indigeneity. Jumping up to the present, we can know that Zionism is not Indigenous anywhere, much less to Palestine, as it is a LAT-based, interpretive, orientation. The Zionist claims of Jewish incumbency in

Palestine do not generate Indigeneity. Zionist claims of nativity are rather of a piece with the settler colonial strategy of eliminating the native.

These considerations also suggest that Israelis could *choose* to be Indigenous to Palestine by choosing to be de-colonial. That would involve an insight that the LAT-based, interpretive violence that Jews and others experienced at the hands of the Nazis is replicated in a LAT-based Hebrew identity state. An Indigenous state in Palestine/Israel would eschew LAT, adopt LE, and allow for a multi-lingual, multi-ethnic, and non-anthropocentric and non-communitarian society. Then, "from the river to the sea, Palestine will be free," will not be perceived as a threat, but part of the de-colonial LE-based Indigenous life shared by people in that region. A two-state solution (assuming that there is any Palestine left given Israel's illegal encroachment) in contrast would be motivated by the ethnolinguistic differences of Israelis and Palestinians, and as it would be based on LAT, it would solve no problems. The idea that Jews need a homeland (and not simply to be at home wherever they live in the absence of colonization) is of a piece with LAT. If we adopt LE, we could not motivate Zionism or any form of nationalism.

5. Conclusion

The conclusion of the main argument of this book is that colonialism and moral philosophy are incompatible exercises. And the coda argument shows that we have a rational obligation to overturn colonization. In this chapter I examine how interpretation, the explanatory force of colonization, is cemented in LAT and creates a colonial history of the West and psychological fragility that depicts outside groups as threats to one's LAT-based moral order, and thereby targets of a genocidal intention. Actual cases of genocide follow through with this *de re* intention. *De dicto* intentions, or intentions in terms of beliefs that one is choosing to or is engaging in a prohibited action, are irrelevant. LE, the explicatory model of thought, accounts for the Indigenous, which consists in the free exploration of moral-philosophical controversy. There are other important differences. LAT encourages an anthropocentric and communitarian approach to values, because language is anthropocentric and communitarian, while LE creates a cosmological approach to thinking and values, where any thing responsible for semantic behavior that could be part of the extension of a thought, defined by an *external* disciplinary purpose, is a person. I explored how these are incompatible, because they involve mutually exclusive approaches to explanation but also thought and value. Colonizers attempt to deal with oppression, if they care to pretend to be anticolonial, by appeal to a common concern for humanity, and frame oppression as an exercise of dehumanization. But this fails to acknowledge that the origin of colonial oppression is the anthropocentrism of LAT. The West, as the dominant colonizing tradition, unique for acclaiming LAT, embodies all of the problems of LAT. As we continue, when we have repeated occasion to criticize the West for engaging in a narcissistic interpretation of everything on the basis of its tradition, we are criticizing LAT. And when we are criticizing LAT, we are criticizing interpretation. The irrationality of LAT is interpretation. The anthropocentric and communitarian preoccupation of LAT provides a veneer for the skeleton of irrationality. Since we have a rational obligation to overcome and put an end to colonization, these considerations show we have a rational obligation to adopt LE and to learn to be Indigenous.

3

Religion

Two Millennia of the White Supremacist Erasure of Moral Philosophy

The Invention of World Religions: Or, How European Universalism Was Preserved in the Language of Pluralism

T. Masuzawa

1. Introduction

It is quite ordinary—*and irrational*—to believe in the innocence of the coincidence that there is something as secular philosophy, which accidentally is the philosophy of White people (starting with the Pre-Socratics, followed by Plato, Aristotle, and their intellectual descendants), and then there is religion, which accidentally, invariably, has an extra-Western origin. Line up world religions and the glaring racial divide is obvious for the only people who seem to have no self-sourced world religion, and need to import it from outside, are European folks. This mirrors our settled way of talking about color. The only people who are treated as without color are White people, and everyone else is colored. World religions are from outside of the European center of the West—Judaism, Christianity, Islam, Zoroastrianism, Buddhism, Jainism, Hinduism, Sikhism, Shinto, Taoism, Confucianism, for example. And what might have been European religion, say the gods and their escapades, as we learn from Homer, gets converted into the topic of Classics. And with the colonial spread of the West out from its starting point of ancient Greece, various Indigenous European practices get wiped out and replaced by Christianity or Islam—with few surviving Indigenous European traditions left, such as the Sámi. This is the same bifurcation into traditions that are acknowledged as having a robust history of moral philosophy—the West—and everything else, which is instead religious or spiritual.

If we explicate, we see that no definition of religion in terms of content or subject matter can adequately explain what religion is. The problem is that for any specification of the necessary and sufficient conditions of religion, we can find uncontroversial counterexamples. A common belief about the religious is that it involves a belief in a personal God and an afterlife. Plato affirms both, but he is not a religious figure. Some prominent examples of what get called religions or religious commitments from South Asia have no commitment to an afterlife and see both a personal God or a sense of a self as something that requires deconstruction or deflation (e.g., Śaṅkara's Advaita Vedānta, or classical Buddhism). Then, there are unusual examples that fall within Hinduism, such as Lokāyata or Cārvāka, that affirms that all existence is material, and that there is no life after death. Similarly, the ancient South Asian philosophy of Sāṅkhya treats reality as an evolution of nature with intellect and mind as emergent properties, with no God. It is one of the most orthodox philosophical doctrines of Hinduism. Said by a White person, it would count as secular materialism. Said by Īśvarakṛṣṇa 2000 years ago in Sanskrit, it's Orthodox Hinduism.

Then, there are derivative ideas about religion that give rise to the idea of doing something *religiously.* Accordingly, religiosity is about a commitment to a practice that one does not deviate from. Jainism is the obvious counterexample. According to classical Jainism, we are all individuals defined by an inherent virtue, which is benign and noninterfering, and hence ideal choice involves *not doing anything.* This results in *sallekhanā*, a fast to death, which is different from suicide, on their account, as suicide is something one does, whereas *sallekhanā* is not doing anything (cf. Soni 2017).

Victoria Harrison (2006), who makes a classic case for no definition of religion being adequate, settles on a Wittgensteinian *family resemblance* explanation. Accordingly, while there is no essence to the religious, the religious forms a continuum of similarity. The problem with this account is that it does not explain why Hinduism seems more similar to Christianity than it does to the entire history of Western philosophy—when "Hinduism" was a word the British gave to the entire history of Indigenous South Asian philosophy. If family resemblances rule the day, the Western tradition of philosophy ought to be a religion too (we could perhaps call it Westernism) owing to its similarity to Hinduism. But that is not how religions are parsed. Nor does it help us to run with the claim that Westernism is a religion too: for then, we have lost a grip on the distinction between the religious and the nonreligious, and we have *hidden* the politics that creates that distinction. For what doesn't get solved by this rebranding of the West as a religion is any historical appreciation of how the West has managed to sit outside of the religious for thousands of years.

The explanation for why religion is not susceptible to an essential definition is that it is an artifact of interpreting on the basis of the West—what gets called religion has nothing to do with its content but with its explanatory subservience to the West. Anything specifiable in terms of some necessary and sufficient condition can be at once religious and nonreligious depending upon its origins. Said by an Indigenous South Asian, the idea that we ought to reduce suffering is the religion, Buddhism. Said by Bentham, it's a form of Utilitarianism. The idea that we ought to do duty for duty's sake is Deontology when said by Kant. Said by Kṛṣṇa in the *Bhagavad Gītā*, it is Hinduism.

This is what I call Secularism$_2$. Accordingly, the secular is Western and anything BIPOC that is subjected to Western colonization is the religious or spiritual. It is the 2,000-year-old global institutionalization of White Supremacy. It cements interpreting on the basis of the West as part of knowledge of the world. Hence, the very formation of religion is irrational, and oppressive. It serves to render Indigenous moral philosophy *inarticulable*. The spread of the idea of religion from the West is the spread of LAT on the basis of the West.

Religion is metaethically significant as it impacts our capacity to engage in moral philosophy via a host of assumptions and commitments. For religion's entire political purpose is to normalize the West's colonialism—White Supremacy—and to treat its anthropocentrism and communitarianism, defined by Western ethnic concerns, derived from its acclaim of LAT, as the default platform for thinking about THE RIGHT OR THE GOOD for everyone. This is created by interpreting everything on the basis of the West. This interpretive activity creates the idea that there are ethical considerations of *this* world (defined by the West) and everything else that is politically disallowed by Western colonization is for some aspirational next world that is the topic of religion. Moral philosophy, the full topic, is redefined as part gobbledygook (this is the religion and spirituality part), which cannot be articulated given the LAT-based constraints of the West. One outcome is the entirely political creation of "religious experience." What religious people experience in this case is a result of their own activity, and their moral and political choice, but via the oppression of the West, which disallows thinking about the same choices as a contribution to how we live. Pushed out of the realm of the articulable, which according to LAT is the anthropocentric and the communitarian, it lives in a fake inarticulability (mysticism, faith), and a real emotionality, constructed by oppression. What is forbidden is what is not consistent with oppression, which is the de-colonial. The de-colonial involves not only a contrast between the colonial and the Indigenous, between interpretation and explication, but a critique of oppression and a correlative greenlighting of freedom. So instead of de-colonization, people who buy the idea of religion talk about soteriology. Instead of moral philosophical reasoning, they talk of faith.

I contrast Secularism$_2$ with Secularism$_1$: free open philosophical dissent—an approach to secularism in keeping with its original definition as "free thinking" (Holyoake 1896). In Secularism$_1$, no doctrine or agreement has to serve as the foundation of social interaction. Secularism$_1$ is Indigenously South Asian, and what the British in time called "Hinduism." In Secularism$_1$, there is no way to identify a position as religious: all options are explicated in terms of their contribution to the debate—and the central debate was dharma, moral philosophy. To identify something as counting as religion requires not only interpretation but the *West*, which functions as the interpretive platform that gives itself the freedom and authority to judge every other tradition in terms of their conformity to or deviation from the *West*. Western "intellectuals" build their careers on the basis of assuming Secularism$_2$. Religion's political purpose is to erase moral philosophy as a de-colonial explicatory exercise and redefine ethics as the ethnography of White people. Religious Studies is then the ethnography of BIPOC traditions.

In the next section, I will explicate the history of the idea of religion. In the third section, I examine what learning about Hinduism has to teach us about religion. It shows us that the concept of religion is entirely vacuous, and it would not exist but for White Supremacy.

These considerations entail that conventional philosophy of religion, concerned with questions of faith, God, and the afterlife, and conventional Religious Studies that studies the social practices of religified peoples, is the continued manufacturing of a mythology of BIPOC intellectual traditions created by White Supremacy. In the fourth section, I consider what the philosophy of race can teach us about religion. In the fifth section, I summarize the argument of the chapter.

2. Secularism$_2$

While it is certainly possible to proliferate categories of colonialism (Shoemaker 2015), if colonization is distinct from imperialism, then there are two main versions. These two versions correspond to the two existential options colonization gives to the colonized: perish or conform. *Eliminative* or *replacement colonization* (sometimes called *settler colonialism*) corresponds to the former. This is genocidal. *Exploitative colonization* corresponds to the latter. Why would exploitative colonialism seem like a good idea when the first impulse of colonization propelled by LAT is moral perspective essentialism and a consequential genocidal intent? Two reasons. First, it may not be possible for those with colonial ambitions to completely wipe out the populations they seek to colonize because there are too many of them. Secondly, it is advantageous for Colonizers to turn a large population of colonized individuals into a source of revenue, cheap labor or surplus wealth. That requires a way of making the colonized feel like they are included—and not marked for extermination—in the Colonizer's plans.

A classic example of exploitative colonialism is the case of British rule in India. The British devised and implemented a plan where the British would buy goods from Indians with tax revenue collected from Indians. Further, if anyone wanted to buy Indian goods, they had to buy them directly from the British in London. According to the Marxian economist Usta Patnaik, with this scheme the British, between 1765 and 1938, managed to drain India of $45 trillion (Patnaik 2017). Just to be clear, the British paid for Indian goods with money taken from Indians, and then sold those goods at a complete profit. At no point did they bear the cost of producing those items: Indians were made to pay the British to steal from them. This not only undermines the Marxist idea that capitalist oppression occurs when workers do not own the means of production (Indians were not wage laborers in this case and the British were not the capitalist who owned the factory who owned the products of labor), but it also shows the benefits that Colonizers can gain from exploitation.

Religion is the *West's* oldest foray into exploitative colonialism. It normalizes BIPOC traditions within *Western* colonization, while permitting those in charge to benefit from this subordination. It is the Colonizer's Noble Lie. Plato identifies the Noble Lie in the *Republic* (that people in an unequal society must be told that their inequality was ordained by a creator God as a way of accommodating everyone's value) so that people would be willing to participate in their own stratification (414b–415d). Religion is the *West's* Noble Lie that convinces colonized people to participate in their own colonization, as though their tradition is valued and appreciated despite its subordination in White Supremacy.

2.1. A Brief History of Three Religions of the West

All world religions are in an important sense non-*Western* with roots outside of the *Western* intellectual tradition. However, some religions acquired their identity as a religion owing to their proximity to historical *Western* power. Hence, a large part of their history is not easy to disentangle from the *Western* tradition. This applies to Judaism, and especially Christianity and Islam. The latter two have virtually no history apart from the West. In these cases, much of what counts as Jewish, Christian, and Islamic philosophy is actually an engagement in Western philosophy.

Like race, religion too has a history, but it goes back almost to the very inception of Western colonization. It was the Romans who came up with the idea of *religio,* where it was contrasted with *superstitione.* We of course get our words "religion" and "superstition" from this distinction. *Religio* was used to mark out a tradition that was acknowledged (not slated for extermination) within the Roman Empire. Jews were acknowledged as having *religio* for instance but early Christians were denied this recognition and were instead persecuted.[1]

Religio or religion is an ancient tool or category that allows for the limited retention and protection of colonized people, while also subjecting them to the colonial rule of the Colonizer. For to acknowledge Jews, for instance, as having *religio* in the Roman Empire is to acknowledge that they are a people distinguished by their own tradition, as recognized by the rulers, but, they do not get to choose the moral and political values that mediate their interaction with the Colonizer: those values are determined by the Colonizer. They are tolerated and recognized insofar as they have something to contribute to the Colonizer's project. Within the context of colonization, this is as close to being protected as one gets. At the start of the institution of religion hence is the interpretation of the colonized tradition in terms of beliefs of the Colonizer. And then their tradition is no longer appreciated as contributing to moral and political debates of the day. Rather it is redefined as not relevant to the question of how people are supposed to get along because those questions are determined by the Colonizer. Religion creates the illusion of imperialism for in the case of imperialism we are allowed to contemplate various options though only one is permitted. Religion seems to introduce the same imperial possibility of being aware of differing religious options though one religion is typically strongly encouraged within specific social contexts. But by defining contrary moral and political options out of scope by calling them religions, that leaves only one moral and political option as what can be contemplated in this colonial space, and that is the option of the Colonizer. Taking religion seriously ensures that only the Colonizer's option is the one we can live by.

Christianity in contrast was seen from the start as a threat to Roman establishment. Indeed, Jesus was tortured to death by the Romans. And hence acknowledging this group as having a *religio* within the confines of

---

[1]   I have my York colleague, Benjamin Kelly, clarifying history of *religio* in Rome. For further sources, see Beard, North, and Price (1998), and Gordon (2008).

the Roman Empire is to apparently legitimize a tradition that has grievances against Roman colonial rule. Such grievances constitute a moral and political criticism of Roman colonization. If we were to restrict our focus to the Gospels that report Jesus's deeds and sayings, his moral philosophy stressed compassion for the oppressed and disadvantaged, gentleness in our interactions with each other, and a criticism of power and establishment that takes the place of personal, transformative moral work of approximating God's expectations. So the crucifixion would on this basis be an evil action, as would colonial oppression on the whole. They exemplify both the violence and condemning judgment that Jesus warned against. But if the Christian population were to be normalized within the empire their tradition would have to not be critical of Roman colonialism. And so the granting of a religious identity to Christians would have to wait for certain modifications, like Paul's gloss in a book aptly called *Romans* (3:9-18). Accordingly: everyone (Jews and Gentiles) is at fault. Hence, Romans in their colonial ways cannot be singled out as especially evil because nobody is perfect. The second addition (once again, from Paul, *Romans* 3: 21-26) is the formulation of a Christian doctrine of Atonement, which casts Jesus's crucifixion as an act of God (not Roman colonialism). With these two additions in *Romans*, Christian doctrine cannot form the foundations for criticizing Roman colonization, because nobody is perfect, and it was God's idea. When Constantine comes to fully recognize Christianity as a religion, but in time the *official religion*, this feature of Christian doctrine survives (for an account of the literature on Constantine's conversion and institutionalization of Christianity, see Lenski 2014). Very few Christians seem to appreciate the extent to which what they consider their religion was most completely created within colonization by Colonizers for the purpose of normalizing colonization (the exception seems to be few progressive Christians, such as @revdrcalebjlines on Instagram).

By the time Muhammad shares his new religion of Islam, ideas of religion, as a political practice that normalizes colonialism and the idea of an official religion tied to state power, were not new. Indeed, it was Constantine's model of a political order based on an official religion that serves as a template for Muhammad. So when Muhammad teaches the new religion of Islam and draws from the Jewish and Christian religions, he is drawing from them *as* religions, which is a creature of Secularism$_2$. We also find Secularism$_2$ in the Islamic distinction between philosophy, which is Western, going back to Plato and Aristotle, and religion, which builds on the extra-Western traditions of Judaism and Christianity. We find it in the idea of the *ummah*—or community of (human) Muslim believers. In this notion, the anthropocentrism and communitarianism of the Western tradition is normalized as basic in Islam, which is the function of religion in Secularism$_2$. This is grounded on the uptake of Islamic thinkers of the idea of *logos,* or LAT, from the West. The Arabic verb *nataqa* means *to speak* or *utter, mantiq* is the word for logic, and *natiq* is often the word used for RATIONAL. For instance, in Arabic discussions of Plato's tripartite division of the soul, the rational soul is often referred to as *al-nafs al-nāṭiqah* (thanks to my former York colleague M.A. Khalidi for this and for more on Islamic philosophy, see Khalidi 2005).

As F.M. Donner notes in *The Early Islamic Conquests,* "Muhammad's career was remarkable not only for his religious teachings, but also for his highly successful pursuit of political power" (Donner 2014, 62). The practice of conquest Muhammad initiates culminates in the conquests of South Asia. David Cook notes that while Muhammad and his followers were initially persecuted for their preaching of Islam, Muhammad in turn waged several military campaigns that culminated in turning the tables against the original oppressors and much more. These Islamic conquests, "wrested control of an enormous territory from Christian and Zoroastrian religious domination and resulted in a linguistic shift in the entire region from Aramaic (and its dialects) and Greek to Arabic." Cook continues to note that the apt comparison is Alexander the Great, "whose victories over the Persian Achaemenid Empire (330 BCE) similarly heralded long-term . . . linguistic shifts (the spread of Hellenistic culture and the Greek language) in the territories he conquered at lightning speed" (Cook 2015, 12). These shifts speak to the spread of a spoken version of LAT, as though what language we speak is important as opposed to how we use it (as entailed by LE). Just as in the case of anti-Jewish racism that we examined in the last chapter where superficially the issue seems to be about religious differences, superficially the spread of Islam looks as though it is about the spread of a religion. But religion is itself a manifestation of interpreting on the basis of the West, which is underwritten by the spoken version of LAT. The spread of Islam is the spread of the West.

The prophet Muhammad within his lifetime (571–632 CE) had consolidated power in the Saudi Arabian peninsula. By the first Rashidun Caliphate (632–61 CE), the empire grew both north and west into Africa. By the second Umayyad Caliphate (661–750 CE) it had pushed further east into Afghanistan, modern day Pakistan and modern day India. These areas were already home to Buddhist and various other Indigenous philosophical practices, such as Zoroastrianism in ancient Persia. These moral philosophical practices were not merely incumbent or· native—they were Indigenous in the full sense of conceiving moral action within a universe of agents with standing beyond the narrow confines of human community delimited by shared beliefs. By 1000 CE, Islamic conquests into modern-day India became periodic and resulted in the establishment of the Delhi Sultanate (1206–1526 CE).

2.2. The *Religification* of South Asia

In exactly the way anti-racist activists in the United States criticize Western colonialism in the Americas but are not thereby promoting a racist view of White people, we should be able to criticize the colonial spread of Islam without being accused or confused with Islamophobia. Criticizing our ancestors entails no criticism of us for we are always free to make different choices from them. So it would be wrong to construe this criticism of the spread of Islam as entailing anything about Muslims. Yet, Western thinkers and modern academics are loath to adopt a critical approach to this colonizing event, in part because their leading intellectuals—and contemporaries committed to Secularism$_2$—were and are deeply sympathetic with the colonial spread of Islam. That is because the colonial spread of Islam is the spread of Secularism$_2$, the White Supremacy that legitimizes the Study of Religion and the erasure of Indigenous resistance to colonialism—as though religion is a thing and not a creation of colonialism. It shows up in the finger-wagging expectation freely articulated by Liberals and Marxists that South Asians should accept religious pluralism, appreciating that their Hinduism (the entire Indigenous practice of Secularism$_1$) is just a religion, like Islam, which should exist within a wider world of Secularism$_2$. They do not say the quiet part out loud, that this expectation is about the subordination of BIPOC Secularism$_1$ to White Supremacy. But Karl Marx and the leading Liberal theorist, John Stuart Mill, pretty much do.

Marx articulates one prominent sympathetic account of the efforts of Western colonization that is influential, at least among Marxists. Marx theorizes India as a place "predestined" to be conquered, having no history at all aside from the history of being conquered. And hence the question is not "whether the English had a right to conquer India, but whether we are to prefer India conquered by the Turk, by the Persian, by the Russian, to India conquered by the Briton." He thought that it was best that the British colonized South Asia as they were the first "superior" people to try to take over India (Marx 1965). On Marx's view, Islamic colonization (conquest by the Turk and Persian—the "Mahommedan" as he puts it) of India was not really a new event: it was just more of the same. Before Islamic rule, there was Hindu rule. It is this story about religion that informs Marx's famous claim in his incomplete *A Contribution to the Critique of Hegel's Philosophy*, not that religion is an oppressive construction of Western colonialism designed to normalize White Supremacy, but that *it is the opium of the people*: "Religion is only the illusory Sun which revolves around man as long as he does not revolve around himself" (Marx 2009). Marx gets this radically wrong. Religion is not what happens when humans do not center themselves. It's what happens when humans do center themselves, by way of the West and its LAT-based anthropocentrism. The "illusory" Sun of religion is actually the de-colonial concern for justice that is disallowed by Secularism$_2$. If humans were to actually live in a better world they would have to de-colonize, which means that they would have to disallow interpretation—except as an error theory. But then they would have to disallow LAT (except as an error theory) and that would mean that there would be no motivation for prioritizing the human. The pain and misery of an oppressed, colonized world is a function of us not affirming our common Indigenous, de-colonial, rational, explicatory interests with a diversity of agents, including the Earth. It is entirely a result of interpreting given LAT.

Marx thinks that the problem with previous Colonizers of South Asia, such as the Turks or Persians, is that after attempts at conquest, they would become "Hindoooized." The British were the first not to let that happen to them, so that is why they are the preferred, *superior*, Colonizer. This is an interesting analysis. South Asia was a vast practice of Secularism$_1$: that is what the British called "Hinduism." So if outsiders get Hindoooized, they are thereby included within the South Asian practice of Secularism$_1$ where everyone gets to participate in the moral philosophical debate and there is no grand colonial order that all have to accept, which on Marx's account is objectionable. It is far better according to Marx that the British establish Secularism$_2$—White Supremacy—in South Asia.

The other reason that South Asianists and academics on the whole don't like to criticize Islamic colonization in South Asia is broadly Liberal and has to do with J.S. Mill. Mill's day job consisted in being a Colonizer with the British East India company, where he wrote daily dispatches (Zastoupil 1994). This allowed him both familiarity with South Asia and supported a colonial interest in controlling it. Mill in *On Liberty* eloquently argues that we ought to allow people to engage in moral experiments and choose their own values, so long as this does not interfere with others. Today, Liberals are likely to think that this moral freedom is an essential part of a secular space. But Mill didn't invent this. These two practices of moral experimentation—*tapas*—and transparency in choosing one's own values—*svādhyāya*—are essential practices of Yoga's Normative Ethics as spelled out in the *Yoga Sūtra* (II.1), circa 200 BCE–200 CE. These practices are so prevalent in South Asia that it is hard to know something about India without seeing that moral experimentation and self-determination of values is ubiquitous. India is after all the land of vast numbers of peoples who adopt unusual life experiments outside of conventional society, and a land of publicly tolerating and venerating a diversity of values and norms, celebrated in art (temple idols) and literature that people are free to choose and celebrate. There is no *a priori* limit on the diversity of such experiments or such publicly celebrated values short of what would undermine others' ability to do the same. Mill, like all Colonizers, is a thief, appropriating this freedom for himself while denying it those he derived it from.

Mill retells this very South Asian, Yogic commitment to experimentation and choosing one's own model of the good as his idea, and puts a Consequentialist spin on this: it's about maximizing happiness on his account. In Yoga, we engage in *tapas* (experimentation, unconservatism) and *svādhyāya* (self-determination) as part of our devotion to Īśvara— Sovereignty—which leads to the recovery of our autonomy (*kaivalya*). So in Yoga we engage in these practices for *non-teleological*, radically procedural reasons. Mill's ethics, in *Utilitarianism,* as an example of the Western tradition, is anthropocentric: denying that human happiness can be equaled to nonhuman pleasure—"better Socrates dissatisfied than a pig satisfied." Yoga, as an Indigenous philosophy articulated against the backdrop of a widespread practice of explication, is not anthropocentric and identifies agents widely as things with an interest in their own independence. However, Mill doesn't of course acknowledge where he got these ideas from—why would he if South Asia was for the taking by the British. Rather, on Mill's account, the freedom to engage in moral experimentation and self-determination of values should only be afforded to the racially mature, unlike South Asians who would be so lucky to have an Akbar rule them (*On Liberty* I.10).

Akbar (1542–1605 CE) was a Muslim colonial ruler of a large jurisdiction in South Asia. While he has a mythic reputation for being tolerant, in his lifetime he compiled "letters of victory" that lauded his conquests over unbelievers in India, which was guided by the genocidal imperative from the Qurʾān to "kill the idolaters [or polytheists] all together" along with the destruction of their temples and places of worship (Zilli 1971, 351–5). More fully, at Qurʾān 9:5: "kill the polytheists wherever you find them and capture them and besiege them and sit in wait for them at every place of ambush" (Sahih International translation). Akbar celebrated his genocidal, eliminative colonialism as justified by the expectations of canonical Islam, and in this way fit the general pattern of colonial violence.

Along with this appropriating argument for moral freedom and thinking that colonial rule is appropriate for South Asians, Mill also makes an impassioned plea against the tyranny of the majority. We often think of this nowadays in Liberal (Western) contexts as a kind approach to minorities. However, in Mill's case, as is the case with Colonizers—especially exploitative Colonizers such as Mill who are not trying to replace the native so much as appropriate their wealth—it's the Colonizer who is the minority. This Millian sensitivity to not judge minorities by standards of the majority is perfectly designed to spare the Colonizer the moral criticism of the global majority. Once you see the Colonizer as the numerical minority, it's hard to unsee this self-serving plea.

What I find remarkable about both Marx's anti-South Asian racism, and Mill's anti-South Asian racism, is the unanimity with which the first Marxist, and a foundational Liberal, thought that the role of South Asians was to be colonized by Muslims—if they are not lucky enough to be colonized by the British. Either way, Secularism$_2$ would be imposed on South Asians, their Indigenous practice of Secularism$_1$ wiped out, which "Hindooizes" everyone. Given that all of this is irrational, an exercise of interpretation, we have to look to oppressive motives for this sympathy for the colonization of South Asians.

Islamic colonization in South Asia was not a singular event. It happened over eight centuries. It caused a general deterioration in public safety due to its genocidal rollout.

Two examples stick out to me as salient in filling out the details of this colonial change in South Asia. The first (in terms of salience) is the martyrdom of Guru Arjan. Sikhism, which I am inclined to identify as South Asia's first native religion—the first South Asian position created with the consciousness of being a religion as per Secularism$_2$—was formed by Guru Nanak (1469–1539 CE), who was born in the Delhi Sultanate. The Moghul emperor Jahangir (1569–1627 CE) had the Sikh teacher and leader, Guru Arjan (1563–1606 CE), tortured and imprisoned with a view to having him renounce his Sikhism. He died a martyr (*śahīd*) (Fenech 1997). What is remarkable about this event is that it introduces into a native South Asian position the idea of martyrdom. As a de-colonial tradition, South Asia has no native concept or discussion of martyrdom.

The *West* is unique among the three ancient traditions of philosophy for beginning with the murder of a philosopher (Socrates) followed by a succession of other killed public intellectuals (Jesus, Boethius, Hypatia . . .). Given LAT, we can see what generates this pressure: its moral perspective essentialism makes not socially conforming a problem that cannot be tolerated. The accusation that Socrates was corrupting the youth and promoting false gods (as we learn in the *Apology*) is the accusation that Socrates was not conforming to community values and expectations. But in South Asia, from the start, what gods to worship and how to raise the youth *was the* question, insofar as unfettered moral philosophy was the basic practice South Asians pursued. So in sharp contrast to the *West*, South Asia has no ancient history of persecuting public intellectuals. Just the opposite: philosophers such as the Buddha or Mahāvīra of Jainism were respected and celebrated for engaging in philosophical experimentation and delivering moral philosophical lessons that brought common practices of violence (such as animal sacrifices) into question. And hence, martyrdom, as in dying for one's faith, is a completely alien idea in South Asia, *until* the Sikh experience with Islamic colonization.

The other salient change under the continuous threat of Islamic conquest is how native philosophy comes to cower in the face of public uncertainty. In ancient times, as we shall see in our chapters on Normative Ethics (Chapters 5 and 6) South Asian moral philosophy was something to be conducted publicly. Moral action as explored in Yoga was recommended as something that has to address public oppression head-on. After the start of Islamic colonization we find the rebranding of "yoga" as something very familiar in the modern world.

We find this in the famous Svātmārāma's *Haṭha Yoga Pradīpikā* (*ca.* 1400 CE) where yoga is represented as something one does indoors, under the tutelage of a human teacher, in a peaceful kingdom. The instruction consists in bodily poses and breathing exercises. If what I have been saying about Yoga seems unfamiliar to you, that is because in all likelihood what you know of yoga goes back to this time of colonial trauma, where yoga is ironically redefined as something one does indoors, under human instruction, in a gentrified part of town. Most notably, whereas classical Yoga, is a process of unconservatism and self-governance that disrupts systemic harm and restores the personal boundaries of persons in public space, under colonialism yoga is reimagined as agoraphobic and something that yields freedom of a yoga studio where one gets to be present and take a break out of one's otherwise oppressive day. Whereas Yoga, the original philosophy, is a de-colonial exercise of devotion to Sovereignty to generate autonomy, yoga is colonially reimagined as a way to cope with the stress of colonization and oppression.

3.　What Hinduism Teaches Us About Religion

In time when the British show up they adopt the Islamic practice of calling South Asians "Hindoos," and decide that South Asians have a native religion that isn't Islam: Hinduism. What the British call Hinduism is nothing short of the entire South Asian tradition. What this means is that it is continuous with the disagreements of philosophy. No position is barred as no position defines Hinduism. Its baptismal moment captures the idea of the South Asian, with no common founder. In my book, *Hinduism: A Contemporary Philosophical Investigation*, I begin distinguishing between *kind* categories (like RED, which collects things that display the category property of red) and *class* categories, like FRUIT SALAD, which are a collection of disparate items that do not, each of them, display the grouping criterion. Fruit salad is a collection of different pieces of fruit. A piece of fruit salad (like a grape, or a piece of apple) is not a collection of different pieces of fruit. Most religions are *kind* concepts: they are defined by some central book or figure, such as the Torah, Jesus, the Qur'ān, and the Prophet Muhammad, and all things that are say Jewish, Christian, or Muslim display some important connection to these defining books or figures. Hinduism in contrast is like fruit salad: it is a collection of all Indigenous South Asian things. Knowing that a position is an example of Hinduism tells us nothing about its content or doctrine, and viewed separately, something Hindu, like say the ten place counting system of 0,1,2,3,4,5,6,7,8, and 9, on the face of it do not display anything of the group trait of being South Asian. If one actually bothers to look and explicate, one sees that no comprehensive view defines what the British called "Hinduism."

Indeed, all four ethical theories explicated in the introductory chapter and which we will return to in Chapter 5—Virtue Ethics, Consequentialism, Deontology, and Yoga/Bhakti—are internal to Hinduism. Yoga as a basic theory is absent in the *West* so the spread of ethical theories within Hinduism is even wider than what we find in the *Western* tradition. While it is common to interpret Yoga's devotional prioritization of Īśvara as Theism, it cannot be Theism as Theism is a version of Virtue Ethics, that prioritizes the goodness of agents: God being the ultimately good agent. Īśvara in contrast is Right. All things considered, *Theism* is a minority position in the South Asian tradition (perhaps only clearly defended by the Nyāya school), and very many "Orthodox" Hindu positions hold atheistic positions on god like beings: and insofar as they are acknowledged they are simply forces of nature, within a naturalistic frame where they have to be factored in a Consequentialist calculus.

If Christianity or Islam are each a fruit, Hinduism is like the produce section of a supermarket—or more like the whole supermarket. But this diversity doesn't just end with ethics. In epistemology too, if we explicate the debates there we find that what competing theories are disagreeing about is THE TRUE OR THE JUSTIFIED. While the famous theories of epistemology we find in the *Western* tradition tend to prioritize truth over justification, Yoga and some other philosophies that get dragnetted into Hinduism prioritize justification over truth (Ranganathan 2018b). In both the case of ethics, and epistemology, as examples, the diversity of theories is greater in the South Asian tradition (Hinduism) than in the *West*. Similarly if we move to ontology and then metaphysics we find a whole diversity of positions both on what there is, and the nature of reality, all within "Hinduism." And of course, logic and aesthetics were also professionally discussed within the spread of South Asian philosophy that gets called Hindu.

If we actually take the trouble to explicate the options that fall under "Hinduism," what we will see is that:

- there is no common essential content that is Hindu, and thus,
- the concept of religion is entirely vacuous, and
- the political purpose of religion is to subordinate Secularism$_1$, free thinking, of BIPOC philosophy, within *Western* colonization.

As a matter of cementing the colonial narrative, which is part of the imposition of the Colonizer's perspective on the colonized it is vital to depict Indigenous reason-based, explicatory practices as weird, mysterious, and religious to legitimize colonization for this ensures that Indigenous people lack connection to their heritage of moral philosophy that could challenge colonization. But it is also essential to the irrational project of colonization to hide Secularism$_1$ and to institute White Supremacy as the default model of secularism the world over: Secularism$_2$. And this myth survives as colonized people who participate in the *West*, the world over, interpret everything on the basis of the *West*, including their own traditions.

What the history of Hinduism as a religion shows us is that *Western* colonialism is the pivotal event, before which South Asians related to each other via philosophical controversies, especially controversies about dharma (*the Right or the Good*) and after which they interpret themselves according to the *West* and treat their religious identities as though Indigenous. In Indigenous South Asia, South Asians did not have religious identities. They have moral philosophical—dharma—identities. Prior to colonization, Indigenous South Asia was a space mediated by explication. People understood themselves not in terms of propositional attitudes that they shared but in terms of the theories they choose that contribute to moral philosophical debate. In this debate were various theories of Dharma, such as the Jain Virtue Theory simply called by its adherents "Dharma," Buddhist Consequentialism called simply "Dharma" by its adherents, and, innumerable theories that span the debates of moral philosophy that after colonization are thrown into the miscellany of Hinduism. The transition from Indigenous moral philosophy to the colonized world of religious identity involves a rupture in the tradition. And this rupture involves adopting an interpretive approach to the tradition, against a *Western* backdrop. Descendants of Indigenous people who are religified no longer have native access to their tradition as they have given up and lost their Indigenous explicatory practices to make room for themselves in a Secularism$_2$ world. This move away from

Indigenous free thinking to a Western colonially mediated understanding of one's tradition as religious, and not an exercise of Secularism$_1$ moral philosophical freedom, happens under the duress of colonization.

One important example of external duress leading to religious identity is the case of Balinese Hinduism. South Asian (Secularism$_1$) influences in Bali have existed for thousands of years. Ancient India was a regional center of research, knowledge, culture, and innovation that had a profound influence on Eurasia, and various areas around South Asia (Dalrymple 2024). Islamic rulers have targeted these areas for control since the fifteenth century. After Indonesia gained independence from the Dutch, and after much of the country had converted to Islam, the constitution guaranteed religious freedom. However, Islamicists in power tried to limit what would be allowed as a religion. Only Islam, Protestantism, and Catholicism were recognized as genuine religions. Other local traditions were recognized as being beliefs only. Monotheism was treated as necessary but insufficient to gain recognition of possessing a religion. In order to avoid being the target of state conversion to Islam, groups required official religious status (Ramstedt 2005, 9). By working with Indian Hindus, Balinese representatives created a uniquely Balinese form of Hinduism that passed the test. In response, the "Balinese had to reinvent themselves as the Hindus that they were already supposed to be" (Picard 2005, 57). They were eventually recognized as supporters of a monotheistic Hinduism that satisfied the Indonesian ministry of religion's concerns (McDaniel 2013).

Far from being an anomaly, the Balinese creation of Hinduism to satisfy external colonial expectations is quite normal in the formation of Hindu self-identity. After all the very idea that South Asians had a shared religion, Hinduism, is one such external, colonizing expectation. The Balinese case provides some insight into why Hindus would bother meeting this threshold: to prevent being the target of further colonization. But it also continues the trend from ancient Rome: religion is a political category created as part of colonial administration of native populations.

Another extreme form of Hindu identity creation can be found in the construction of the Hindu Right (Hindu nationalism), or sometimes commonly called "Hindutva." This position requires several colonial innovations to get off the ground. First, one had to have the categories of religion, such as Islam and Hinduism, facilitated by colonization. Via British colonization, the very doctrine of LAT is transmitted. And this leads to the invention of a "Hindu" language—Hindi—written in the South Asian script, Devanagari, and a Muslim language—Urdu—written in an Arabic script, out of a common spoken language: Hindustani. With this linguistic understanding of what it is to be Hindu, it is only a matter of time before a

LAT-based, Hindu nationalism is formed, complete with moral perspective essentialism, which depicts anyone external to this Hindu national identity, such as and especially Muslims, a problem (for more on this development, see Sharma 2007, 2011). And indeed, Muslims are hence on the receiving end of the genocidal intent of Hindu Nationalists.

In general, the colonization of South Asia by the *West* in the form of Secularism$_2$ constitutes a loss of ancestral, Secularism$_1$, explicatory skills to understand oneself and others in a world of moral philosophical diversity. With this loss of explicatory skills comes a move to oppressive forms of social interaction and a difficulty in engaging in moral criticism of national moral identity—as we observed on Planet Ethics. The shameful state of the study of religion typically treats the end result of this historical process as the topic of Religious Studies. What would be historically responsible is to study, historiographically, the creation of religion as an essential part of the rollout of White Supremacy.

4. Race and Religion

Secularism$_2$, as the oldest form of White Supremacy, is sustained by interpretation—irrationality—on the basis of the *West*. As noted, what it creates is not a mere *rebranding* of BIPOC intellectual traditions. It creates a colonial distortion of BIPOC intellectual activity as though *it* is outside of the scope of reason. In some perverse way, this is true of religion if understood as an artifact of colonization: as it is a result of interpreting BIPOC traditions, and interpretation is irrational, the resulting religion (the BIPOC tradition interpreted) is irrational. But that's just an artifact of oppression: not the reality of the Indigenous tradition that was subsequently colonized.

The parallels between the creation of religion as a colonial distortion and race are salient, and should have already been explored by anyone interested in Religious Studies or the philosophy of religion. That would be objective. It would elucidate the objective diversity of what gets lumped in religion, and allow us to identify the interpretive cause of this categorization as a false, White Supremacist, narrative of what is intrinsically much more rational.

4.1. Race

At a critical juncture in European colonial expansion with the advent of the Atlantic Slave Trade, which saw Africans taken as slaves to Europe and North and South America, beginning in the sixteenth century, a racial theory that codifies colonial expansion is developed by Europeans. François Bernier (1625–88), credited with creating the modern concept of race, divides humanity into races, and assesses races he takes to be intrinsically dark in terms of the deviation from the race of White people. Others such as Carolus Linnaeus (1707–88) and Johann Friedrich Blumenbach (1752–1840) follow in this exercise with progressively entrenched views about the value of races and their connection to biology. Racial theory was not originally a mere anthropological exercise of dividing humans into phenotypes. It was a political exercise that put White people at the top of a hierarchy and everyone else at a lower point: the more people seemed to conform to the White stereotype, the higher up they were, the more they deviated, the lower down. If we were to ignore this history, we might come to think of race, as many racists do, as a natural feature of human existence, not constructed out of colonialism but reflecting deep structures of personality, and propensities driven by biology. Similarly, if we ignore the history of religion, we could similarly continue to believe in the natural religiosity of BIPOC, and the superior free thinking of the Western tradition.

In an overview of the options in the philosophy of race, I follow Ron Mallon's account (2004, 2006, 2007, 2016) and Michael James's (2016). What is *explicatorily* useful about this overview is that it divides the options along two lines of debate. On the one hand there is the metaphysics of race: one could adopt the view that there is no such thing as race as there is nothing in nature corresponding to our ideas of race (*racial skepticism*), or that race though not natural is socially created (*racial constructivism*). Racial skepticism is critical of the ordinary notions of race, according to which the distinctions between Black, White, Asian etc. correspond to heritable traits that explain behavioral and cultural differences across races. Science has not vindicated racial naturalism and has in fact provided more evidence that it is not true. The racial skeptic hence rejects that there is anything in reality corresponding to race. Racial constructivism claims that given beliefs about race, humans create racial distinctions that often have real-life implications for everyone.

A third metaphysical option is possible—*racial population naturalism*. This is the idea of race that contemporary science investigates when, for instance, scientists are interested in whether diseases correlate with certain populations, or certain allergies or medication intolerances are also correlated with certain populations. This last notion of race is outside of typical race talk and has to do with markers that are typically not even visible but testable given modern science.

Then there are two normative views that one could take on race. One could adopt *eliminativism*. Accordingly, we should simply drop talk of race all together and work to purge it from our understanding of humans as there is no evidence for it—and if there is evidence for it in the sense of racial population naturalism, it will not correspond to essentialized notions of races that treat it as the explanation of personality or cultural traits (Appiah 2006). In contrast there is racial *conservation*. Constructivists often support conservation, for "since society labels people according to racial categories, and since such labeling often leads to race-based differences in resources, opportunities, and well-being, the concept of race must be conserved, in order to facilitate race-based social movements or policies, such as affirmative action, that compensate for socially constructed but socially relevant racial differences" (James 2016).

4.2. Religion

Naomi Zack in her *Philosophy of Race: An Introduction* (2018) notes that we can find ideas of race in early Western writers insofar as they identify groups of humans defined by common ancestry in terms of certain traits. But our concepts of race were formed starting with François Bernier (1625–88) at a time when Western colonization was dividing the world into Western colonizing powers, and the BIPOC colonized. Our race concepts hence come with a hierarchy and this is economically encoded in the world today as colonial states are vastly more well-off than colonized states that are typically racialized.

The observation that religion as a category was created by Western colonialism starting with the Romans as a way to preserve a population for exploitation while shielding itself from ethical criticism points to a parallel history. And the outcome is that religion *racializes* intellectual traditions, the way that our concepts of race racialized bodies. And just as White people are apparently without color and everyone else is colored, White people are without any surviving native religion: all religion is from outside of the West.

But the appropriation of BIPOC traditions as religions changes how they are taught about, understood, and valued. They are no longer explicated as sources of moral philosophy that could critically challenge colonialism but interpreted according to the Western tradition, rendering them morally toothless in the face of Western colonization. If a religion is appreciated as having moral philosophical content, it is acknowledged as such because the moral teachings associated with the religion are consistent with the anthropocentrism and communitarianism of the West: everything else is the spiritual content.

As in the case of race, does the evidence support religious *skepticism* (the skepticism that there are such things as religions), some type of religious *naturalism* (the idea that religion really tracks something out there) or religious *constructivism* (the idea that religion was just made up)? If we explicate, we can see that religion is a fiction and this leads to skepticism about the topic. But if we interpret according to the West, then we construct religion out of colonized BIPOC traditions. Neither provides any support for there being any natural reality to religion, though that is certainly the myth we buy when we interpret on the basis of the West.

Should we *eliminate* talk of religion or *conserve* it? Again, if we explicate all we would ever find are the disagreements of philosophy, so it simply disappears. But if we interpret according to Secularism$_2$, we have to conserve it as part of the global system of White Supremacy. This shows that while there is no way to be accurate about what religion is (as it's a fabrication), we can be precise about religion.

Here is where the entailments of race and religion diverge. In the case of racialization, and especially racialization against the backdrop of a White Supremacist hierarchy, the farther people deviate from the White paradigm, the more they are disadvantaged. This explains why the darker one is the more one suffers in this racial hierarchy. Affirmative action and other such programs are plausible responses to this type of injury as the very practice disrupts deference to this hierarchy. In changing the racial distribution of office holders across various rungs of power, we would be disrupting the hierarchy that links power and race. Religion is a kind of racialization of BIPOC intellectual traditions. But this description, I now realize, is insufficient. Unlike race, religion is not a hierarchy with the Western at the top and the BIPOC on the other end.

Religion operates within a mutually exclusive disjunction between the Western and the BIPOC. Secularism$_2$, this disjunction, is not a hierarchy but a bifurcation. Religion is not a spectrum on which the Western tradition sits, as race is a spectrum on which Whiteness sits. Religion is the name for what is outside of the West. The West is thus like Boethius's God who sits outside of time and space and can judge all of human history at once—without having any impact on what it knows. In this profound global colonization, the West becomes the ahistorical tradition and what it discerns is also ahistorical, like religion—apparently universal but not for it as it has no native world religion—apparently a timeless feature of human experience, but at the same time discernible only when the West discerns it. As a result, Secularism$_2$ is a remarkably pernicious and normalized form of White Supremacy, which treats White people and their intellectual activity on the basis of their tradition as *outside* of actual human history. Every proclaimed secular state in the world today—and every religious state for that matter—is based on this White Supremacy as they are all based on the Secularism$_2$ creation of religion and the secular. It creates this bifurcation that elevates the West to the timeless by paradoxically treating the West's history as universal human history: what we all really have in common. By way of Secularism$_2$, White humans—and the humans prized by the West, especially able-bodied, cisgender White men—become universal humans, and everyone else is a deviation. It is violent, for it depicts people outside of this mythic universal human history as polluting. Any thought from BIPOC traditions is depicted as religious and a threat to the secular order. *Even if* the same idea can be found in the West and outside, it becomes dangerous to the secular public order when sourced from BIPOC traditions—a threat that can be neutralized if it can be shown to also have some *Western* origin.

Here, we can see the toxic conflation of racial hierarchies, with the bifurcation of the West that is depicted as secular, and the BIPOC as religious. What this introduces into race, which is a set of differences on a spectrum, is a recalcitrance of the explanatory superiority of White people. Whiteness becomes more than mere bodily presentation: it becomes explanatory authority. In the next chapter we shall explore this in detail where I will describe it as "White Irrationality." It is a form of extraordinary stupidity that irrationally advantages White people.

Given this bifurcation, philosophy can then be conflated with the ethnography of White people as their cultures, values, and assumptions are somehow abstract and universal enough to be everyone's moral values and assumptions. Religious studies is then the ethnography of everyone else who pollute this pristine space of universal humanity. Philosophical Apartheid I identified at the start of this book is no accident but a deliberate creation of Secularism$_2$, Western colonization.

4.3. Two Aspects of Religion: The Western and Everything Else

People who hail from colonized traditions have to contend with the religification of their ancestors' practices. De-colonizing our relationship to these traditions has to provide a way for us to make use of them in Secularism$_1$ practice—otherwise we continue the practice of Secularism$_2$. This is especially challenging for traditions that self-understand as religions and have no significant pre-Western history, such as Christianity and Islam. To this end we should distinguish between two aspects of what gets called a religion. First is the *Western*, colonizing aspect that renders the religion subordinate to the *West*, as an alien alternative that poses no threat to its LAT-based history of anthropocentrism and communitarianism, and its conflation of the *West* with the content of public options that are permissible almost everywhere to act on in a world of White Supremacy (Secularism$_2$). Then, there is what lies outside of the *West*, and its history of anthropocentric and communitarian colonization, which motivates interpreting these traditions according to the *West* to declaw and render toothless any possible Indigenous criticism of the *West*'s colonization. This politically converts what would be de-colonial into the soteriological, and what would be Indigenous, reason-based moral philosophy, into faith. When this process is complete, religious identity has a nationalistic focus, exemplifying the anthropocentrism and communitarianism of LAT-based *Western* colonization. This is so normal it is hardly noticed. Churches often have linguistic or ethnic identities over and above religious identity: the Anglican Church, or the Greek Orthodox Church, for example. In the United States, Christian Nationalism is taking over many Christian institutions. Synagogues in North America are often fronts for Zionism. Gurdwaras in North America often are seats of Khalistani Sikh Nationalism. Modern Hindu temples especially outside of India without roots in precolonial South Asian traditions are often associated with some version of Hindu nationalism. And Islam is often associated with state politics insofar as Islamic states often have a version of Islam that they claim. Buddhists in Asia (in Sri Lanka and Myanmar) have emerged as nationalist forces who problematize non-Buddhists.

What we could call the *Religious Left* is an approach to religion that treats it as a basis for moral philosophical options. Those who engage this option are better understood as moral philosophers who adjudicate a religious tradition they identify with as a source of premises, for conclusions. As they treat religion as a source of reasons they are not committed to defending every reason in a religious tradition, and they are also able to find common cause with others, drawing on different traditions, for similar conclusions on the basis of different reasons. It is a de-colonial exercise insofar as it celebrates moral theoretical diversity.

Within this broad approach identified as the Religious Left people who draw upon their religious traditions for moral considerations often do not feel compelled to defend every premise and conclusion of their tradition. The Religious Left does not so much look to a precolonized tradition for guidance (for in some cases, there is no such thing, such as the case of Islam or most of what is called Christianity), but looks to the colonized, religified tradition, as containing moral reasoning. Sometimes, this approach is called *progressive* or *reconstructionist*. An interesting example of this I see online is Muslim veganism. Islam contains prescribed practices of animal slaughter, and yet some Muslims choose to look at their tradition not as something that has to be accepted wholesale, but as a source for guidance that allows them to use some moral commitments (such as compassion and a concern for animal welfare) as grounds for criticizing other traditional commitments. This is de-colonial as these Muslims are choosing their reasons, as opposed to simply believing everything passed down to them. People with religious identities all over the world can be found engaging moral philosophically with their tradition in this way. It involves choosing an explicatory approach to one's tradition as opposed to an interpretive approach. Muslims do this all the time when they decide not to act on *Qur'ān* 9:5, which directs them to kill all polytheists or idolaters.

I would also note that most people who identify as scholar-practitioners of a particular religious tradition are often in this group of the Religious Left *because* they treat their traditions as providing reasons for choices. Moreover, scholar-practitioners of one tradition can be excellent scholars of other traditions, because they are inclined to treat traditions as a source of practical reasons. This conflicts with the idea that the best informants about a religion are those inside the practice itself. What counts in favor of one's research skills is the ability to explicate, and that is not the same as what beliefs or outlooks are native to one's upbringing or life.

What we could call the *Religious Right* is an approach that treats a religion as identical with the expectations of a LAT-based community, and problematizes other traditions by way of moral perspective essentialism. It is xenophobic and irrational as it is an exercise of interpretation. This is a very standard approach to religion where it is treated as a foundation for ethnonationalism.

These two options take different approaches to something very much like the Euthyphro Dilemma. Socrates in articulating this dilemma in the *Euthyphro* asks: is something right because it is loved by the gods, or do the gods love something because it is right (10a)? We can recast this dilemma as the question: is a reason worth taking seriously because it is traditional, or is a tradition worth taking seriously because of the reason? This dilemma pushes the Religious Right in one direction, of opting for the first notion that a reason is worth taking seriously because it is traditional as determined by one's beliefs, and the Religious Left in the other direction, that a tradition is worth taking seriously insofar as it acknowledges certain reasons.

In addition to the Religious Left and Right, we should also acknowledge a third category of precolonial traditions that are posthumously called religious. These are Indigenous, LE-based traditions. They lack the anthropocentric and communitarian core that is the normalization of the West. They are already formulated as contributions to moral philosophy. In this case, the reason-giving nature of the position and it being traditional coincide. They require no de-colonization. Rather, we have to de-colonize our approach to them and treat them as contributions to moral philosophy, which they are. Most classical South Asian positions fall into this category. An important sign of such traditions is that they are not formulated as what we must agree to but as contributions to a debate on the right choice and good outcome. We learn about them not by inheriting religious practices but by studying the history of moral philosophy.

5. De-Colonizing Our Past

Secularism$_1$, which the British called "Hinduism," is the free explication of all possibilities. If we engage in this, we never find any account of religion: all options are explicable and intelligible insofar as they are part of the debate. This reflects the Indigenous approach to thinking, LE, where every thought is the common disciplinary purpose of contrary perspectives in a disagreement. Secularism$_2$ arises from interpreting everything on the basis of the *West*. This bifurcates the world into the Secular *West* and the religious everyone else. Here, we see through human history the incompatibility of colonialism and moral philosophy. This is not a mere academic incompatibility: actual human history that humans inherit is structured on the eradication of the public practice of moral philosophy and its replacement with the cultural expectations of *Westerners*. That is why we are saddled with religion. Within the normalization of White Supremacy, Secularism$_2$, pleas for all to adopt a secular approach are patently racist, for "secular" here is the *West*. Maintaining the legitimacy of religious identity is no less problematic. Rendering this explicit is an act of de-colonization. What this shows is that we couldn't arrive at the world we live in characterized by religious identity if we stuck to explicatory practices characteristic of Indigenous traditions and necessary for the exploration of moral theory. To recover the world that we lost, we need to adopt explication, render explicit the options of pre-colonized peoples, and reinstitute the public practice of moral philosophy: Secularism$_1$. To fail to do so would be irrational.

4

Gatekeeping, Peer Review, and the Normalization of Appropriative Stupidity

*Forever when we had Black History Month we had some White jerk in the
back say, "When are we going to have White History Month?"
. . . And when we have White History they immediately outlaw it. Because
we actually don't want White History Month. We want White Mythology Month.*

~~Baynard Woods~~, author of *Inheritance: An Autobiography of Whiteness*

1. The Paradox of Intentional Ignorance

This chapter concludes our exploration of Metaethics, the logical, semantic,
and epistemic requirements and constraints on participating in moral
philosophy. This chapter brings together the implications of the previous
chapters to answer larger, broader questions of oppression, which is an
interference in the public practice of moral philosophy. The question to be
answered here: how is it, even though oppression is *so stupid*, it manages to
survive? How is it that interpretation does not shoot itself in the foot and die
off the undignified death it deserves? One would imagine that a practice of
not-reasoning that leads to an irresponsible approach to thought and data
would lead to those who adopt it to have lives of self-sabotage. And yet,
colonialism and oppression dominates, not simply intermittently, but over
millennia.

In Chapter 1, I explained how interpretation (explanation in terms of
propositional attitudes), is the essence of irrationality and thereby deviates
from reasoning, and how this irrational failure is also a social failure that
manifests as colonialism and oppression, not to mention narcissism and
a lack of empathy, which requires reasoning. There, I also introduced the
idea that LAT's conflation of thought with language conflates thinking with
believing, creating and entrenching interpretation. In Chapter 2 I argued not
only does LAT generate interpretive pressures leading to genocidal intent and

eliminative or *replacement* colonization, the West is unique in acclaiming LAT, leading to it being the dominant colonizing tradition of the world. In Chapter 3, I reviewed the global outcome of the West's acclaim of LAT. It spread and spreads because it interprets everything on the basis of its tradition, and this is manifested in its rebranding BIPOC traditions as religion or spirituality. This results in the West's exercise of *exploitative colonization*. In this process, the West creates a global institutionalization of White Supremacy, as Secularism$_2$. The artifact of this global colonialism is religion, which serves to normalize the outcomes of LAT-based interpretation, including anthropocentrism and communitarianism. The flip side is that anything that could be de-colonial is reimagined as mysterious and inarticulable and depicted as speaking about an aspirational next world—nothing that is relevant to now. Just as race racializes BIPOC bodies, religion racializes BIPOC intellectual traditions. And all of this has the global outcome of the eradication of the public practice of moral philosophy. But, the latter phenomenon of religification is also more toxic and more recalcitrant than the mere racialization of bodies. Secularism$_2$ that produces religion constitutes a bifurcation, not a mere racial gradation. The result is that the West and its people, White people, are granted an explanatory authority as universal humans, while BIPOC intellectual activity is depicted as not different in degree but in kind. The combination of the bodily and intellectual prioritization of the West results in what is sometimes called "Whiteness" and what I will here discuss as "White Irrationality."

The second section answers the question of how, despite its *demonstrable idiocy*, interpretation can survive as a strategy because it is appropriative. In the third section, I compare interpretation and explication in open competitions. Because interpretation is appropriative, and not *disallowed by anyone* (present company excepted), it survives and wipes out explication. This explains how the Western tradition that brings us colonization and genocide, and begins with Plato and Aristotle providing moral justification for social inequality, is somehow also the tradition that gets credit for ideas of egalitarianism and human rights. Western moral thinkers start theorizing about egalitarianism and autonomy (beginning in the 1600s) after the West's genocidal phase of eliminative colonialism (starting in the 1500s) in Turtle Island and elsewhere because they are literally appropriating these concerns from colonized people.

In the fourth section, I respond to the objection that my characterization of the West as an irrational—interpretive tradition—is wrong. In the fifth section, I conclude.

This chapter also returns to a theme set out in the first chapter—that the epistemic failure that characterizes Philosophical Apartheid is the same oppressive power structures we live within a world of colonization. These are identical phenomena as oppression and colonization are the social manifestations of the irrationality of interpretation. So while this chapter will switch to questions of how the academy is regulated by peer review, these same dynamics account for oppression in public practices of gatekeeping. Insofar as we have a rational obligation to overcome colonization, we have the same obligation to clean up the normalization of oppression in the academy. If we can do it there, we can do it anywhere.

1.1. Emotional Fragility and Tyranny of Interpreters

As preparation for what is to follow it is worth noting that interpretation is an emotional failure that manifests as oppression. Interpreters confuse thinking with propositional attitudes like belief. Attitudes are noncognitive—they are neither true nor false. Insofar as emotions concern how we feel about various things, attitudes are emotional states (for a discussion, see Epley 2018). Hence, when interpreters are engaging in explanation by way of propositional attitudes, *they are emoting*. In other words, interpreters are emotionally disregulated. Here are some ordinary examples.

When I was a child growing up in Toronto in the 1970s and 1980s, all I would have to say is, "I don't eat meat," for adults to get very angry. If others were happy with their choices, one would imagine that they would happily endorse the propriety of meat eating. But instead they betrayed a discomfort at the topic and anger at me for making a choice to skip the meat. It was as though my simply identifying my choice was enough to show them that *there was a choice to be made*, and because they were interpreting, they treated their belief about the topic (not their choice) as the final word. From their perspective, I wasn't allowed to make this choice: no one is.

Similarly, these days, someone announcing that they are transgender, or they have pronoun preferences for how *they should be addressed*, meets with all sorts of outrage from many corners. Someone asking to be called "they" or "she" or "he" in accordance with their gender identity is not demanding that everyone be called "they," or "he" or "she." And yet, one would think that it was the third-party interpreter who is being hard done by, if we were to listen to their complaints about respecting people's pronoun choices.

Another example of this phenomenon of interpreters reacting badly to what doesn't conform to their outlook is the case of the US 2020 Presidential election. Poll workers explicated the voter data, rendering explicit the controversy between competing candidates and the final tallies of votes. This determined that Biden won that election. Trump, in contrast, claimed that he won the election. Trumpies, people who believe what Trump says, believed this claim of Trump and then interpreted the outcome of the election in accordance with this belief. They were happy when jurisdictional outcomes conformed to their outlook, but at a loss and upset when it didn't, leading to the invention of *ad hoc* conspiracy theories to account for the difference between their expectations and the data. And many participated in a violent riot on January 6, 2021, while the results of the election were being officialized in Washington, DC. What is notable about the Trumpy is their emotional instability occasioned by the divergence between their propositional attitudes and the evidence. In this case, rioters acted as though *they* were the ones under threat when they were the ones unleashing violence on US Capitol Hill police officers and politicians. In these cases, and countless others, what we are observing is the interpreter's confusion between various propositions they have attitudes toward (desires, beliefs, etc.) and who they are, such that the divergence between reality and their propositional attitudes is perceived as an existential threat.

1.2. White Irrationality

I titled this introductory section "The Paradox of Intentional Ignorance." The paradox is the observation that:

- at once, interpretation is a metaexplanatory and metaethical choice that is cognitively incompetent—literally irrational —and yet,
- it not only survives, it dominates.

An aim of this chapter is to account for the seeming success of a strategy that is not rational and is oppressive.

The surviving interpretive strategy in our world is *Western* interpretation. I call it "White Irrationality," deliberately, to bring attention to ways in which this structures a world of oppression. It is irrational because it is a form of interpretation. It is racist because it privileges what the *Western* tradition celebrates, which has become White, cisgendered, able, well-to-do, heterosexual, men. People who are bodied—or oriented—in ways that deviate from this paradigm (like women) are in proportion to this deviation marginalized and oppressed, with nonhuman persons being categorized as non-persons, *born for oppression*. Nonhuman persons can hence be treated as commodities and as though they are not agents deserving of considerations afforded to humans. Nonhuman persons include animals but persons of different biological sorts, such as the Earth, ecosystems, rivers, and various other agents whose behavior is semantically significant—enough to be part of the extension of thinking on the Indigenous, explicatory (rational), LE model. In the case of humans, the assumed picture of the paradigm person also freezes a behavioral range that is defined as ability, and then any deviation is defined as a disability—even if there are advantages to this deviation. Disability and the consequent group of disabled people are hence both constructed and oppressed via their interpreted deviation from the assumed norm. This ensures that their idiosyncrasies are never accommodated, while the idiosyncrasies of "able" people are. Economic oppression is also a phenomenon that is kept in place by White Irrationality. Economic success depends on one's interpreted position within a world of Western colonization. Economic success is not a mere matter of one's activity within a context of White Irrationality: it has to do with the value ascribed to one's activity and this is often also a function of all the ways one is valued within a context of White Irrationality. We could simply call this *Western Irrationality* and not talk about Whiteness, but it would hide the ways in which the tradition celebrates White bodied human-people and their ancestral beliefs in ways that are systemically oppressive. As noted in the previous chapter, the same philosophical position articulated by a White person on the basis of the Western tradition counts as secular, and when it is articulated by a BIPOC on the basis of a BIPOC tradition, it becomes religious or spiritual. The former is permitted in public secular spaces, while the other is seen as a threat to the Secularism$_2$ order and has to be marginalized. This sets moral philosophy from BIPOC traditions in a different category from other anti-oppressive philosophical projects.

One can be an anti-racist or a feminist and still operate within the anthropocentrism and communitarian space of Secularism$_2$, thereby posing no real threat to the institutionalization of Western colonization and White Supremacy. Feminism and anti-racism on the basis of the West—usually expressed as a form of humanism—will be permitted to some extent but also thereby ineffectual to the extent that it depends upon the very infrastructure of oppression it seeks to overcome. But drawing from the disappeared moral philosophy of BIPOC people rebranded as religious is to draw on ideas that are polluting to the infrastructure of oppression in our world— Secularism$_2$, White Irrationality, the Ethnography of White people, and its anthropocentrism and communitarianism. It is maximally threatening and hence barred by ordinary Philosophical Apartheid by the two-prong ignorance and indifference of professional philosophers and the subjugation of BIPOC philosophy to people outside of philosophy. My Brownness, and the philosophy I draw from owing to its Brown origin, is polluting according to Secularism$_2$. On its account, it's all Hinduism.

Secularism$_2$, global White Supremacy, also provides the infrastructure for regional forms of oppression, say for instance casteism, in India. Caste, the usual story goes, is an essential part of Hinduism, and Hindu society. To the extent this is true, it is true of a thing made up by the British—Hinduism, the religion (as opposed to what the British posthumously called "Hinduism," which was the entire history of Secularism$_1$). And hence casteism is a creature of *Western* colonization—White Irrationality—which is Secularism$_2$. This generalizes: any time a regional form of oppression functions within the religious or spiritual—the *West's* words for the BIPOC—it is oppression within Secularism$_2$. Secularism$_2$, White Irrationality, constitutes a global interpretive structure that keeps regional forms of interpretation in place and locked. Local change is not possible without disrupting Secularism$_2$, and that is a global order. One can fight this cementing of local religified oppression but the only way that can work is by rejecting White Irrationality and its infrastructure of interpretation.

In Chapter 2, I did note that the Chinese commitment to the Orthographic version of LAT problematizes some groups such as the Uyghurs and Tibetans who do not participate in Chinese orthographic identity. However, China also adopts Secularism$_2$ via its official Marxism—a creature of *Western* colonization—and this allows for the problematization of these groups as religious (Islamic and Buddhist) within a wider secular (Secularism$_2$) China. This regional oppression is also a manifestation of the global White Supremacy of Secularism$_2$, and hence White Irrationality.

White Irrationality is simply our world's manifestation of interpretation as a global colonizing force. Because the *West* uniquely begins with LAT, uncontested, and LAT is an interpretive model of thought, it grows into a global colonizing tradition. Because oppression is a cost borne by people in proportion to their deviation from the paradigm of the global colonizing tradition, we have to acknowledge the ways the paradigm White person plays an explanatory role in accounting for how much oppression people suffer in proportion to their deviation from this standard. We can and should appreciate that it is underpinned by interpretation: get rid of that and the entire structure collapses. But we cannot ignore its *Western* flavor and roots without losing track of how the degree of oppression is generated. We cannot ignore its *Western* flavor and roots without failing to appreciate how it is spread and normalized.

Finally, I call this "White Irrationality" to bring attention to the way in which *Western* interpretation provides an *irrational* advantage to White people and people who can approximate what is celebrated in the *Western* tradition. This advantage can serve to overcome disadvantages that an individual experiences in proportion to their deviation from the paradigm person of the *Western* tradition. As it is irrational, the advantage it confirms seems almost supernatural.

1.3. Three Costs

Most humans today, and for centuries, including most racialized people, adopt White Irrationality as their interpretive strategy of survival. One way this shows up is in the prioritization of the White Colonizer's (often Victorian) sexual mores by colonized peoples (such as South Asians) when their own Indigenous traditions were sex-positive. The other way it shows up, of course, is in the gullible, wholesale, adoption of Secularism$_2$—the religification of BIPOC traditions, and the concomitant adoption of anthropocentrism and communitarianism as the secular option. This internalization of White Irrationality, by choosing interpretation, poses problems for BIPOC in three ways.

- First, internalizing this strategy that de-celebrates one's own tradition, orientation, and body—regardless of what other upvalued traits it displays, like for instance, being male, able, or straight—is a challenge for it involves internalizing a system of oppression that devalues oneself as a matter of origins. This is an ongoing, unrelenting stress.

Stress is known to cause inflammation, which causes disease. Scientists are now starting to study epigenetic inheritance and the impact on future generation health outcomes on the basis of the trauma of former generations (Švorcová 2023). It is no accident that racialized people in the geographic west have a higher incidence of metabolic disorder and South Asians (colonized for a millennium) have a higher incidence of cardiovascular disease. To fully see those regularities, you have to explicate the history of colonial oppression, and you will have to keep track of populations who have survived centuries of deprecation. For now, these ailments are treated as private costs to individuals, medicalized, and disassociated from the history of oppression, making treatment and control elusive.

- Secondly, BIPOC will often lack very many of the *Western* beliefs necessary to excel at the strategy of White Irrationality owing to a lack of doxastic inheritance for obvious cultural reasons. So while very many people who are not of *Western* descent participate in the anthropocentric and communitarianism of the *West's* doxastic commitments (most BIPOC do insofar as they buy Secularism$_2$), they do so at a significant disadvantage to themselves, thereby ensuring and continuing their own oppression.

They will have to make up for their doxastic shortfall while suffering the personal consequences of internalizing their own deprecation.

- Third, White Irrationality as a form of interpretation is irrational. Internalizing this strategy by racialized people is irrational and undermines their own capacity to de-colonize.

1.4. Irrational Advantage

Not only does White Irrationality promote people of *Western* descent in proportion to their conformity to its archetype, its beliefs are easily inherited passively via enculturation if one is of *Western* descent (White folks, generally). White people or people in proportion to their conformity to the personal expectations of the *West* do not suffer the first two costs suffered by people who deviate from these *Western* expectations. The third cost of irrationality it would seem is borne by anyone who interprets.

However, maddeningly, it serves to advantage people who do not suffer these first two costs, as these are the people who are promoted by *Western* interpretation.

- So paradoxically *it is as though* the irrationality of interpretation is not a cost suffered by White people who interpret or others who can conform to its expectations.
- It is as though a benefit—which is likely why White—Western— philosophers are so keen to defend interpretation.

This last point is important. Interpretation is irrational, and hence it has no rational defense. Hence the only salient motive we could find for White intellectuals to upvalue interpretation is its *racial* benefit for White people in a world of White Irrationality. As representatives of the tradition that brings us colonization and White Supremacy, White intellectuals are beneficiaries of interpretation. Their defense of the indefensible—interpretation—is hence wholly self-serving and racist.

It is easy to confuse this argument with various proposals based on identity politics. It is not uncommon for people to claim that everyone has some presumed advantage when they are speaking about their own heritage and ancestral tradition, and hence by extension European descendant individuals should not study BIPOC traditions, and rather BIPOC scholars should speak for their own tradition. This is the kind of thing one would believe if one bought LAT, which is the premise of *Western* colonization. For only in such cases will people's linguistic or cultural heritage be an epistemic advantage. If we switch to LE and our de-colonial analysis we can see that colonization is an equal opportunity phenomenon and that people from colonized traditions face significant and unique challenges in accessing an explicatory connection to their ancestral tradition—a connection deprived to them by intergenerational trauma and the localization of White Irrationality via colonization. And indeed, anyone who works on explicatory skills and is willing to do some research can become a credible researcher on anything. One's ancestry and pigment have nothing to do with actual epistemic success. The argument here is rather that in this irrational world, White people have an irrational advantage to interpret everything on the basis of the *West*, including and especially traditions that are not theirs ancestrally, to the exclusion of explicatory research. But this generalizes—White people will have an irrational, unjust advantage in almost every public arena.

This phenomenon is widely evidenced. As I write this, a senior White man, twice impeached, found liable for sexual abuse, who led a riot against the Capitol that he ran as president—live on TV—and was under investigation and prosecution for numerous other crimes, has threatened to prosecute political rivals, a convicted felon, who appointed an anti-science conspiracy theorist as secretary of health, and a wrestling promoter in charge of education, was elected as the president of the United States. His history of racism and misogyny is well-known. His opponent, a capable, career civil servant with no history of scandal or criminality (she was a prosecutor), lost—she was Black, South Asian, and female. Whatever the faults of the latter, one wonders how anyone could have voted for the former. White Irrationality predicts that people will vote for him not despite his faults but because his faults typify the *Western* tradition's history of violence, racism, and misogyny. The more he is able to *exemplify* White Irrationality, its irrational callousness and cruelty, the more he will seem like a safe bet to those who participate in White Irrationality. No failure of his counts against him (to date of writing this) as they are all signs of White Irrationality. The same dynamic explains why people by and large prefer a White interpreter to be the person they turn to learn about BIPOC intellectual traditions. These irrational deficits do not count against the unqualified White academics who write on Indian philosophy in Indology, Religious Studies, or Yoga Studies: they count in their favour. The more a White person explains by way of their beliefs, the more likely they will appear trustworthy. The more a Black or Brown person reasons, the more they will appear a threat.

As it is easier for people of *Western* descent to participate in White Irrationality without suffering consequences, namely, White people, while most everyone the world over who buy Secularism$_2$ participates in it too but with associated self-deprecating, belief-lacking, costs, there becomes the Illusion of White Supremacy. Somehow White people as a group (or people who can approximate the *West's* preferences) are just better in every respect—smarter, more beautiful, more interesting, and safe to be around, as they conform to the global colonizing expectation. This promotes a global Stockholm Syndrome where everyone seems to engage in an irrational sympathy for the *Western* tradition and its luminaries—despite their faults. And as long as people are irrational and choose to interpret, they treat the entirely believable facts of the world—including the global success of White people—as the content of all explanation. So White Supremacy and the outcomes of White Irrationality are reified by the adoption of interpretation as though a natural fact, while it is interpretation that created this irrational advantage.

- This analysis entails why anti-White racism and blaming White people is confused.

The resulting White Supremacy and White Privilege of White Irrationality is a system property of *Western* interpretation which almost all humans participate in. What keeps this together is *interpretation*. Get rid of that and one gets rid of the whole system.

White Irrationality provides a bizarre advantage to White people—especially White men, though White women can take advantage of it too, and often try—for being incompetent and irrational. BIPOC people—and White people who do not try to take advantage of their Whiteness—are held to a higher and often impossible standard. They cannot be promoted for exemplifying the irrationality of the *West*. So they instead often aspire toward standards of perfection, for which they will likely fail and even if they achieved would not be grounds for promotion in competition with people who can take advantage of being an irrational White person. This shows up in ordinary, everyday, collegial contexts in the *West* where White people—especially White men—can make mistakes, sub-perform, and are upvalued and promoted, while for everyone else who fails by *Western* standards or chooses not to participate, there can be no mistakes. You don't get a second chance. Everything you do is dangerous. Often, when engaging in the same behaviors as White men, women and racialized individuals are judged more harshly (American Sociological Association 2019). These are symptoms of the problem, not the problem. White people are not the problem. The problem is interpretation.

1.5. Costs of Not Participating

White Irrationality is an error, which explains how our world functions. But it is not an account of all possibilities.

> Very many people, including very many White people, do not participate in White Irrationality as they reject oppression in all of its forms, wholesale—including the oppression of nonhuman persons.

Benefiting from White Irrationality requires participating in it. If one rejects interpretation and hence oppression in all forms, one no longer participates in it and its many benefits start to run out. Any White person who situates themselves against this historical process of White Irrationality becomes a problem for it and will be treated as such. A White person who stands up for animals in factory farms, and victims of White Supremacy—including the humans of Gaza—will find out pretty quickly how they are no longer a beneficiary of White Irrationality (I think of the remarkable Greta Thunberg as an example—a White public figure famous for environmentalism and veganism who lost the spotlight when she stood up for Gazans and spoke about the connection between various forms of oppression). Of course, this is one reason why many (most) White people wouldn't take such a stand— and most people who participate in White Irrationality (including racialized people) wouldn't either. That is because White Irrationality makes it seem as though freedom is a *zero-sum game*—to agitate against other's oppression because of White Irrationality risks one's own irrational advantage and relative freedom afforded by White Irrationality.

It is worth noting that because (as we shall see) interpretation is appropriative, it can in time appropriate the positions of its victims. And then it will come to pass *One Day, Everyone Will Have Always Been Against This* (the excellent title of an important book by Omar El Akkad). I see signs now that the widespread *Western* tolerance for genocide in Palestine is starting to wear thin and perhaps one day it will be what everyone says they were against. But as I write this now, the vicissitudes of White Irrationality are propping up that campaign, as the genocide is nearly complete.

While White Irrationality gives White people a positive motive to participate—a net advantage over every other group, which allows White people to succeed by being irrational in ways promoted by the *West*—it provides a negative motive for everyone, including BIPOC, to participate: to not risk losing relative privilege or freedom. Relative advantage for BIPOC to participate in White Irrationality consists in the positioning of humans over nonhuman persons such as nonhuman animals or the Earth. And hence, it is very common for racialized humans to frame the oppression they experience as "being treated like an animal" or for genociders to frame their justification of genocide in terms of the animality of their victims. This is crystallized in the *West*ern distinction between human rights and animal rights. Racialized humans typically buy White Irrationality as a means of articulating their aspirations of being acknowledged for their humanity. Indigenous humans have the good sense to know that they are animals, and don't participate in this nonsense. While indeed it does provide a net advantage for White people to participate, the irrational costs associated with White Irrationality, owing to its interpretive foundations, are borne by poorer White people. We find this explored in the aptly titled book by Jonathan M. Metzl, *Dying of Whiteness,* in which Metzl explores how poor White people in rural Southern America vote against social policies (like universal health care) that would advantage them out of fear that enabling those policies would also help Black people. Rich White people (in these same places) vote in the same way, but they will not suffer the same consequences as they can privately afford what such programs would offer.

This de-colonial analysis of oppression as the adoption of a shared doxastic outlook explains what is sometimes called *epistemic injustice.* Miranda Fricker, beginning a conversation about this, identifies two varieties of epistemic injustice (Fricker 2007). Testimonial injustice arises when prejudices deflate the importance of a person's testimony. Hermeneutic injustice occurs when there is a gap in interpretive resources that puts a person at an unfair disadvantage in making sense of their social experiences. According to the argument pursued here, White Irrationality creates the infrastructure for the prejudices that diminish the testimonial importance of many agents in proportion to their deviation from its paradigm person. It also disadvantages those who lack interpretive resources to articulate their experiences. The argument of this book entails that the solution to these problems is de-colonization by the adoption of explication. We don't solve this problem by closing the hermeneutic (interpretive) gap. We dissolve it by explicating.

2. Interpretation: Epistemic Mimicry and the Appropriation of Epistemic Labor

This section has two purposes. The first is to explore to the end the interpreter's confusion. While interpretation is stupid, this claim is not an *ad hominem* argument, which would be the claim that we should ignore the interpreter because they have nothing to contribute. We get to see it's irrational, and an epistemic failure (stupid), by treating it as worthy of explication, only to arrive at dead ends. The second is to show how, despite its irrationality, it survives because it is a system of appropriation. This will help us answer the question of how interpretation survives despite its deficiencies. And this will certainly add to the conclusion that the only reason Western thinkers adopt it is the oppressive, appropriate benefits it yields.

2.1. Unpacking the Confusion of the Interpreter

Interpreters claim that all explanation is explanation by way of one's propositional attitudes. I noted that there are two problems with this. The problem is that either this claim (a) transcends the limits of our own attitude or (b) in making it we are just expressing our perspective. If the former, we are committed to something that contradicts the relativism of the claim that we are always explaining by way of our propositional attitudes. If the latter, it's unclear why anyone else should care. Secondly the idea that all explanation is explanation in terms of one's propositional attitudes is *easily* refuted by the example of explicating a valid argument with premises and a conclusion one does not belief, desire, fear … But there is a residual worry—how is it that we can identify an argument as valid. Doesn't this require some belief about what validity is?

Now, one way to refute this worry is to notice that we can come to *learn* about validity by inspecting a variety of arguments and inductively generalizing about a subset that has a peculiar property that we call "validity." If this is the case, then we do not have to have a belief in validity as a condition of identifying an argument as valid: we can discover that. This is why it takes time to learn about reasoning. One needs to be given many examples and an opportunity to identify this thing called validity. And then over time one develops a personal inductive library and a generalization about validity— the property where *if the premises are true, the conclusion has to be true*—that provides us some confidence about the topic. But this generalization is not a reason: it's the conclusion of an inductive reasoning process. It provides confidence, but not justification as it's the outcome of inquiry. We know this because every new argument requires us to look at it afresh to discern whether it has or lacks this peculiar property of validity.

If a belief in a proposition that enshrines validity is required to identify an argument as valid, then we have an answer to the question: why did you identify *this* argument X as valid? One could say: I know what validity is (this criterion of validity I believe) and that's my reason. Ok. If that is the case, then the believed proposition that enshrines validity (which the interpreter believes) should *entail* that an argument is valid, for then the proposition would function as a reason, and the identification of the argument would be the conclusion.

Let us assign, *if the premises are true, then the conclusion has to be true,* the letter V, which will symbolically stand for the criterion of validity. We call arguments valid that meet this criterion. If we needed to assume this in order to determine whether an argument such as Modus Ponens (*If* P *then* Q. P. *Therefore* Q.) is valid, then at least Modus Ponens (MP) would follow from V. But this is what we get if we try to put this into practice:

(1)   V.
(*Therefore*) *If* P *then* Q. P. *Therefore* Q.

Conclusions have to be propositions that can be true or false in order for an argument to be valid. What is listed in the conclusion is an argument. It cannot be true or false as it is not a single proposition. So assuming the truth of V does not get us to Modus Ponens. Moreover, if the assumed truth of the criterion of validity does not do anything to get us to Modus Ponens, then the belief in the criterion of validity is one more step removed from pointless. I take this to be a general refutation of interpretive claims that all explanations depend upon some prior belief that bears upon or illuminates the object of knowledge. Even if we somehow treated the entire conclusion as a proposition, we could name, MP,

(1)   V
(*Therefore*) MP

we do not have a valid argument, which is to say that the conclusion (MP) does not follow from the premise (V). We know this because for all possible assignments of truth values to V and MP, there is at least one where V is true, and MP is false.

There is no way to save the interpreter's intuition that we need a prior belief to make sense that an argument is valid. Here's the problem:

(1) If a belief is required to understand that an argument is valid, then the resulting argument should be an entailment of a belief (a believed proposition).
(2) But no argument is an entailment of a belief for no argument is a proposition that could be entailed by any believed proposition.

(*Therefore*) No belief is required to understand that an argument is valid.

I think the interpreter might have something like this in mind.

(1) MP is an argument where if the premises are true the conclusion has to be true.
(2) Validity is the name for an argument where if the premises are true the conclusion has to be true.

(*Therefore*) MP is a Valid Argument.

Yes, this argument is valid. The second premise is a modification of V, but it's actually different—it's a linguistic definition of "valid argument," not the criterion of a valid argument. But even if it were the same thing, the problem remains: how can we figure out that this argument is valid? And we are back to the problem that we can't figure it out by using the criterion of validity as a reason as no argument is a proposition that follows from a reason.

If we buy LAT, we think incorrectly arriving at the discovery that MP is a valid argument is a proposition for we can represent this discovery as a linguistic claim that we believe. We can say "MP is a valid argument" and confuse that with what we discovered. LAT hence deceives us into confusing representations of what we know with what we know. And having changed the subject to a linguistic representation treated as the proposition, we are led to think that our attitude toward it is central to its epistemic relevance. And then we are no longer in a world of knowing but in a world of believing.

If understanding and belief are two different matters, knowledge as an example of understanding is not as Edmund Gettier (following Plato) famously put it, a kind of belief, true or justified (Gettier actually criticized this model but also somehow made it the default position in Analytic epistemology). But for the same reason, knowledge is not any kind of propositional attitude. Timothy Williamson for instance has claimed that knowledge is a specific kind of propositional attitude, one that is *factive* (Williamson 2002, 34). A fact is a true proposition so on this account knowledge is an attitude only to true propositions. But when I know that an argument is valid I don't know a true proposition nor do I have an attitude to a true proposition.

(1) If P then Q
(2) P

(*Therefore*) Q

To know that MP (this argument) is valid is to know a bunch of *variables* for propositions (P and Q) that relate to each other validly. The object of knowledge is the argument form, and discerning the valid relationship between the premises and the conclusion is like having a really in-depth appreciation of the shape of an object, like a potato or a rock. I may thereby know many false—non-factive—propositions that comprise the valid argument I know. Knowledge of an argument is *de re*—about the thing, the argument—not *de dicto*, about the proposition, about the argument. If knowing this argument was a factive state, then this argument and its property of validity would be a true proposition. But it is not a proposition. It is an argument.

One major strand of Western epistemology, especially as we see it celebrated in the Analytic tradition, tries to frame all knowledge as an exercise of an agent, S, knowing a *proposition*, P, where the P is the subject of some special attitude. But this can't be enough. On a more traditional account, the proposition is standardly thought to have to be true, and we need some supporting condition—justification, or warrant—*because*, otherwise, we're left with a nonrational state of having a positive feeling about a thought, P (whether belief or an attitude to a factive state), as though knowledge. Justification here *functions as an expiation* for the irrationality of the propositional attitude that is the content of knowledge. This is the kind of mental gymnastics one has to enable to make sense of interpretation as though it isn't an exercise of irrationality. But it is. And one sign of this is that it does *not allow us to simply know* anything. We always have to know a proposition *about* a thing and its properties. What is not normally appreciated is that this leads to an infinite regress. Consider the case of knowing that P is false. How can I know this? According to the interpretive model, I know a true proposition, P_1, that I have some emotional relationship to (an appropriate attitude to), and the content of that proposition is the claim "P is false." But if I need a proposition to scope over P and its truth value to know it, then I will need to know another proposition, P_2, whose content is "P_1 is true," to have the right kind of attitude to, and so on.

Notice that this problem is not solved by adopting what is sometimes called a "knowledge-first" approach where knowledge is analyzed as a special propositional attitude to a true proposition (not merely a belief). The problem again is that when we know, we know things. Treating it as an attitude toward propositions recasts knowledge as an attitude toward representations of things and their properties. And this would lead to the same regress (YS IV.21-22). Similarly, as all of the criticisms of interpretation pertain to propositional attitudes, we could reword the argument above, where we note that the validity of an argument does not follow from a believed proposition, to an argument where we note that the validity does not follow from an attitude to a true proposition, for an argument is not a proposition that follows from other thoughts. The knowledge first story is still a version of interpretation (explanation in terms of propositional attitudes): it's just not one based on belief.

If knowledge is *objective*—that is about things that we can observe from differing perspectives—knowledge is not a matter of propositional attitudes. A propositional attitude is a view of a thought from the perspective of the *attituder*. That's not objective.

Western authors who claim that humans are special because humans engage in linguistic representation and thereby propositional knowledge, rendering humans rational to this extent, are mistaken.

- Even in the case of knowing logic, knowledge is not propositional knowledge.
- Knowledge even in the case of logic is knowledge about things, like arguments.
- What people—humans, dogs, the Earth—know, are things, and some of those things are thoughts.

We can certainly know propositions, but when we know them, we know them as things, with inferential properties. We may or may not know that they are true. And often the propositions that we know are false.

Language actually gets in the way of reasoning by changing the subject to our representations. Language helps humans in thinking not because it facilitates thinking: it facilitates the record or storage of thinking that has to be representationally deflated by reason. Language is the human way to offload, into public record, thinking. Concluding that linguistic meaning is thought is like thinking that the grooves on vinyl or dots on a CD is music. That's not music: it's a representation of music. To listen to (liberate the) music we have to reverse the process of encoding. Similarly to liberate thought we have to reverse the encoding by LE, which identifies thought content as the disciplinary use of a representation. And this allows us to distinguish between our proprietary ways to record thought (our language, for instance) and others' ways to do the same.

These considerations also help us see how interpreters fake understanding. They do so by having attitudes about linguistic representations of what can be known. They can memorize for instance the criterion of validity, and various inference rules. But the difference in the case of the interpreter is that they will *choose not to reason* about propositions they disagree with. They hence mimic reasoning, but do not reason. They mimic learning, but do not learn. That's why *no* Western author ever bothered to explicate South Asian moral philosophy. That requires reasoning about propositions one does not agree with as a Westerner. That's why it's easier for Westerners to fall back into the familiar old beliefs of White Irrationality, itself a form of interpretation.

2.2. Inquiry: Two Accounts

Inquiry itself can be modeled either as an interpretive endeavor or as an explicatory endeavor. The standard approach to the study of BIPOC traditions is a case in point in interpretive mimicry of inquiry. In this case, beliefs from the Western tradition, created by its colonial rollout, including Secularism$_2$, are the frame imposed on BIPOC traditions, and then only what is consistent with the frame is counted as research.

There are softer versions of the interpreter's project that do not so fastidiously hold on to all beliefs as gatekeeping criteria. A reflective equilibrium strategy would allow us to consider new beliefs that contradict old ones, and we could then revise the list of propositions we are willing to endorse by accepting something new and jettisoning something old (Goodman 1954, 63–4; Rawls 1971, 20). This would allow us to not treat our doxastic commitments as a hard barrier to acquiring new beliefs; it would leave our beliefs intact, on the whole, as a constraint: whatever new beliefs we accept must fit with the ones we keep.

Donald Davidson's thought also exemplifies a kind of softening of interpretation. Earlier he was a proponent of the Quinian account of applying the principle of charity where we must try to maximize agreement between ourselves and those we are trying to understand (Davidson 2001, 101). Later he retreats from this formulation and instead suggests that the point of charity is to render the total behavior (linguistic and other) of a speaker or author intelligible (Davidson 2000, 23–4; 1996a, 66–7). Toward the end of his career, he understands these ideas in terms of our need and capacity to triangulate with others in common linguistic contexts, allowing us to fix the content of what we say and believe via this social interaction (Myers and Verheggen 2016). It is true that Davidson's view comes close to what I advance as LE. But there are huge differences. Davidson is committed to the importance of language to fixing objective content, and hence nonhumans and small children cannot participate in this. As well, it's an account of triangulation that depends upon interpreting others, which is far removed from LE.

Both of these softened approaches to interpretation do not solve the problem of interpretation which is that it conflates the perspective of the epistemic agent(s) with an acceptable explanation. If it is our belief that must on the whole adjudicate any new belief, or if it is our belief that render an object of explanation intelligible, we're not really any more free from the irrational force of propositional attitudes. The appropriative implications of interpretation are hence not expunged by this approach—every other person and their reasons would be appropriated by the interpreter as the interpreter's to explain by their beliefs.

An explicatory approach to inquiry in contrast is not concerned with truth, and hence it is not concerned with what we are willing to endorse as true (our beliefs). It is concerned with objectivity, namely, what we can disagree about. This is because whereas an interpretive approach based on one's beliefs is *first-person*, an explicatory approach is always a *third-person* account. We engage in this third person perspective when we evaluate whether an argument is valid. And hence would engage in this when we can imagine what follows from a data set or reasons whether or not we believe them.

Accordingly, the first level of explicatory inquiry concerns rendering explicit, via deduction, options that entail conclusions that are controversial relative to competing options. The second level is inductive: here we identify the topic of dissent as a generalization of the topic given the representative sample of options determined at the first level. The third level corresponds to IBE. At this third level, we want to identify the best option out of possible known options that explains the disagreement. Such a theory would have to explain why the same objective phenomenon is viewed differently given differing perspectives. It would have to explain for instance that what the blind men are feeling are the same elephant, or conch. This third level of theoretical explanation might find that the best explanation is one of the many surveyed at the first level, or it may require an innovation that adds to our appreciation of the first level options. The best theory here is not necessarily the true theory. We might find with the fullness of time that our appreciation of the first-order options expands, rendering a different second-order induction, and necessitating a different third-order explanation. In fact, we need not take a position on truth to undertake inquiry through these three levels.

When for instance the Covid-19 pandemic started, there were multiple theories about the new illness, including the idea that it was just a bad flu. But there were observations about the progression of the disease that didn't fit that diagnosis. And so several theories were considered that accounted for some of the observations of the disease. Once there were enough conflicting theories about the disease there was some way to pin the objectivity of the disease (which is what the conflicting theories differ about): this would take us to the second level of inquiry. The third level consisted in developing an account of what everyone was disagreeing about that explained the disagreement. And this involved the formation of a new theory about a novel virus: SARS-CoV-2. The success of the theory had to do with its capacity to explain why the disease would superficially look like a flu or a cold, though it was neither and had properties and symptoms not captured by traditional diagnoses.

In physics, there is a first level disagreement between Quantum Mechanics and the macroscopic theories like Einstein's Relativity, not to mention older theories, like Newtonian physics. Einstein's Relativity and Newtonian Physics predicts that events are continuous and deterministic, while Quantum Mechanics accounting for microscopic events describes them as not local and probabilistic (meaning that events separated from each other can display connections that require them to be described together even though they are not spatially connected). This first-order disagreement sets out the second-order objectivity—the thing, namely, physical phenomenon—that is the topic of dissent. And then at the third level what is required (and not yet obviously produced) is a theory that will account for this first level disagreement, generalized at the second level.

If we adopt the explicatory approach to philosophy I recommend, we would explicate the first-order diversity of theories of dharma, theories of the *tao*, and theories of ethics. This would allow us to notice that at the second level the first-order theories are dissenting about THE RIGHT OR THE GOOD. And there are four basic theories: Virtue Ethics (the good produces or conditions the right), Consequentialism (the good justifies the right), Deontology (the right justifies the good), and Yoga (the right conditions or produces the good). And then at the third level the successful theory would explain the disagreement about THE RIGHT OR THE GOOD. There is no mystery about which theory allows us to do this: Yoga. From top to bottom Yoga allows us to first determine that there is a first-order disagreement via its foundational argument for explication, and thereby accounts for what we are disagreeing about. As a normative ethical theory, it claims that moral practice is about choosing our own values, while not being constrained by prejudices or assumptions. And this also describes what makes the disagreement on ethical theory possible. This shows that ethics, moral philosophy, and philosophy, are no less objective than physics or biology. In fact by beginning with explication and the contrast with interpretation, Yoga constitutes a meta-normative starting point for all inquiry. The illusion of ethics being less objective a discipline than physics or biology is a function of the interpretive, nonsense approach to inquiry, where everything is assessed by way of the propositional attitudes of the inquirer. If that's what ethics is about, then surely it is not objective. And if our propositions about ethics are just what we say in our language, given its peculiar cultural and political history (weaponized by LAT as we saw in Chapter 2), then indeed there is nothing objective about moral claims. But the problem here is not the topic but the method of inquiry. Interpretation is inquiry in name only for it cannot allow us to learn anything that we do not have the appropriate propositional attitudes towards.

And it is not simply that moral philosophy is objective, in the sense that we can find that it has objectively nothing to talk about. Just the opposite: it sorts through controversies of THE RIGHT OR THE GOOD. And the best explanation of these controversies is the ethical theory that allows us to appreciate the controversies. This is by no means an ordinary way of thinking about moral questions. But it is isomorphic with all cases of explicatory inquiry. And when we get to the third level of explanation, we are still dealing with argument, and explanation. There is no single proposition to believe that is true. It's *de re* all the way down.

A very naïve objection to the objectivity of ethics can be found in the idea that we have empirical senses that can underwrite empirical science but we lack a moral sense (Kagan 2007). This is a red herring. Most of what scientists talk about is not observable. Rather good science is possible because it explains what is objective, which we can disagree about from differing perspectives. And we can likewise disagree about ethical claims and ethical theories from differing ethical perspectives. Good moral philosophy takes that as its topic. Bad moral philosophy prejudges the topic by conflating it with the ethnography of White people. End-state Colonialism, complete with skepticism about ethics, is a further artifact of White Irrationality. It relies upon interpretation which problematizes inquiry by conflating it with our perspective.

2.3. Fake Learning, Hepeating, Appropriation, and AI

In this section, I want to address how interpretation, a nonrational, and irrational, method of explanation, manages to survive as an explanatory strategy. The main problem with interpretation is that it seems unable to learn. If one has to only accept what one believes, then one's willingness to believe will constitute a constraint on what one is willing to entertain. To answer how an interpreter can nevertheless do something like learning, consider the phenomenon of *hepeating*.

This portmanteau that combines "he" and "repeating" was coined by the astronomer Nicole Gugliucci and friends: "My friends coined a word: hepeated. For when a woman suggests an idea and it's ignored, but then a guy says the same thing and everyone loves it" (Gugliucci 2017). This is an example of what Fricker calls testimonial injustice. What I find important about this example is that it is a case where the man, repeating what a woman has said, mimics learning something, but he is credited with the innovation while she, who made it explicit, is not. So mimicry is in this respect a case of the appropriation of what is explicated. What is the process by which this happens? I think we can certainly identify cases where this appropriation is conscious and planned out in advance. But if you have ever observed hepeating happen, you will have noticed the utter cluelessness of the man engaging in hepeating. In cases that it is most flagrant, it is seemingly unconscious as the hepeater does not even react to what is originally said by the female explicator: it's as though she said nothing. How does one come to appropriate what one is not aware of?

Our focus on the mechanics of interpretation can fill out the details of this *intentional* process. This process is illuminated by four components of a propositional attitude generated by LAT. There is (1) the content (what she said or did), then (2) a linguistic representation about this content as though a thought, then (3) an attitude toward this alleged proposition, (4) and then the agent who has an attitude toward this linguistic representation as though a thought. In treating knowledge as a relationship to the linguistic representation as though a thought, LAT creates a firewall—the linguistic representation—that prevents awareness of the origins of the content of the representation—for knowledge is described as an awareness of the representation or claim (*de dicto*) not the thing (*de re*). And in this lack of awareness of the origins of the content of a representation, the interpreter thereby appropriates the content, encoded in the representation as though their belief, their desire, or some other propositional attitude. Explicators based in LE wouldn't confuse their representations with a thought, and moreover, they would be aware of the history of representation as something that has to be deflated as part of thinking. And so explicators would be very interested in rendering explicit the ideas and thoughts of anyone. But the interpreter driven by LAT renders the origins of content that is represented in language out of view. This is to repeat an earlier observation that LAT and its interpretive method is ahistorical, pretending that what is linguistically encoded is not itself a result of a historical process of agents choosing. Interpreters hence *appropriate* as a matter of course. Insofar as LAT encourages interpretation, LAT-based cultures will facilitate the rampant appropriation of the intellectual labor of explicators. The result of course is a mediocracy that combines the appropriated epistemic labor of explicators, with the ignorance of the interpreter.

The interpreter is by the same mechanism susceptible to appropriating the fear of their oppressed group as their own fears. And so we should not be surprised that descendant societies of White Supremacist colonization (like the United States) act as though they are under threat by the influx of migrants or immigrants—even when the migrants are descendants of displaced Indigenous people native to their colonized lands.

All interpretation in our world occurs within the global practice of White Irrationality that marginalizes people in proportion to their deviation from the assumed paradigm person in the *Western* tradition. One's place in this hierarchy of marginalization, *if one interprets*, provides motive to be aware of one's equals and betters, but to ignore those further marginalized. Hence, men would on the whole hepeat women. But White folks would, within this hierarchy, appropriate from BIPOC for there would be nothing in the exercise to shine a light on BIPOC importance relative to one's place as a White person. Everyone would look up to the White man as the original thinker in this case, though they are likely the ultimate beneficiaries of the appropriative activity of interpretation. Hence, Philosophical Apartheid seems natural and normal.

This explains how interpreters, despite being irrational, can benefit from reasoning—not unlike generative AI. For while they do not reason, they can steal the explicatory work of others and they also internalize explicatory strategies within interpretive limits. And while the political project of imposing one's own beliefs on others as a mode of explanation does not account for the origins of egalitarian ideas (as this project is oppressive) if the process of interpretation simultaneously allows for the interpreter to appropriate the propositional content of the people they are colonizing, they can bring about a *colonial-exchange* where the colonized is saddled with the oppression of the Colonizer while the Colonizer appropriates the egalitarian and freethinking ways of the colonized—again, not unlike generative AI that "learns" off of training data. In this interaction, the Colonizer is better off for the interaction and the colonized worse-off. This is structurally the same as the worse-off position a female colleague is when she is repeatedly hepeated and the men around her are promoted on the basis of this appropriation. And as an example of colonization, there will be no public record that credits the female colleague with her epistemic labor.

And hence it should not be a surprise to us that just when European Colonizers—interpreters—were engaging in genocidal settler colonialism and other forms of appropriative colonialism around the globe, they were also appropriating the intellectual labor of the Indigenous people they were colonizing who were in contrast to their oppressive ways free and not interested in the project of colonization. This enrichment of ideas, in addition to the wholesale theft of capital from colonized peoples, explains the remarkable boom in technological and cultural accomplishments at this time in Europe. It also explains how, all of a sudden, when Europeans were militarily oppressing everyone else, their intellectuals started articulating theories of egalitarianism and equality of persons. As noted in Chapter 3, this is indeed what J.S. Mill did in formulating his particular form of comprehensive Liberalism: he appropriated the epistemic labor of South Asians rendering explicit their practice of Yoga, and represented it as *his* idea that we ought to structure a society where individuals can engage in moral experimentation while determining their own conception of the good, while denying that South Asians were sufficiently mature to engage in this themselves. And indeed, this is the story of Liberalism on the whole (more on this in Chapter 5): ideas of egalitarianism and freedom that were originally alien to the *Western* tradition become standard in *Western*—White—ethical thinking just as Europeans were colonially crushing BIPOC in a process of *colonial-exchange.*

The similarity between generative AI and White Irrationality cannot be exaggerated. AI models, especially generative ones like diffusion models and large language models, are typically trained on massive datasets collected from the internet, which often include copyrighted works by artists and authors without their explicit consent. Both AI "training" and White Irrationality mischaracterize the appropriation of others' epistemic labor as though an epistemic innovation on the part of the appropriator. Both do so insofar as both are exercises of interpretation, which treats what is observed, and thereby believed, as the content of further explanation, which merely mimics and reifies the original content. There are differences. At the moment AI is a tool. Colonizers acted for their own ends in appropriating the intellectual labor and capital of the colonized. But the remarkable readiness of people in a world of White Irrationality to credit AI with *actual intelligence* is a symptom of a failure to appreciate what learning actually is, and thereby what oppression amounts to. Interpreters confuse oppression with learning. And in this ready inclination to treat AI as intelligence, interpreters are greenlighting the use of AI to replace accountability. As has been observed by AI researchers such as Joy Buolamwini, racism, sexism, colorism, and various forms of discrimination are coded into computational systems, and AI is bad at recognizing dark skinned people (Buolamwini 2023). This was preceded by the important work of Safiya Umoja Noble in her *Algorithms of Oppression: How Search Engines Reinforce Racism* (2018). None of this is surprising if we appreciate that what counts as "artificial intelligence" is merely a computerized form of White Irrationality. Recently, in an article aptly called "The Illusion of Thinking: Understanding the Strengths and Limitations of Reasoning Models . . ." researchers at Apple relate that at a certain level of complexity, known AI models suffer a complete collapse in accuracy, even when supplied the correct strategy (Parshin Shojaee et al. 2025). Given what we know about interpretation, this is not surprising: interpretation only seems reasonable insofar as it repackages content it has appropriated. But this is insufficient to think, which is to explicate. Thinking, as opposed to propositional attituding, is a metaethical, meta-explanatory choice. To use AI as a tool could be responsible so long as we appreciate that it's stupid, like all interpretation. To treat it as intelligent is to continue the project of the *West's* colonization.

Of late it is not uncommon to hear prominent leaders of the AI revolution either worrying about its ethical implications or claiming that as it can learn, it can also be taught morality. But if AI "learning" is really an exercise of interpretation, complete with the appropriation of epistemic labor, then AI can never be ethical. It will always be oppressive and unable to explicate moral-philosophical controversy. It will be very much like our LAT-based nations on Planet Ethics: preoccupied with the perspective it has confused with the content of thought, which would generate a genocidal intent to disallow what is not consistent with it. And like on Planet Ethics, it might even have internalized, as part of its code, rules of beneficent moral behavior. That wouldn't stop it from generating genocidal intentions to those who do not participate in its flavor of morality.

3. Peer Review and the Self-Appointed Gatekeepers of White Supremacy

The academy is not an alternative reality disconnected from the politics of the world. All the forces of oppression that structure our world, like White Irrationality, are reified and maintained by the academy because there are no rules or prohibitions against interpretation in academic institutions or in academic publications. As academic appointment is based on academic accomplishment, including publication, and there are no institutional policies against interpretation, those who are promoted by conventional academic means are promoted by participating in White Irrationality. Peer review is no protection against this corruption: it is how it is implemented. Without concerted effort to ban and criticize interpretation, the West and its LAT-based tradition dominate by shutting out Indigenous people. And as interpretation is itself an activity that can and does appropriate the epistemic labor of explicators, the academy, in allowing these very same forces of oppression that constitute the world we live in, is largely an exercise of appropriating the epistemic labor of explicators while prioritizing the Western tradition and its tradition of White Irrationality. Allowing interpretation free rein results in a hobbled academy that produces very little good research. Instead, the very people whose methodology is irrational and responsible for oppression are allowed to engage in oppression by peer review. They are hence allowed to block the airing of research that would shine a light on their incompetence. Requiring the explicatory practices of disciplinary research, including moral philosophy, would put this to an end.

3.1. The *Gatekeeping Game*

To consider how this could come to pass that the anti-rational, pro-oppression, model of interpretation has come to dominate our intellectual lives and our politics, let's consider the game of *publish or perish*. For the sake of not making the discussion cumbersome, I will talk as though belief is the propositional attitude that interpreters are working with but it could be any propositional attitude, including an attitude to only true propositions. The results will be the same because they are outcomes of employing propositional attitudes. When this same decision structure operates publicly outside of the academy, where similar decisions about the candidacy of others for various positions are made, we could also call it the *gatekeeping game*. This is a game comprised of contestants (authors in the academic case of publish or perish) and reviewers. To simplify things let us begin assuming that both populations of contestants and reviewers are split between interpreters and explicators. Let us give the interpreters a slight advantage to compensate for their self-inflicted disadvantage. We know they have trouble reasoning. If they had to defend themselves by way of argument, they would likely fail as that requires thinking and instead they do propositional attitudes. But they can believe propositions that, as a set, comprise various valid arguments, and these propositions can be the ones they are interested in defending. As noted in the previous section, they can mimic learning and reasoning. Explicators reading the writings of these interpreters will be able to render explicit various arguments that are implicit in their writings. That is, explicators could treat the artifacts of interpreters who accidentally say things that comprise valid arguments as contributions to the first-order options. And if the beliefs that interpreters are willing to defend are the ones that can get by explicators (as interpreters are epistemic parasites), they will in general engage in writing that quite accidentally can be explicated as providing reasons for a conclusion. In a *Westernized* world, these beliefs will be *Western*. Explicators in contrast are more independently minded. They aren't given to simply repeating propositions that are familiar: they will pursue strange arguments too! They may draw on propositions that are alien to the *Western* tradition. Let us assume that half of the explicators in any round of the game accidentally share the *Western* doxastic commitments of the interpreters, so on interpretive grounds, their submissions can be accepted. Finally, to survive the game two reviewers, one explicator and one interpreter, have to accept the submission:

	# of authors	Explicator Reviewer Acceptance	Interpreter Reviewer Acceptance	Survivors
Explicator Authors	100	100	50	50
Interpreter Authors	100	100	100	100

If only the survivors of one round of *publish or perish* are allowed to play the next round, then all the interpreters will survive. However, only half of the explicators will survive one round: the ones whose propositions complied with the beliefs (or other relevant propositional attitude) of the interpreter. If you play this game recursively, after seven rounds, explicators are completely eliminated. All the interpreters will survive.

Insofar as *publish or perish* is meant to determine who is fit to continue participating in the competition, then every successive round determines who survives to participate again. No one gets to survive this game by repeatedly failing rounds. Even if failing a round does not automatically result in elimination, those who do not fail a round have a competitive advantage over those who do, and those who are judging the competition keep track of the score.

To this game, it makes no difference what propositional attitude the interpreters employ. It could be an attitude to only true propositions and it would have the same results. I have played this game with differing proportions of interpreters and explicators and I found that it does not matter how few interpreters there are. They could comprise a minority of the contestants at the start. However, in the long run, with survivors of previous games making up the new batch of contestants, the explicators will be eliminated given the constraints that only half of the explicators will defend what the interpreters endorse and that the interpreters appropriately produce what can be explicated by explicators. What if the reviewers themselves were derived from the pool of successful contestants? As long as interpreters have an advantage that explicators do not, namely, that they will cull explicators who do not conform to their propositional attitudes but they will always appropriatively endorse what can be explicated, they will over time eliminate all the explicators. Interpreters—like all Colonizers—are like an invasive species. Little wonder interpretation is the backbone of colonization. The only explicators that can survive are those who manage to buy the propositional attitudes employed by the interpreters and never deviate from them, which is effectively to give up on explication and to adopt the strategy of interpretation. These explicators will try to hide themselves in plain view. They will avoid speaking up and bringing attention to themselves as critics of the dominant interpretive strategy. But they will also end up supporting the politics of interpretation as they will do nothing to disrupt it.

There is a catch for the success of the interpretive strategy.

- In order for it to work, interpreters have to share an outlook that they employ in interpretation.
- If they employ attitudes to widely different propositions, they will eliminate each other.

So in order for interpreters to avoid being eliminated by other interpreters, they have to converge on a shared outlook. Given the history of *Western* colonialism, in our world, the shared outlook consists in the facts of a world structured by *Western* colonization. As noted, White people have a net motive to participate in this irrationality, and everyone has a negative motive to avoid losing their space in the privilege hierarchy to maintain it. Hence, White Irrationality becomes a group project for interpreters, something that all interpreters, even those who are disadvantaged by White Irrationality, endorse for fear of being eliminated by other interpreters.

- The academy as something governed by Publish or Perish, with no prohibitions against interpretation, is a free, unconstrained exercise of White Irrationality.
- This is displayed as Philosophical Apartheid.

Given the prevalence of the success of interpretation, how does anything good ever get published? (Or, asked about the *gatekeeping game*, how do worthy candidates who do not exemplify the celebrated paradigms of White

Irrationality get any social recognition?) If the pool of reviewers is equally comprised of interpreters and explicators, and two reviewers are drawn randomly, with a 50/50 chance of an interpreter or explicator being selected, then there are four possible combinations: (1) Interpreter and Interpreter, (2) Interpreter and Explicator, (3) Interpreter and Explicator, (4) Explicator and Explicator. If success requires the approval of both reviewers, then only in the fourth option could an explicator with something new and important squeeze through—if an explicator has the courage, energy, patience, and material conditions to adopt the long game while constantly being rejected and eliminated by the *gatekeeping game*. Success may come, but never as quickly as those who adopt the strategy of *Western* interpretation, and if the speed of one's success is a factor that determines whether one can stay in the game (if for instance you have to show success in gatekeeping within a certain window after entering the game, say after education and entering the job market), then the game is designed to ensure that people who are interested in explicating without restricting themselves to the outlook of the dominant tradition will not only be less successful but failures. Moreover, if the pool of reviewers is also derived from the pool of survivors of the *gatekeeping game*, then over time there will be less explicators, and it will be more unlikely that any one of your reviewers, let alone all of them, will also be explicators. If you are an explicator in this world, you have to adopt the strategy of the tortoise while others try to be the hare. And this may not always be possible, if meeting one's material needs requires success in gatekeeping or publish or perish. The entire system is set up to attrite the explicator. This ensures that academic tenure is almost never possible for the explicator for it is unlikely they will be able to show academic results in the short schedule. This encourages academics to be interpreters.

In philosophy—and especially the peer review of Indian philosophy—an explicatory reviewer is rare.

In any discipline, the explicatory reviewer simply wants to know if the author followed proper explicatory procedure. In philosophy they want to see that: (a) the contribution is on topic for the publication, (b) the submission does what it says it's going to do, (c) it provides an argument— valid, and possibly sound—(d) the author explicated the positions they draw on, and finally (e) the submission makes a contribution to one of the three levels of explication. There are very many ways for a contribution to fail on explicatory grounds, but *never* is one of those that the author considers propositions the reviewer disbelieves. An actual explicatory contribution can be improved and never has to be jettisoned. Interpreters in contrast on top of being irrational—or because of it—throw up all sorts of stupid roadblocks to publishing good work. The interpreter reviewer assesses a submission on the basis of what they would like to see, based on their beliefs and preferences. In other words, they make review not about the objective features of the submission—which we can converge on as we disagree—but rather on the basis of the propositional attitudes they identify with. And in this state, they approve of what is in conformity with the propositional attitudes they identify with and are alarmed by what is not in keeping with it. And this may even take the form of seemingly well-meaning, sympathetic review, where the reviewer believes they are helping the author by recommending revisions based on their beliefs. This is narcissistic, oppressive, and irrational.

Because interpreters do not reason, interpreters will want whatever you attribute to an author to be literally inscribed by the author, but in ways that they interpret. And when faced with an argument that relies on propositions they do not believe, they read it as an effort of the author to claim something that is to be taken on face value and simply believed (they miss out that the point of the proposition in an argument is to be the content of reason, not belief). This disposes interpreters to act like *fact checkers*, as though the truth of what is claimed is the value of the scholarly contribution. And interpreters assess truth in terms of their attitudes. The interpreter reviewer for this book (as though playing the stereotype of what occurs in Philosophical Apartheid) recommended a complete rewrite that removed all the discussions on ethics, though the book is on moral philosophy. The point was to avoid engaging in the argument, which is not about the reviewer's beliefs. They believed they were being helpful. They were playing their part in White Irrationality that sanitizes South Asian discussions about ethics out of view.

As interpreters in a world of White Irrationality draw on beliefs from this tradition and as the literature is largely policed and filtered to echo these beliefs, one way the interpreter polices submissions in accordance with their beliefs is by expecting anything new to conform to what has already been peer-reviewed and published—or to engage in an impossible interpretive unseating of those beliefs. Interpreter peer reviewers can hence make it seem as though it's not their beliefs that are being used to police submissions: they claim rather that the author has not responded to the literature, not as part of an exercise of academic honesty but as though for the new contribution to be considered the old ones have to be refuted or problematized. Explication is not about refuting the truth of received opinions—it's about elucidating the objective. But the interpreter can't understand what that means. The explicator just wants to elucidate the possibilities of research. The interpreter needs their beliefs as epistemic credibility and would expect them to be refuted if anything new is to be considered. The expectation that all explicatory novelty has to refute received published opinions is a roadblock that serves to never consider innovation.

These problems are especially prevalent in philosophy. Tim Crane's excellent "The Philosopher's Tone," an article on the problems of peer review in philosophy, is actually an exposé of how interpretation runs amok in this field (Crane 2018). Such problems include an implausibly low acceptance rate, as though there is something dangerous about publishing something that makes false claims, and the bizarre and prevalent assumption that because a reviewer can think of an objection to a submission that is sufficient grounds to reject the submission or demand revisions. This is exactly what an interpreter would assume for they see acceptability in terms of their willingness to believe something (or have the appropriate attitude to a proposition), and so their objection to a proposal appears to them as evidence that it is unacceptable. Meanwhile, objectivity would require dissent and disagreement: quality academic work should contribute to such debates.

Novel non-Western options have an additional challenge: they cover material not widely known in the literature. So they often have a double burden to educate the reader while exploring the topic. The requirement by interpreters that such an exercise consist in a lit-review, and not merely requirements of academic honesty, is a way to ensure that such a contribution would needlessly balloon in size and then be unpublishable for reasons of length.

This also shows the ways in which their project, and hence the project of intellectuals wrongly given academic posts, who gained that position by interpretation, are epistemic parasites as interpretation is an exercise of epistemic parasitism.

Philosophers writing on classical figures in White philosophy, and those deemed to be classically or canonically Western, get to just focus on the argument. Russell, Frege, Wittgenstein, Davidson, Husserl, Heidegger, or Derrida themselves just followed their concerns and referred to others when relevant to their case. I used to naively believe that this was because in this case what we have is explicatory scholarship. But now I see that this willingness to engage in the writing of these authors without the mediation of lit-review (and their own willingness to do the same) has to do with these Western authors being central to the interpretive project of the West. The farther you are from these central White authors in your thesis, the more you have to do lit-review, for the more you have to demonstrate that what you are talking about is acceptable to White Irrationality. "Scholarship" here is like having the appropriate immigration documents to show that you are not an illegal migrant. The farther you are from the White core, the more you have to justify your presence with documents.

These considerations of unchecked interpretation allowed to take over and normalize White Irrationality in peer review show that academic freedom is an illusion. Academics are supposed to be free to pursue research topics without censorship in the interest of knowledge, research and discovery. But what actually happens given unchecked interpretation is that academics are permitted to pursue a narrow range of topics, the Overton Window of the academy set by the vicissitudes of White Irrationality. Whatever falls outside of this, like South Asian moral philosophy, or Palestine and the ongoing genocide, is erased.

Outside of the academy, in the *gatekeeping game*, these same options exist of White Irrationality and explication, and the same power dynamics will come into play. If you have the good fortune of being assessed by an explicator they will be interested in your epistemic work in making options clear. If you are assessed by interpreters the outcome depends on how you present. If you seem like a paradigm example of what the West values, people will treat you as not requiring justification or legitimation. What you say and how you present constitute the doxastic evidence that satisfies others. The farther you deviate from these examples, the more you will be discussed, and the less you will be directly engaged as a person. And in this discussion about you, as opposed to engagement with you, you will be judged in terms of White Irrationality.

A chief way to hide that this evaluation is an interpretive exercise is to construct a peer review or upward feedback questionnaire with numbered responses, as though that makes the result scientific and quantifiable. Quantifiable data isn't the result of research though; it's the beginning of research. Data has to be explained: it's not the explanation. And so such exercises get inquiry backwards. We have plenty of evidence of how this works. The American Sociological Association, in amassing several studies, shows that student upward feedback discriminates against Women, and People of Color, even when these people display behaviors and processes evident in White male teachers. As a result they have recommended that these not be used to compare candidates for rank and promotion (American Sociological Association 2019). And yet upward feedback, generated from the administration of questionnaires, is used in industry and in the academy to grade employee success, and for assessing tenure and promotion. The expectation that we submit to this as part of employment review is a constant terror designed to maintain the apartheid of a *Western* world. It is a terror designed to ensure that people low on the White Irrationality privilege list are penalized for being responsible, when a White person being irrational would have been preferred.

3.2. Things Must Be Better in the Sciences?

One might object that the interpretive problems with peer review noted are peculiar to the humanities, or social sciences: peer review in the sciences would not fall for that as it's a serious discipline (ha ha). Responding to this concern is important or it shows how prevalent the problem is. And the classic work that sheds light on the same phenomenon occurring in the sciences is Kuhn's *The Structures of Scientific Revolutions*.

According to an idealization of scientific method, scientists propose hypotheses with testable implications. If they observe evidence that contradicts the testable implications, the hypothesis is falsified. The test is formalized in (1): *If* the hypothesis P is true, *then* we will observe Q. The falsifying evidence is found in premise (2): we observe *Not* Q. And this leads to the *conclusion*: Not P. That's Modus Tollens. According to Kuhn, this is not what happens at all in science. Rather if we look at the history of science, it is characterized by successive paradigms. A paradigm is a scientific culture with its own language, and LAT explains how such paradigms function. When a paradigm sets in, what follows is "normal science." Scientists apply its assumptions in empirical work and importantly they do not take disconfirming evidence as epistemically dispositive. Moreover according to Kuhn, what counts as the evidence is itself an entailment of the paradigm. Kuhn paints an interpretive picture of scientific activity where the evidence is not processed independently of the scientist's outlook: it's rather defined by that outlook (Kuhn 1970, 206). According to Kuhn, old paradigms are not refuted by the contradictory evidence (Kuhn 1970, 76). Scientists rather construct *ad hoc* explanations to explain away inconsistent evidence. New paradigms take over not because they are demonstrated to be superior. Rather old interpreters die off and are replaced by new interpreters with their own paradigm.

Two epistemic norms describe what Kuhn describes as the activity of normal science. First is the expectation that any new information that is worth taking seriously has to *cohere* with what is already believed as part of the paradigm. Second is the commitment to *doxastic conservatism*: we ought to prefer our old way of looking at things over new possibilities. Both norms help the paradigm-based scientist resist new evidence that does not fit with their commitments.

Both the coherence strategy and the strategy of conservatism are motivated by a concern for belief. If we treat scientific knowledge as a set of beliefs, then we will not be able to tolerate anything that doesn't fit with our beliefs and we will also conservatively hold on to our outlook because they are our beliefs.

If we were to bring our explicatory considerations into the picture, we would note that there is no logic-based requirement that any new information has to cohere with what we already are committed to. The expectation that new information cohere with old information is tantamount to outlawing Modus Tollens, which is weird as it's logically valid. Similarly, there is no logic-based reason to conservatively prefer the propositions we are already committed to. That is tantamount to confusing beliefs with what we can think about.

One way to read Kuhn is as providing a description of how scientists operate. Some have noted that this is challenging as Kuhn appears to normativize this description of science as an interpretive affair by calling it "normal science." But for us we can note that it is an exercise of interpretation as it is governed by the beliefs that constitute the paradigm: and as Kuhn describes it, it's LAT-based. Science could and does operate according to an explicatory model of dissent across first-order empirical theories, leading to a second-order induction of the objectivity of the question and a third-order IBE about the second-order disagreement. When science moves forward, it operates according to explicatory considerations. As interpretation is not formally banned in academic spaces, we ought to expect that all the same forces of White Irrationality operate in the adjudication of scientific literature, resulting in what Kuhn calls "normal science." An Indigenous approach to science would in contrast prioritize the three levels of explication by disallowing LAT and preferring the explicatory model of LE.

4. Objections

The criticisms that I have been directing at the *West*, and White Irrationality, are criticisms that they deserve in virtue of being exercises of interpretation. And the reason that the *West* gets special mention is that it has taken over as the predominant interpretive tradition. And I've argued that the reason the *West* becomes this global colonization tradition is that it alone acclaims LAT. The reason I have been unrestrained in my criticism is that interpretation is a choice, and the fact that an entire colonizing tradition makes a bad choice, consistently, renders it worthy of criticism. There is no advantage to coddling Colonizers. Being nice to them won't make a difference. But there is an advantage to explicating their faults and stupidity is one of them.

An objection to this approach is that the criticism has been uncivil. What we have before us is a disagreement about how we can frame thought, say, between LE and LAT. And instead of appreciating that disagreement, Ranganathan has resorted to name-calling. This is mistaken. I have rendered explicit this disagreement between interpretation and explication as methods of explanation. In modern times and in English, no one else has. It is the interpreter who is incapable of acknowledging a disagreement because they confuse their perspective with the thinkable. They are folks who would sooner engage in genocide than merely allow a philosophical debate to be explored by all concerned. Calling interpretation stupid is, all things considered, a kind, gentle, and compassionate response to its violence.

Here's a follow-up objection. If any epistemic failure is stupid, then it's unclear how this is a particularly insightful or useful criticism as it seems that no one is perfect and we all make mistakes. The response to this is to note that there is an important difference between a mistake that is a result of circumstantial factors—like fatigue, oppression, or even a lack of exposure to relevant data—that one is more than happy to correct, and an error that one is committed to and unwilling to correct. Insofar as someone commits errors as a result of circumstantial challenges (including natural circumstances like environment or genetics), it is hard to call this an epistemic failure of the agent: it is rather better explained by external factors (like oppression) that interfere with the epistemic success of an agent. And in such cases agents can overcome their mistakes by getting back to their explicatory practices. That is a challenge, and not an assured success. But recovering explicatory practices would be how anyone has to correct this external imposition on their autonomy. This willingness to self-correct (however fruitful that intention) is a sign of intelligence, not stupidity. In contrast, the interpreter is *committed* to being irrational. They like that. That's their jam. And if you call them on it, they will try to defend it tooth and nail by interpreting. That's stupid as it represents an enduring, stable, epistemic failure as a result of personal choice that is not a result of circumstance. It is a result of their choice at the metaethical level to be irrational. As it's their choice, it's their fault. They deserve to be ridiculed and humiliated for that—especially given its oppressive outcomes. The oppressive problems of the world: their fault.

Another objection is that the very formulation of "White Irrationality" is racist, and unfairly impugns White people. In response, first, we should note that racism relies upon the privileging of the importance of one race over another: *identifying* the global phenomenon of White Irrationality does not privilege any race over any other. In fact, it is a criticism of exactly this crime of racism. Moreover, nothing in identifying this phenomenon entails that: (a) White people have to participate in White Irrationality, or that (b) only

White people are guilty of White Irrationality. Race like religion is a construct of colonialism. Ultimately neither race nor religion is objective: they are a creation of a dominant perspective. But participating in White Irrationality ensures that we treat fictions of Western colonization, like race and religion, as though they are real, and the political motivation for this irrationality is to consolidate privilege within the oppressive hierarchy of White Irrationality.

A lingering discomfort I suspect many readers have concerns my wholesale criticism of the Western tradition. It seems to throw the baby out with the bathwater. The objection based on this concern is that my criticism of the West is inaccurate and overgeneralizes a few features of the tradition. My response is to note that the features of the West that I criticize—namely, its being based on LAT, and the resulting anthropocentrism and communitarianism, glued together with interpretation as a methodology—are major themes of the tradition. A further entailment of these trends is that what is celebrated in this tradition is a confusion of thought with belief, and the promotion of interpretation. So even when we find a thinker like Quine, who criticizes propositional attitudes, he's remembered for recommending that we interpret.

One way to rephrase this objection is to complain that the charge that the West is irrational does not comport well with its long and storied history of rationalism. The response is to note that the West's history of "rationalism" isn't really rationalism but interpretation.

In Plato, in the *Republic*, rationalism is the idea of the Divided Line and that reason pertains not to what we experience but to numbers and ideas, which are superior to empirical observations. Plato is mistaken. We can reason about anything as it is content neutral. Restricting reason to abstractions is an interpretive constraint. Similarly, Descartes is often identified as the iconic Rationalist. But for Descartes, reasoning out of an exercise of skepticism is made possible by the *cogito: I think therefore I am.* That is a belief he cannot doubt. Reasoning is not believing. And yet Descartes would have us understand reason as what builds on this propositional attitude. This is stereotypical: when Western authors talk about reasons, they talk about their beliefs.

Descartes' posthumous student Edmund Husserl is to be credited with an important contribution to thinking about reasoning, namely, his "Prolegomena to Pure Logic," which begins his *Logical Investigations*, where he engaged in a sustained criticism of *psychologism*—the notion that logical laws are psychological states. Psychologism is an interpretive account of reason. Husserl is correct to criticize it and many of his criticisms are important. And yet, when we look to his subsequent work on phenomenology for which he is known, in the *Logical Investigations* to start, he constrains analysis to the first-person perspective, and then adds to this the idea of the *epoché*, the bracketing the question of existence of what one is thinking about. This avoids having to deal with the objectivity of the meaning or ideas one is analyzing and to treat it as given, and self-justifying. But this brings the exercise back into the realm of propositional attitudes, as it is answerable to one's gaze at a representation, whatever its content. In other words, his phenomenology is an exercise of psychologism, which conflates the operation of the mind with what is rational. Moreover, this *epoché* is exactly what occurs in interpretive appropriation: the hepeater, as an example, engages in bracketing the question of the objectivity of the content that is perceived and instead worries about his representation *as though his idea.* So all the while Husserlians are engaging in an *epoché*, they are colonizing and appropriating some one else's epistemic labor. High points of the Continental tradition continue this remarkable confusion. Heidegger, who was Husserl's student, breaks away from him by defining humans as interpretive agents—*Dasein*—who engage in a projective existence. This saves Husserl's claims of the given but by explaining them as projections. While Heidegger says many things, it's unclear what premise would entail his claim of the inescapability of interpretation that was not question begging. Or put another way, how could Heidegger ever escape his own subjectivity to figure this out?

Heidegger's famous student, Hans Georg Gadamer, tries to fill in these gaps by providing something like an argument. In his classic *Truth and Method,* Gadamer restricts his research to reviewing famous *Western* intellectuals. Gadamer stresses that many intellectuals who claim to rise above the prejudice of the past fail to appreciate the ways their history and assumptions condition their positive claims. This review shows that all explanation is explanation in terms of what one already believes, which he calls *prejudice*, or judgment in advance of all the facts.

In Section 2.1, Unpacking the Confusion of the Interpreter, of this chapter, I dealt with all the obvious refutations of this argument. And really the simplest way to show it is false is to point out that anytime someone is explicating an argument that relies on premises that they disbelieve, they are engaging in a form of understanding that does not rely upon their beliefs. If we look more closely at Gadamer's effort to argue his case, it's atrocious. Arguments that lead to generalizations are inductions, and hence if we were to view Gadamer's argument as an induction it would be weak. One cannot draw strong generalizations about what all people are capable of on the basis of a sample of a few White men. That is, even if Gadamer's conclusion is true, his narrow sample does not support that conclusion. Another aspect of his position is the universal claim about prejudice as indispensable to all explanation. This leads him to claim that criticisms of prejudice, as exemplified in the Enlightenment, are in fact a prejudice against prejudice (Gadamer 1996, 270). Gadamer writes as though confessing one's prejudices expiates their influence (Gadamer 1996, 362). This is nonsense: unless we choose to explicate, being transparent about our beliefs that we use to interpret changes nothing. Now we're just transparently bullies. That Heidegger was a Nazi is a case in point. He confessed his prejudice. That didn't stop him from being a Nazi. It emboldened this politics of genocide.

In Chapters 1 and 2, I reviewed how LAT, and interpretation, is assumed and defended in the Analytic tradition. The Analytic tradition of philosophy is especially paradoxical as it at once values reason and argument, but on the other hand is *extremely* Western, assuming LAT without defense. It is assumed even when authors in this tradition claim to be distancing themselves from the idea. Consider Bernard Williams' *Ethics and the Limits of Philosophy*.

Williams dreams up a similar scenario to Planet Ethics. He asks us to consider *hyper-traditional societies*, and given LAT, every society on Planet Ethics is hyper-traditional. Members of these communities are homogeneous and "minimally given to general reflection" (Williams 1985). What is different about Williams's thought experiment is that he is unreflective about models of thought, and while he pours scorn on framing issues linguistically because it fails to provide an account of the social dimension of ethics (Williams 1985, 127–31), his thought experiment requires LAT. What Williams asks us to do is to consider a hyper-traditional society and ask whether they could have moral knowledge? There are two varieties of knowledge: the unobjective (which consists in knowledge of cultural participation) and the objective. He concludes that hyper-traditional societies can be understood as having nonobjective ethical knowledge as a kind of cultural competence. But this competence relies upon the exercise being non-reflective and merely accepting cultural norms as cementing nonobjective ethical knowledge. If people in these contexts actually start reflecting on the arbitrariness of their cultural practices, it will undermine their capacity to unreflectively participate. And hence, "reflection can destroy knowledge" (Williams 1985, 148–52).

Williams doesn't appreciate this but his criticism is a general indictment of the Western tradition that conceives of thought in cultural and linguistic ways. If reflection destroys knowledge in the case of ethics on William's account, it does so because reflection asks us to transcend the boundaries of the cultural and the linguistic. If thought is linguistic, then knowledge about science will also be destroyed by reflection. This anti-intellectual, pro-social conformity picture of knowledge ("normal science" as Kuhn puts it) is entirely a creature of LAT. As all Western philosophers—every single one of them—Williams doesn't raise the question of whether there could be other ways to model thought. (He oddly claims to reject LAT but provides an argument that depends on it.) Indigenous thinking, in LE, is not about explanation in terms of our cultural representations. It's about deflating their representational significance to explicate possibilities in a world that exists on an ecological and cosmic scale. Williams' musings about hyper-traditional societies, however, describes the *West* and its uncritical dependence on LAT. And given that reflection destroys *what we thought was knowledge* on the basis of LAT, then *Western* philosophers are motivated to be unreflective and to participate in White Irrationality for fear that reflection will destroy what was called "knowledge." And here we can hear Lao Tzu in the background pouring scorn on "knowledge." If that's all knowledge is—cultural competence—we don't need it.

This theme of simply assuming LAT and then endlessly observing outcomes of the theory is ubiquitous in the *West*, but *always* without any appreciation that LAT is just *a* theory of thought, not the only option. For instance, Charles Travis in his *Objectivity and the Parochial*, writes, "By 'parochial'" I mean to refer to features of our thought which are . . . marks of the human . . ." (Travis 2010, 138). Further he pinpoints this problem in language: "If the reach of our representing (at least in language) is fixed by agreement—by shared capacities for acknowledgement, shared sensibilities . . . then the parochial *permeates* our thinking" (Travis 2010, 14). This holds true only if we assume LAT, for if we assume LE, the representational character of any semiotic device we use to think is deflated. But the point in referencing this is that Travis is assuming LAT without defense, which is so ordinary in the *Western* tradition. How does this come to be in print? By a process of peer review that is dominated by White Irrationality that simply greenlights all the assumptions of the *West*. An explicator reviewer would require that this passage be rendered explicit as assuming LAT. But if it did, there would be no grand point to make about the parochialism of thinking: only the parochialism of LAT and the *West*.

When we move to our penultimate chapter on Applied Ethics, we will have an opportunity to review the canon of *Western* moral philosophy. There we will see that it is dominated by the themes of anthropocentrism and communitarianism: ethics is retold in the *West* as practical challenges of living with other humans in community. This and all the other ways in which the tradition confuses reasons with propositional attitudes point to a common origin in LAT, which is interpretive but also anthropocentric and communitarian. The *Western* tradition is easily stereotyped because it is so narrow in the range of options it considers. Alfred North Whitehead called the *Western* tradition a "series of footnotes to Plato" (Whitehead 1978, 39). But it is better explained as an interpretive unpacking of LAT, with a Greek starting point. The problems it perennially comes back to, such as the tension between the objectivity of our propositions and the seeming parochialism of language and our human ways of representing possibilities, are interminable given the uncritical acceptance of LAT. And if those are the limits, then colonialism is a way to solve the problem by treating the limits of our culture as though a maximal rendering of the possibilities—which everyone must either conform to, resist, or perish under.

5. Conclusion

Colonialism is an outcome of the irrationality of interpretation: both arise from LAT as an interpretive model of thought. And given that the *West* uniquely acclaims LAT, the resulting interpretive irrationality that dominates the world is White Irrationality. I call this "White" Irrationality to bring attention to the ways it provides an irrational advantage to White people. It also serves to explain all forms of oppression in a world of *Western* colonization: oppression is thereby the marginalization that befalls an agent in proportion to their deviation from what the *West* values in an agent. Nonhuman agents are treated as born for oppression in this regime. Regional forms of oppression are held in place by their subservience to colonial artifacts like Secularism$_2$ by White Irrationality.

While LAT-based interpretation is irrational, dysfunctional, and can solve no problems, it nevertheless survives as a practice of epistemic parasitism. Peer review in the academy—and gatekeeping outside of the ivory tower— is not a quality control that prevents White Irrationality. In the absence of prohibitions against interpretation, peer review and gatekeeping are dominated by White Irrationality. The combination of the appropriated epistemic excellence with the stupidity of the appropriative *Western* tradition creates a pervasive epistemic mediocracy that characterizes the academy and all public interaction—at best. Those who win by "merit" in this context are those who win by virtue of the mediocracy that prefers the appropriative and irrational over the intelligent and responsible. It is no surprise thus that universities tend to crumble in the face of fascist and authoritarian expectations because they have been churning out students who have succeeded by excelling in unchecked interpretation who later staff universities, and oppressive governments. Universities, and the academy on the whole, are already compromised. The fascist dictator is just the final straw. What is inconsistent with all of this is a public practice of moral philosophy, which White Irrationality disallows. To normalize a public practice of moral philosophy would require explicating and thereby disallowing interpretation. We have a rational obligation to pursue the latter.

Part Three

Normative Ethics

5

Conventional Morality

Good Character, Good Outcomes, Good Rules

1. From Parochialism to Indigenous Moral Philosophy

This is the first of our two chapters on Normative Ethics, which concerns theories of THE RIGHT OR THE GOOD. The findings of the previous three chapters on Metaethics will serve as a background as we move to think about how normative ethical questions, about THE RIGHT OR THE GOOD, are limited and constrained—colonially—by interpretive pressures, that are generated by LAT. This continues our investigation of the thesis that moral philosophy and colonization are incompatible—and that we have a rational obligation to overturn colonization and its generated oppression. When we think about the options of the *West*, LAT with its anthropocentrism and communitarianism plays a very important role in creating the distinctive flavor of *Western* Normative Ethics. It accounts not only for its beginning moral theories that were radically authoritarian, but it also explains, via its appropriative function as a form of interpretation, that it comes to enrich itself and become a tradition of Liberal theorizing *via* colonization. For genuinely anti-oppressive moral theorizing, we'll have to look elsewhere.

LAT-based colonizing traditions are parochial (narrow, local) because they base the possibilities of moral and political thinking on the culturally encoded. At the start of the *West*, what we learn from Plato is that the possibilities of a LAT-based community rest on shared beliefs—even if that means that everyone has to be lied to—and an aversion or rejection of outsiders (*Republic*, Book X). *Logos* or reason is the same as speech, and so the person who can best articulate the community's language is the one who is reasonable. Plato calls that person the philosopher. But the philosopher for Plato is a kind of autoethnographer, uncovering the universals (the forms) supposedly revealed by one's language (*logos*), lit by the light of the Good. Socrates in Plato's story argues that we need a "Noble Lie" because it would seem that without such a story no one would buy the unequal and hierarchical structure necessary to sustain this convergence (*Republic* 414b–c). Plato is often depicted as both a rationalist and a realist who treats categories as transcending social practices. What is not usually noted is that Plato thinks that it is the actual language of the philosopher (not the foreigner's language or culture) that reveals the morally essential. This is parochial. As we saw in Chapter 2, this is also genocidal.

On Aristotle's naturalization of Plato's inequality, it does not require motivation or a Noble Lie as its justification is part of the social structure that we find ourselves in, and ethics is really about navigating that structure—hence it's political science (the science of getting along in one's city or community) (*Nicomachean Ethics* I.3). And the person who is qualified to take the job of autoethnographer, who understands the values of the community, is the one who has been properly raised by those values. Moral knowledge is hence knowledge about the cultural expectations you are raised with.

The same patterns can be observed in the LAT-based philosophy of Confucius in the Chinese tradition. In the *Analects*, Confucius assumes patriarchy (the superiority of the older to the younger, and of the male to the female) and then theorizes the man of humanity (*jen*) as the one who is in a position to tell everyone how to coordinate via propriety (*li*).

LAT-based parochial traditions set up a tradition of authoritarianism and social conformity for two related reasons. First, we learn our first languages in positions of vulnerability from elders who are stronger than us. Modeling thought on the basis of language builds in patriarchy—in the sense of deference to the older and the authoritative. Secondly, communicating successfully with language in social contexts largely concerns fitting into social expectations. The Western, English, words for THE RIGHT OR THE GOOD, "ethics" or "morality," come from the Greek (*éthos*) and the Latin (*mores*), terms which mean something like "custom." And hence the LAT-inspired foundations of modeling thinking as such give rise to theories of THE RIGHT OR THE GOOD that build into their foundations expectations of social conformity. This is itself a variety of parochialism that defines THE RIGHT OR THE GOOD in terms of the vantage of someone who treats the thinkable as what is culturally encoded in language. The meta-parochialism of LAT is the absurd expectation that all moral theorizing (its moral perspective essentialism) has to conform to this.

Ironically, Europe's tradition of authoritarian moral theorizing begins to crumble because of the second phase of its colonial outgrowth. The first with the spread of Secularism$_2$ was largely an exercise of exploitative colonialism leading to "religion" and the spread of the *West* as a political foundation for global colonization. But in the modern period, it is layered with campaigns of eliminative colonialism. And now, we find an Enlightenment concern for equality as *Western* colonialism begins to destroy Indigenous peoples by appropriating their freedom. As noted, interpretation mimics learning by appropriating what it comes in contact with. So Europeans all of a sudden valuing freedom when they colonize Indigenous people is not surprising: Colonizers are appropriating Indigenous ways while denying those very ways to them. But where were these ideas coming from? I have noted that Mill's comprehensive Liberal ideas come from South Asia. David Graeber and David Wengrow in *The Dawn of Everything* (2021) show that another source was Indigenous people—the Wendat—who lived in what is now Canada. I shall summarize their findings.

Graeber and Wengrow focus on the French settlers and missionaries accounts of Indigenous peoples of Turtle Island, specifically in modern-day Canada. The Wendat people figure large in their account as there are many historical records of French interaction with them. Both the Wendat and the French Colonizers who interacted with them agreed that the Wendat and other Indigenous peoples lived in generally free—unconstrained—societies and Europeans did not. What they disagreed about was on whether personal freedom was desirable. Of course, in time, freedom becomes a dominant theme of the American and French revolutions. And in philosophy, individual freedom becomes the theme of modern moral philosophers. But at the time of these initial interactions, Graeber and Wengrow observe that modern readers would find more sympathy with the described Indigenous peoples and their way of life than the exceedingly oppressive, hierarchical, French Colonizers who had many restrictions on personal freedom based on social status, the role of women, sexual mores, and a high tolerance for poverty within their own society and among their own people. All of this struck the Wendat as absurd. There were other peculiar features of Wendat society that caught Europeans by surprise. While indeed there were leaders among Indigenous people, the leaders had no coercive power. So if they thought that their community or society should take some particular action, they would have to persuade others. And given this dynamic, people spent much of the day arguing with each other in community commons about what was to be done. Plato envisioned a functioning society as one premised on shared beliefs imposed from on top. Indigenous people took up the challenge of arguing and persuading each other in light of open debate. Given our investigation in the previous three chapters on Metaethics, we should not be surprised by the cultural differences between oppressive and Indigenous traditions.

- In the case of Indigenous traditions, disagreement and debate are a good thing.

This is what we would expect given LE. The very structure of thought on this account is controversy.

- For the irrational Colonizer and oppressor, disagreement and debate are a bad thing.

This is what we would expect given LAT, as we saw in Chapter 2.

On the one hand, it seems like a weak counter-example to these observations that the White Supremacist, Colonizer J.S. Mill, who championed public debate, stole his model of open intellectual activity from the very Indians he deemed too immature to handle it. On the other hand, just observing that Mill couldn't allow South Asians to have a say in moral debate, as they were too racially immature, says a lot about how moral philosophy is a threat to colonization. If the lowly colonized people could join the discussion, the Colonizer no longer has any peculiar authority to govern them.

Whereas the White Colonizer thinks it is his job to decide if South Asians can be trusted with intellectual freedom, the reality, as reviewed in Chapter 3, is that South Asians have a long history of Secularism$_1$ openness to free thinking—to the extent that they had to be colonized by Secularism$_2$ to put this intellectual freedom to an end.

Graeber and Wengrow also make much of a historical philosopher and diplomat of the Wendat people, Kandiaronk, who was widely regarded by the French and others who interacted with him as the brightest person they had met. Graeber and Wengrow identify him as the person called "Adario" by the traveler Baron de Lahontan, who wrote *Dialogues avec le sauvage Adario*. Graeber and Wengrow note that European scholars tend to dismiss this as pure fiction, while Indigenous scholars take this to be based on actual interactions with Kandiaronk. Moreover, they are concerned to motivate the idea that it is from such figures that European thinkers derived their concern for freedom, and that for *some* reason, they stopped crediting Indigenous people as the source of these ideas.

Given the analysis of interpretation as epistemic mimicry that appropriates the intellectual labor of explicators, we shouldn't be surprised by the appropriation of these Indigenous ideas by modern Europeans—and a feature of this appropriation is the *colonial-exchange* where Indigenous people are forced to conform to the colonial expectations, and the Colonizer takes Indigenous ideas as their inventions. *Colonial-exchange* does something incredible: it treats *ideas and reasoning*, which are *not proprietary*, as the proprietary intellectual accomplishments of the Colonizer. In this way, moral and political *ideals are stolen from Indigenous people*. Also, our previous analysis of the game of peer review and gatekeeping shows how we get stuck in political ruts—something Graeber and Wengrow are keen to fight against: it is because interpretation, the appropriative activity, is permitted as a strategy that interpreters have to converge on a shared doxography (or set of propositional attitudes), and in our world, White Irrationality supplies this shared outlook, complete with the appropriated intellectual labor of Indigenous people. That's our rut. What is important about our investigation with respect to Graeber and Wengrow's exploration is that we have a *singular explanation* for:

- colonization,
- the appropriation of Indigenous intellectual ideas in the form of their moral theorizing,
- and the political stagnation Graeber and Wengrow were hoping to undo by considering Indigenous ways.

The explanation is:

- interpretation.

In the following sections of this chapter, I want to draw from another Indigenous tradition of moral philosophy—the South Asian tradition. Graeber and Wengrow take pains to argue that the Indigenous people they spoke of valued freedom, but were not necessarily egalitarian as they apparently tolerated slavery. The ancient South Asian tradition in contrast is radically egalitarian and also deeply concerned with freedom because its beginning question is not, how do we work together in a human society, as was Plato's worry, but rather, what possible room is there for agential freedom in a world causally determined by natural states? That way of framing the starting point of moral theory strips away natural attributes that differentiate us in a world of inequality (such as attributes of sex or species) and places them within the realm of the natural causes. Normative moral theory is then what retrieves freedom for us—but it speaks not to us as defined by our natural attributes, but in terms of moral interests. In the third section, I will ask the question of how oppression and inequality can be recreated in a tradition that starts out criticizing oppression? An answer to this is to be derived from the *Mahābhārata*. It explicates the creation of oppression via the model of the rigged game of dice: people concerned for maximizing expected utility while demonstrating their virtue and willingness to play by good rules are easily manipulated into participating in their own oppression. The gamble involves suspending serious moral-philosophical inquiry while chasing after goodness. What this prevents is serious consideration about the right: justice, fairness, procedure. Instead, they tacitly consent to their oppression by focusing on good outcomes. In the fourth section, I will consider the Yoga tradition's analysis and response to this challenge of getting ourselves out of oppression of our own making. I close with an analysis of how South Asians, under colonization, gambled away their freedom by giving up on moral philosophy and by adopting Secularism$_2$. South Asians, like all people under exploitative colonization, are agents. While indeed we can and should blame colonizing traditions for their irrationality, Indigenous people can give up on their Indigeneity by trying to cooperate with Colonizers with hopes of recovering what is lost. Then they no longer have an explicatory connection to their past: they interpret themselves and everyone via the West. To de-colonize, we will all have to look to the precolonial traditions of moral philosophy to recover what was lost.

2. Hiding Indigenous Normative Ethics in Plain Sight

Explication is research and what research reveals is history, especially when we are explicating debates and the evolution of ideas. Sometimes, the ideas that pop on the scene are a hard break from what was there before. Secularism$_2$, and the idea of religion, for instance, represents one such hard, dramatic shift from an earlier way of carving up issues. This is not only a historical disconnect: it's a methodological disconnect, which involves interpretation, and especially White Irrationality. The earlier way, prior to colonization, in South Asia, was purely based on explication, and we can see this as the only way to make sense of the diversity of theories of dharma is to appreciate that they were contributions to a disagreement about THE RIGHT OR THE GOOD.

In addition to South Asian dharma philosophers developing and advocating for Virtue Ethics (the Good character produces or leads to the Right choice), Consequentialism (the Good justifies the Right choice), and Deontology (the Right choice justifies the Good action, or omission), they also developed and defended Yoga/Bhakti (the Right, devotion to the procedural Ideal of the Right, produces the Good). This span of moral theorizing exceeds what we find in the West, it is also internal to what the British called Hinduism. Every theory of dharma is a theory of Normative Ethics. But what the South Asian theories of THE RIGHT OR THE GOOD point to is a common worry or concern, which each is a solution to. The worry is how moral freedom is possible in a world of causal determination.

2.1. From Hard Determinism to Moral Realism

If we go back in the history of surviving recorded South Asian philosophy we find the earliest records being the Vedas, an Indo-European corpus, authored over a thousand years, in South Asia. Like other ancient Indo-European texts it spoke to a cosmos governed by nature deities (*devas*). But unlike in Homer where these deities are capricious, in the Vedas, they are presented more uniformly and as acting in a system of interdependent natural forces, held together by a cosmic moral norm: *Ṛta*. This is the view we find in the early portion of the Vedas, known as the *Mantras* (chants) and *Brāhmaṇas* (ritual manuals). Here the paradigm is Consequentialist. Votaries are described as desiring favorable outcomes, such as freedom from illness, victory over enemies, and pleasing the forces of nature is conceptualized as the means. This paradigm was not without evidence. The *Brāhmaṇas* show appreciation that the fire of the sacrifice to which offerings were made to the deities is the same as the fire in our bodies. Both demand to be fed, and failure to do so leads to illness and death. The authors of the Vedas betray their moral confliction at this system, which requires that they procure a sacrificial victim, on whom the very outcome they wish to avoid (death) is inflicted on so that they could appropriate the victim's body for food. Persons here understood themselves as animals needing to feed the natural forces that constituted their physiology. While *Western* interpreters are loath to acknowledge this, the early Vedic people were naturalists. They thought the universe was explained by the operation of natural forces. The *devas* were literally forces such as fire and wind.

The Vedic tradition develops into a remarkable criticism of this earlier stage in repudiating Consequentialism, but also naturalism. We find in the latter part of the Vedas, the *Āraṇyaka* (Forest Books) and the *Upaniṣads* (the Dialogues), a move to what would best be described as *procedural metaphysics* with the identification of Brahman—Growth, Expansion, Development—as the ultimate substance, of the Ātmā, or self (for a review of this development and its inversion, see Ranganathan 2018c). According to this inversion, moral explanations are better understood by way of the procedural requirements of existence: teleological explanations fail to appreciate the explanatory priority of the self, or agent, in their own life.

As the tradition was moving away from this early naturalism, a formal philosophy, Sāṅkhya, showed up on the scene. Sāṅkhya distills the politics of the early Vedic practice but in ways that are chilling to agential freedom. According to Sāṅkhya, perhaps the most ancient of systematic South Asian philosophies, and recorded much later by Īśvarakṛṣṇa in the *Sāṅkhya Kārikā* (200 BCE–200 CE), the universe is an evolution of nature or matter from an indistinct state into increasingly complex states. Not only bodies, but also sensory organs, mind, and intellect are emergent properties of this evolution. Sāṅkhya acknowledges persons, *puruṣa*, but only as passive spectators. Persons are acknowledged because when we reduce the objective aspects of our existences, including our bodily and psychological constitution, the only thing that is left over is a subjectivity. And this subjectivity is numerically distinct across organisms. The main implication of Sāṅkhya for moral theory is that choice is an illusion. When we feel like we are choosing and doing, that is actually our natural—material and psychological—constitution evolving according to prior causal states of nature. Our experience is hence epiphenomenal, including our experience of deliberating and choosing. Not only are our bodies causal states of the natural universe, so too are our psychological and cognitive states, which comprise a *subtle body*. This is loosely associated with states of the physical body insofar as the psychological and cognitive properties can be more unchanging despite rapid and more radical bodily changes. As a consequence, subtle bodies can survive the death of gross bodies, and cause new bodily states to be animated by them. All of this happens within the material realm of nature according to deterministic considerations.

Sāṅkhya is an argument for hard determinism. And moreover it is an argument for a kind of moral illusionism. Moral properties like virtues, for instance, lead to beneficial outcomes, but these virtues are actually natural properties of a natural world, determined by antecedent states of nature. So they are nothing we can cultivate or rely on.

As a starting point for moral theory, Sāṅkhya is humbling. Any possible virtue that you wish to advertise as part of your identity is actually part of the natural world, not you. Any aspect of your biology that distinguishes you is really just a function of natural causes, and nothing you can claim credit for. No *ism*, whether ableism or racism, has a fighting chance here as any ability or racial feature we may be proud of, or scorn, is nothing anyone can take credit for. Humans, with big brains and opposable thumbs, are no different than grasshoppers or scorpions when it comes to ourselves: biological differences across organisms are differences on the side of nature, not differences with respect to the agent's predicament of lacking freedom in a coercive universe. And if we are to find something distinctive about us as agents, it will hence not be on the side of natural difference, but the moral requirements of observers. Moral theory as a response to Sāṅkhya is theory for all observers. And thus the South Asian tradition is remarkably anti-speciesist but also anti-ableist as species and ability have everything to do with our natural endowments, not our moral interests.

Sāṅkhya's hard determinism was not generally seen as a threat by South Asian moral philosophers because they were not trying to reduce the thinkable to a singular perspective, which is encouraged by LAT. Given LAT, thinkers feel all sorts of pressure to reconcile normative terms with descriptive terms, as part of a coherent and consistent linguistic frame. This either results in giving up on the project of morality as it seems nature precludes it, or LAT-based thinkers, in colonial fashion, taking moral credit for all sorts of natural endowments that they had no hand in producing, as though their natural talents are who they are. Given LE, South Asian philosophers were free to acknowledge as a given that there is a conceptual and explanatory difference between natural, causal explanation (that is deterministic), and normative explanation (that is evaluative and prescriptive). This reflects the familiar distinction between the *is* and the *ought*. Causal explanations account for how things are: these are natural explanations. Ought explanations account for agents as things responsible for their lives. This background distinction ends up being celebrated as basic in Yoga, where persons are distinguished substantively from natural explanations, and the normative challenge of life is to integrate natural aspects of our existence into the normative requirements of agency. It plays a broadly important role in Indian moral theorizing: the tension between the *is* and the *ought* is depicted as the room for the life of normative beings in a causal universe.

Moral Realism is the idea that there are mind-independent moral facts. In the South Asian context, Moral Realism is the idea that there are opinion-independent correct ethical choices, and that there are consequences to all choices beyond one's perspective. Opinion is a psychological state, and psychological (mental) states are generally reducible to natural, causal, states, according to the Sāṅkhya background everyone was working with. If moral considerations are distinct from causal considerations then we ought to expect that morally correct choices are not constrained by causal considerations such as opinion. The nexus of interaction between the moral realm of explanation and the causal realm in this tradition is action: karma. When we agents act, we introduce into the causal realm a process with consequences, much like causality, but with a moral valence. Action can be good or bad, right or wrong. And in introducing causal chains with moral attributes into the causal nexus, they can linger beyond our psychological awareness. Hence, karma has a way of catching up to us.

In (generally) not feeling any particular need to reconcile the causal and the normative, South Asian moral philosophers developed robust forms of Moral Realism, which White Irrationality described as spirituality or religion.

- The reason South Asians were so enthusiastic about moral theory was that it was how the freedom of the agent was recovered and explained in a universe that is otherwise causally hostile to freedom.

Moral philosophy was pursued in academic texts, like the *Yoga Sūtra*, and then popular literature meant for a non-academic crowd. Moral philosophy, especially of a more accessible sort, was hence explored in art and literature. Given LAT, it is difficult to understand how a moral value could be a person. But given LE, agents constitute the content of thinking and many foundational moral values are persons—especially if they personify the stated interests of a person. And given the backdrop Moral Realism, these moral values as persons are taken seriously as mind-independent moral realities. These candidate moral realities are, given the preceding considerations, not reducible to psychological states of opinion, as they are normative, and not causal. And this is why our devotional practice to them as our values is necessary to unlock their impact on our lives. Otherwise, they remain unrealized norms.

Kṛṣṇa, as someone who engages in moral theorizing but at once speaks as a cosmic norm, in the *Bhagavad Gītā*, is outside of the scope of LAT-based imagination. Whereas LAT-based moral philosophy is often geared toward motivating social cohesion, the *Gītā* is a discussion of moral philosophy as society is falling apart, on the precipice of war—which occurs on a battlefield called the "Field of Ethics" (*dharmakṣetra, Gītā* 1.1). Kṛṣṇa is an *avatāra* of Viṣṇu, and Viṣṇu along with his consort, Lakṣmī, and their devotee, Ādi Śeṣa, the cosmic serpent, correspond to the three basic practical values of Yoga: Viṣṇu is unconservatism (*tapas*) depicted with external projections of his activities that do not bind him, such as the disk and mace; Lakṣmī is self-governance, depicted as a lotus sitting on herself and hence governing herself (*svādhyāya*); and Ādi Śeṣa is devotion to Sovereignty, who devotes himself to these two essential traits of Sovereignty as they float together over an ocean of external influence (*Īśvara praṇidhāna*). This famous image brings together the normative theorizing of Yoga, with its three values, and the metaethics of Yoga as a practice that gets us away from external influence in one famous picture of the three floating in an opaque ocean (It's YS II.1 over YS I.2–4). (For more, including pictures, see the open access Ranganathan 2022). It is hence no accident that Viṣṇu shows up to articulate this discourse on Yoga in the *Bhagavad Gītā*, and is name-dropped in important canonical articulations of Yoga (such as in the *Kaṭha Upaniṣad*). Explicated thus, the stories of these three deities constitute thought experiments of these basic moral values in different practical contexts. While Viṣṇu and his crew are associated with procedural ethical theories, Śiva, the ideal observer, and his partner, Śakti, who is the range of his experiences, are associated with teleological ethical theories, whether Consequentialism or Virtue Ethics. And hence, stories that report their escapades are thought experiments about teleological values. Westerners will want to rediscribe all of this as religion because they do not like moral philosophy and would rather interpret on the basis of their anthropocentrism and communitarianism. And they will hence prefer non-philosophers in Religious Studies who also lack any interest in moral philosophy to instead study the culture and practice of people who identify these values as important to them. Most readers are hence both familiar with these topics and figures via colonialism but unfamiliar with the Indigenous, de-colonial significance of studying them in moral philosophy.

2.2. **Four Normative Theories of** *THE RIGHT OR THE GOOD*

The classical South Asian tradition responds to the challenge of Sāṅkhya with four basic ethical theories: one more than we have in the Western tradition: Virtue Ethics, Consequentialism, Deontology, and Yoga/Bhakti. Unlike their Western counterparts, none of these options are anthropocentric or communitarian. Here, I will engage in a general explication of the salient South Asian versions of these theories. More detailed explorations are available.[1]

The earliest and most influential Virtue Ethics from classical times is Jainism. Virtue Ethics is the view that the good character or agent is the condition of right choice. According to the Jains, agents, what they call *jīva*-s, are comprised of three characteristics: consciousness (*caitanya*), bliss (*sukha*), and virtue (*vīrya*) (Jaini 1998, 104; see also 102–6 for the other innate qualities). When *jīva-s* do not appreciate their intrinsic virtue, the act for further ends, which results not only in harm to other *jīva-s*, but an enmeshment of the *jīva* within the realm of natural causation by action. The way out of this problem is to choose in conformity to virtue, which is to choose not to do. This not only results in the cessation of harmful acts, but it also leads to the remission of confusion and enmeshment with natural causation, leading to a freedom for the individual characterized by *dharma*, described as a principle of motion. This is the Jain picture of moral freedom. Jain Normative Ethics hence recommends not getting involved in anything, for getting involved leads to action contrary to intrinsic virtue. This culminates in *sallekhanā*: a fast to death, which is distinguished from suicide,

---

[1] For more on this topic, see the *Bloomsbury Research Handbook of Indian Ethics,* or my edited Level 1, MA course in moral philosophy as part of the government of India's rollout of online support for graduate education (Ranganathan 2016).

which is an action aimed at ending one's life. Jains were the most intense critics of ritual violence, and defenders of the rights of a diversity of agents with different natural attributes to be spared harm. India's long tradition of vegetarianism and veganism is a result in no small part to the influence of Jain ethics. Jains call their entire doctrine "Dharma."

The earliest and most influential Consequentialist ethics from classical times is Buddhism. Consequentialism is the view that the good end, justifies the right, choice or action. Buddhists respond to the Sāṅkhya view by denying its claim that we are outside observers of a matrix of dynamic causation, passively viewing life events unfold. There is no outside, permanent self. Rather, what looks like natural causation is agential, which is why classical Buddhists call various components of causal reality "dharmas" or "ethicals." We as individuals are not anything other than a certain type of physical and psychological causal stream in a world that is completely caused by prior events (a principle known as *dependent origination*). Our suffering arises through subjective motivations of desire, which try to solve for the aims of an autonomous agent, which does not exist. This leads to choices that produce coercive outcomes and are experienced painfully. Responsible choosing arises from abandoning desire (*taṇhā*) as a motivation, that cause suffering. Dharma, Buddhist doctrine, is in its classical form a Consequentialist view that the Good of suffering-diminishment justifies actions that are instrumental to this end. And the chief such action is the abandonment of desire as a motivation. Moral freedom is possible because we embrace our reality as continuous with the realm of dependent origination. The end we transition into, *nirvana*, is a state of continuity with dependent origination without desire.

The earliest influential Deontological view from classical South Asia is what Kṛṣṇa in the *Bhagavad Gītā* calls "Karma Yoga," the discipline of action. Deontology is the mirror opposite of Consequentialism: it claims that the good choice or action, is justified by a right procedure or choice. While there are many good things one might do, only some count as one's duty. Kṛṣṇa uses the term "dharma" for one's duty and famously claims, better one's own dharma poorly performed than another's well performed (*Gītā*, 3.35, 18.47 see also 2.38 and 2.47). He often also speaks about it as *action*: intentional behavior—*karma*. Action, or karma, is morally distinct from mere behavior compelled by natural factors. How do we figure out what our duty is? While we are all forced to behave by natural causes (*Gītā* 3.5), obligatory action is what we do when we are not propelled for the sake of outcomes but rather because it is the thing to be done (*Gītā* 3.6). This activity has the characteristic of being good or best (*brahma*), context transcendent (*nityam*), and of the nature of sacrifice (*yajñe*), which requires renouncing good outcomes for the sake of a diversity of agents (*Gītā* 3.15).

Kṛṣṇa describes our specific duty in terms of one's natural, sociological, particulars, including what are at some points described as *varṇa* categories, often translated as "caste." In today's language, *varṇa* captures the social endowment we are born into, with familial knowledge of economic activities. On the modified Sāṅkhya model Kṛṣṇa is working with, all of this is not intrinsic to us but determined by natural factors. We hence take back our freedom from external coercion by perfecting the activity of these contexts, in a way that sustains ourselves, and contributes to a wider world of diversity. This argument with Sāṅkhya operating in the background is an argument for all agents. Any agent, regardless of species, is born into a context with certain endowments, which constitutes the context in which they can perfect an activity that sustains themselves, those that depend on them and contributes to a world of diversity. Karma Yoga so understood is an ecological ethic. It subverts our natural context (as defined by external pressure) by modifying it into something that sustains us and allows us to contribute to the ecology we survive in. Kṛṣṇa punctuates the species transcendent nature of moral action by identifying his duty—speaking as the procedural ideal of action— as what maintains a universe of agential diversity (*Gītā* 3.22–24). Kṛṣṇa— unconservatism—then functions as the general form of duty, and then anything that is our duty participates in this general form. Kṛṣṇa's dutiful behavior involves re-establishing the moral order, repeatedly (*Gītā* 4.7–8). But it is also what we are doing when we are each perfecting our contribution to a world of diversity by way of our own duty.

Kṛṣṇa also makes a case for a theory he calls "Bhakti Yoga," which is essentially the theory of Yoga we find in the *Yoga Sūtra*, and other texts. Yoga is the mirror opposite of Virtue Ethics, which prioritizes goodness in the production or conditioning of right choice. Yoga prioritizes the Ideal of the Right, Sovereignty, as the basic procedural ideal. In being devoted to this ideal, we practice its essential traits: unconservatism and self-governance. The good is simply the perfection of this practice, which in practical terms is our own autonomy. Whereas Karma Yoga treats external pressure as what has to be subverted to allow an agent to thrive and contribute to a world of diversity, Yoga (Bhakti Yoga) is far more disruptive. Both Deontology and Yoga are procedural ethical theories that prioritize the right over the good. But Yoga defines the right thing to do independently of goodness. That means our proper and required practice may be bad, and involve the destruction of conventions that are good on some account. Whereas Deontology concerns good activities or choices, which are properly justified, Yoga is concerned with doing the Right, which may not be good in any sense. However, in time, it becomes good because it is the perfection of that practice. Whereas Karma Yoga is subversive, altering our natural context and pressures so that we are accommodated, Yoga/Bhakti is disruptive to social pressures and constraints as it is about activity in deference to a procedural ideal all people share, and nothing particular to our context.

Yoga's Metaethics in the *Yoga Sūtra* provides a response to Sāṅkhya's hard determinism, the idea that we have no moral freedom given the reality of causality. Hard determinism is just one possible explanation, and our responsibility as autonomous agents is to explicate and isolate options so we can choose. Hence, those who *choose to believe* the Sāṅkhya story that hard determinism makes no room for agency have actually exercised their agency in service of an outlook that undermines their agency. A truly ethical practice consists in giving up on interpretations in every context (YS IV.29) so that we secure our agential autonomy. Failing a basic ethical practice, we use our agency to interpret by empowering propositional attitudes to create a prison of psychology (YS II.3).

Like the other three (South Asian) ethical theories, Yoga too is not based on human agency. Being human is a natural trait, and agency in contrast is a normative trait. The predicament that agents are in is the same regardless of species. And the solution for all would be the same too. Yoga is more radical in many ways than other ethical theories from this tradition that put stock in our inheritance in a natural universe. This can and should be disrupted by a devotional practice to Sovereignty, which agents of any species *ought* to engage in. So whereas Buddhists, for instance, in redescribing the realm of causality as a moral realm of dharmas have to accommodate natural causation that constitutes our mind and body as morally relevant to us, Yogis do not: my mind, body, senses, and intellect are natural endowments that I have to steer and control as part of my normative challenge—they do not define who I am. I have to define them by my choices.

3. In for a Penny, In for a Pound

The four ethical theories reviewed, albeit briefly, reject the notion that there is a relevant moral difference, from the vantage of moral theory, between agents on the basis of natural constitution. They are egalitarian for this reason: whatever suggestions they have to maximize moral freedom are the same for all agents. But also they are anti-oppressive insofar as they think about moral action as something that has to make room for the agent in a world that is otherwise causally oppressive. Given this as the cultural starting point of South Asia, how do South Asians come to create states of oppression? How do Indigenous people walk themselves to states of colonization? A Yoga-based answer to this is to be found in the *Mahābhārata*.

It is quite ordinary to treat the *Bhagavad Gītā* as a stand-alone text. But it is not. It's a part of (and even a later interpolation in) the *Mahābhārata*. This epic tracks the fratricidal animosity of two groups of royal cousins. The Pāṇḍavas, who are the five sons of Pāṇḍu, are good but not perfect. Their cousins are the Kauravas, who are a hundred sons of Dhṛtarāṣṭra, and evil and jealous. Dhṛtarāṣṭra is the older brother of Pāṇḍu, and his children would be the heirs to the throne. However, Pāṇḍu's wife, Kunti had sons before Dhṛtarāṣṭra could father children. The Pāṇḍavas, the eldest being Yudhiṣṭhira, the middle and famous son, Arjuna, and the other three brothers, were known for their valor and prowess in war. The Kauravas, jealous of their popularity, hatched several plans to get rid of the Pāṇḍavas, which failed, until they invited them to play a game of dice—which happened to be rigged by the Kaurava's uncle. The Pāṇḍavas as warriors felt that they could not say no as refusing a challenge was incompatible with the valor of the warrior. Yudhiṣṭhira bet for the brothers, and nothing went well for them. Yudhiṣṭhira managed to bet their property away, then their own personal freedom, and then the freedom of their common—beautiful and intelligent—wife, Draupadī.

Draupadī was brought to the court where royalty and dignitaries were in attendance of the game. There she was molested—sexually assaulted! As she was brought to the court, she delivered many devastating moral criticisms of the Pāṇḍavas and all in attendance. She pointed out that if Yudhiṣṭhira had lost his own personal freedom first, he was not in a position to bet her freedom away. Next she excoriated the elders in attendance who were moral guides to the Pāṇḍavas and the Kauravas: teachers and warriors who had set the standards for the boys as they aged. Now they—elders, all men—sat dumbfounded and unable to assert their moral authority as an injustice was unfolding in front of everyone. In this mix, Draupadī was *the only person willing to engage in moral philosophy*. Everyone else wanted to avoid the topic. The onlookers, like the Pāṇḍavas, seemed unable to extricate themselves from the travesty that they saw unfolding in front of them. (Kṛṣṇa, who shows up later in this story, and was absent during this event, tells Draupadī later, according to one version, that if he were there he would have killed everyone for what they were allowing to happen to her.)

Whatever the foolishness of the Pāṇḍavas, Draupadī was an innocent victim, and yet she was suffering the brunt of the loss. When challenged to speak up about the injustice of the turn of events by Draupadī, the elders gave voice to platitudes about the difficulty in pronouncing on dharma, it being a subtle and difficult matter to determine—even though all in attendance were uncomfortable and incensed by the turn of events, *including the Pāṇḍavas.*

While Dhṛtarāṣṭra was not known for virtue or valor, he was not able to bear the cries of Draupadī in being mistreated (he being depicted as a simple hedonist who didn't like the unpleasant sounds), and so as the reigning king, he annulled the game, restoring Draupadī's freedom. Ridiculously, the Pāṇḍavas played the game again. They wagered and lost thirteen years of freedom in exile, the last year which had to be incognito, lest they be found and have to repeat the thirteen years again.

The rigged game of dice is a model for conventional morality, but a critical model as something that can be manipulated. Conventional morality is constituted by (1) Virtue Ethics, (2) Consequentialism, and (3) Deontology. These are the three main ethical theories of the *Western* tradition. They are also found in the South Asian tradition, as noted, but the latter also has Yoga—from whence we learn about explication as a basic metaethical commitment. According to conventional morality, moral luck rules the day (outcomes that one does not control, which one is nevertheless morally bound to) *and* it consists in giving up control to the gamble. Conventional morality is the morality of (1) good character, (2) good ends, and (3) good rules. The game of dice allowed Yudhiṣṭhira to (1) demonstrate his valor as a warrior, (2) strive toward good ends (projected utility) of winning, while (3) participating in good rules of the game.

Explication is itself a radically procedural approach to understanding options: it is an exercise of the Right. In focusing on the Good, conventional morality hence excludes the procedure of explicating options, and hence it excludes the activity of engaging in moral philosophy. In contrast, it is an exercise premised on beliefs about the *goodness* of the exercise. It is an exercise of interpretation. It is entirely worth noting that each of the three contributing ethical theories to conventional morality has things to say about the Right. If we were to explicate the contributing moral theories, we would see this. But this activity of rendering clear moral philosophy and its theoretical diversity is locked out of conventional morality. Instead, conventional morality as modeled by the game of dice is a self-justifying system that excludes procedural concerns. The goodness of the expected utility justifies participating and endorsing the goodness of the rules, and taking up these prospects of goodness makes it an easy way to display one's own goodness as a participant. Engaging in this activity is an interpretive endeavor as it rests upon many beliefs about the goodness of the self, the outcome, and rules that agents participate in. These beliefs are part of why moral conventionalists do not reason about the moral-philosophical aspects of their choices.

As the game goes on, there is ample evidence to the horrified onlooker that Yudhiṣṭhira is not valorous but foolish, that only one side is reaping utility, and not everyone is playing by the same good rules. Yudhiṣṭhira's beliefs are his prison. He is interpreting. From Yudhiṣṭhira's perspective, to depart from the game would be to reveal oneself to lack the valor one claims to have, to fail to see the project out to the projected utility, and to renege on one's commitments to play by the rules. So his own commitment to Virtue Ethics, Consequentialism, and Deontology provide independent reasons to stick with the game.

The Yogi, in contrast, unconcerned with these three ethical markers, and committed to not treating beliefs as the foundation of action, would as a result of their devotional practice be required to disrupt the unfolding convention the moment they realized it was an exercise of oppression contrary to their devotional practice to Īśvara. In the spirit of Yoga, one could enter the game with some moral-philosophical end in mind as one's own self-determined value. One could participate in the game for the sake of valor, outcome, and good rules as values one self-determines. But as one is also committed to unconservatism, one will reevaluate and also feel no urgency to continue the game. The basic context-independent commitment to Īśvara would always take precedence over one's contextual commitments.

The rigged game of dice is an explication of the dynamics of how well-meaning people create oppression because of their focus on the Good and how this creation of oppression brings along with it innocent victims, like Draupadī. It is also a criticism of how conventional morality is misogynistic, and patriarchal: both are moral aberrations that are not corrected in conventional morality for it lacks any serious concern for the Right. As the participants are concerned with the Good, innocent victims are collateral damage, and those who have benefited from the exercise—the old and often men—sit and watch in silence as injustices unfold in front of them.

In this case, the injustice of moral convention is not an accident, disconnected from the goodness of the participants. Yudhiṣṭhira was fabled for being righteous, scrupulous about moral considerations, and the person who would never compromise principle for convenience. He is like the stereotypical Kantian who could never tell a lie. And yet, he's the one who is the author of the Pāṇḍavas's misfortune. He is the author of this misfortune for his preoccupation with goodness creates a moral blind spot, and this spot occludes questions of the Right, detached from all teleological considerations. Unwilling and unable to engage in thinking about the Right and the Good, his calculations are outside of moral philosophy. Conventional morality, structured by a lack of concern for the Right, depicts all choices in terms of benefit but also loss of benefit. What it prevents is the idea that it may be better to be right than win by conventional expectations. So as the Pāṇḍavas continue to lose, Yudhiṣṭhira continues to participate in hopes of regaining the good he desires.

It seems as though we are far from our discussion in Chapter 2, where we considered LAT-based societies. But there is an important similarity. These LAT-based societies on Planet Ethics each have their own conventionalized morality that underwrites their moral semantics. And as ethics is conflated with these conventions, what is locked out of this model is the radically procedural concern of Yoga: explication. For to engage in that activity unseats and deflates the credibility of conventionalized moral expectations. So we have a historical explanation of why some traditions become LAT-based. The more their commitment to conventionalized morality, the less divergence there is between their linguistic practice and their moral practice. And hence in time, the interpretive activity of the conventional moral expectations will be indistinguishable from their linguistic practice. Traditions that head down this road are focused on the Good, and do not make room for thinking about the Right independently of the Good. Indigenous traditions as departing from LAT in contrast make room for thinking about the Right independently of the Good.

4. The Genealogy of Manipulation

4.1. Arguments About Goodness to Avoid Challenging Oppression

The game of dice was an interpretive exercise for the Pāṇḍavas that involved beliefs about the morality of the arrangement, but the Kauravas in contrast did not believe that the game was fair: they were rigging it. But they too were motivated by a different set of propositional attitudes that had to do with their resentment to the Pāṇḍavas, and their desires to get the better of them. As long as everyone was involved in their own exercise of interpretation, moral philosophy was not a priority. The only person in the ordeal who critically engaged in moral philosophy was Draupadī, searching for the principles and arguments that would justify the fate that she was victim to, and finding nothing. Her cutting engagement in moral-philosophical dialogue and criticism was an act of resistance that cast the unreflective and largely agnostic responses she received—from men—in a sharp light. The oppressors were not engaging in moral philosophy but the innocent victim was.

After the exile was over and the Pāṇḍavas returned, the Kauravas refused to give them back their previous territory nor any space to live. This meant that war was inevitable, despite the Pāṇḍavas' every effort to broker peace. Both sides sought Kṛṣṇa's help: he offered himself or his army. The Kauravas took his army. The Pāṇḍavas chose Kṛṣṇa. Kṛṣṇa played the role of Arjuna's charioteer in the battle. The *Bhagavad Gītā* is the moral philosophy discourse and dialogue between Kṛṣṇa and Arjuna prior to the battle.

In what is likely the earliest articulation of Yoga the philosophy, in the *Kaṭha Upaniṣad*, we find Death articulating the model of the chariot to the remarkable boy Naciketa, who suffers an untimely death and is facing the question of Death ahead of time. In this dialogue, Death teaches that like a chariot, we are comprised of many components: the horses are like the senses, the mind is like the reins, the charioteer is like the intellect, the car is like the body, and in this we sit. When we allow our senses, the horses, to drag us here and there, we land in trouble. But if we can guide the senses via the mind, and the mind via the intellect, we are practicing Yoga, and this takes us to the realm of Viṣṇu (unconservatism). In the *Gītā*, situated in a chariot, Kṛṣṇa's role as the charioteer renders him the intellect and what he delivers is a lecture on moral philosophy, but the philosophy of Yoga in particular. Arjuna as the passenger is the self, who in this state of crisis has to turn to his intellect to sort out his conflicting interests.

In the impending battle, Arjuna will have to fight not only the Kauravas who are his enemies, but also loved ones and elders who for reasons of professional obligation have to side with the Kauravas, though morally their sympathies are with the Pāṇḍavas. In response to this crisis, Arjuna articulates three arguments as to why he should not fight. Each argument highlights the three contributing moral considerations of conventional morality of good character (Virtue Ethics), good outcome (Consequentialism), and good rules (Deontology).

Arjuna articulates a Jain Virtue Ethics argument. Accordingly, evil people motivating this war are bent on fighting because of their lack of virtue. If Arjuna should fight, he would be no better. Therefore, he should not participate in the war (*Gītā* 1.38–9).

Arjuna articulates a Buddhist Consequentialist argument. War leads to suffering, and that on balance, though there may be some good outcomes from winning the war, even then the bad outcomes of suffering outweigh the good. Therefore, he should not fight (*Gītā* 1.34–6).

Arjuna articulates a Deontological argument. Arjuna claims that war undermines the social fabric that protects women and children. Undermining the virtues of this social fabric is wrong. Therefore he should not fight (*Gītā* 1.41).

Kṛṣṇa first responds with three, relatively unserious, arguments that make use of the same theories. He claims for instance that fighting is a valorous (virtuous) exercise for warriors (*Gītā* 2.2–3, 2.33–7). He claims that even dying in battle is a good thing (*Gītā* 2.36–7). As for the Deontological worry, Kṛṣṇa responds that we're all eternal anyway so you don't have to put too much stock into safe practices (*Gītā* 2.11–32). Therefore, he should fight.

Kṛṣṇa's more serious response consists in providing a wedge between teleological theories and procedural ethical theories. If the oppressive mess that the Pāṇḍavas found themselves in was structured by expectations of utility, recalibrating moral practice as a radically procedural matter, unconcerned with Goodness allows for a way forward that does not render Arjuna vulnerable to the same pressures.

To this extent, Kṛṣṇa makes a case for three procedural ethical theories.

As noted, Kṛṣṇa does make a case for the Deontology of Karma Yoga. And whereas the Deontology of conventional morality are the supposed good rules of the gamble that one has reason to conform to, in Karma Yoga, one finds the goodness of one's behavior by giving up on any concern for outcome, and by focusing on activity as a way to sustain oneself in a world of diversity while also creating support for one's dependents. In giving up any concern for further outcome as part of the reason for conforming to one's own duty, Karma Yoga provides some protection against conventional moral expectations motivated by a promise of good outcome.

Bhakti Yoga, or the Yoga of the *Yoga Sūtra*, also urged by Kṛṣṇa, is a more radical departure from the elements of conventional morality for no part of the formulation of the right thing to do depends upon Goodness. The right thing to do is to be devoted to the Right. It is via a procedural devotion to a procedural ideal—Īśvara—that we create a wholly new good, namely our autonomy, and a safe space for others to engage in the same devotional practice.

Jñāna Yoga is the third ethical practice suggested by Kṛṣṇa: it is entirely metaethical. It consists in an appreciation of the reasons for abandoning teleological considerations in favor of procedural considerations.

Kṛṣṇa shares two important facts about himself, as unconservatism (*tapas*) and speaking on behalf of Īśvara (Sovereignty). The first moral fact about himself is that he has to return periodically to reset the moral order (*Gītā* 4.7–8). The moral order as locked in conventional morality is vulnerable to manipulation and degradation by moral parasites. That's what happened to the Pāṇḍavas as they were playing the game of dice, itself a metaphor for conventional morality. To reset the moral order requires eliminating moral parasites and allowing for the establishment of moral conventions that are parasite free, which is an unstable state, waiting for manipulation by parasites. Once moral parasites show up, the moral order starts to crumble and what is really going on is a state of war between the conventionally moral and the parasites—the conventionally moral are the last to be aware of this. Kṛṣṇa, unconservatism, has to return to start the cycle again.

The second important moral fact that Kṛṣṇa reveals is his function as unconservatism as an essential trait of Sovereignty. Viewed morally the universe is the space of uncoerced moral action. This is consistent with, and in no way contradicts, the reality of a universe that is both good and bad, but also a universe in flux. Kṛṣṇa reveals this as his cosmic form, which Arjuna has trouble viewing at first (*Gītā* 11). This is an entailment of Yoga's radical procedural focus. There is no incompatibility of doing the right thing and being bad. Conventional morality's obsession of goodness creates oppression. Coming clean about one's procedural obligations to disrupt what is wrong also involves coming to terms with the way doing the right thing is not only a departure from ordinary ideas of goodness. It also involves being willing to work on things, which is to accept one's teleological imperfection as a given. This is an important moral difference between Theism, a version of Virtue Ethics, that prioritizes God as the ultimately good agent, and Yoga that prioritizes Sovereignty as the ultimately Right ideal. There is no problem of evil for a procedural ideal. But an all Good, Knowing and Powerful God seems quite incompatible with the evil of the universe.

4.2. Being Bad but Right as the Response to Oppression

After the moral philosophy chat on the battlefield that is the *Gītā*, and once the war commences, Kṛṣṇa counsels the Pāṇḍavas to lie, cheat, and steal to win the war, even telling them to forget "dharma" (*Mahābhārata*: 7.164.68) while fighting in the battlefield known as the Field of Dharma. And indeed they do win, though the Pāṇḍavas who are at heart conventional moralists never feel free of the guilt of winning at that cost. Kṛṣṇa consoles them by noting that there wouldn't have been a victory any other way (*Mahābhārata*: 9.60.59). If we assume conventional moral standards, then these departures from conventional morality are moral transgressions. Kṛṣṇa's counsel in contrast shows that conventional morality was actually the means by which the Pāṇḍavas were oppressed. And whereas moral parasites want others to abide by these conventional expectations to take advantage of them, devotees of Kṛṣṇa want to reset the moral order and rid the world of moral parasites. One gets rid of moral parasites by not playing by conventional moral rules, but also by engaging in a different kind of moral practice—Devotion to

Īśvara or Sovereignty (Kṛṣṇa in this case). And this is a moral practice that is devoted to an interest we all share. So both the devotee of Sovereignty and the moral parasite do not abide by conventional morality: but the parasite is in it only for themselves, while the devotee of Sovereignty has our shared interest at heart. One of the implications of this narrative is that good people are to blame as much as moral parasites for the problems of the world. And these problems can only be done with if we switch to a radical focus on the Right, without any fidelity or concern for Goodness. Doing the right thing is messy, and it involves upsetting people who have gotten used to their privilege in conventional society.

Many of these theses show up in an egoist form in the writings of Nietzsche, who was aware of "Hindu" literature (D. Smith 2004). We can add him to the list of leading *Western* theorists who appropriated Indigenous moral theorizing. Nietzsche's idea of the Übermensch, or the superior person who leaves conventional moral expectations is everywhere in South Asian moral philosophy, including the *Gītā*. The idea of eternal return in *Thus Spake Zarathustra*, for instance, is articulated by Kṛṣṇa as his fate. The idea that we need to *go beyond good and evil* (the title of one of Nietzsche's books) is the central theme of the *Gītā* as it urges Arjuna not to give up on morality but to adopt a procedural focus of right and wrong, in contrast to good and bad. Finally, in the *Genealogy of Morals*, Nietzsche depicts an analog of the game of dice, he calls *slave morality*. It is the morality of mutual consideration and compassion which displays the supposed virtues of the participants, aims at good ends for all concerned (if nothing else ascetic ends), and is constituted by the good rules of mutual obligation. The problem is that this is the kind of morality that we would adopt if we assumed that our place was one of subservience. Nietzsche in response, like Kṛṣṇa, advocates for a self-affirming (noble) morality as opposed to one that denies the self. This part of Nietzsche's analysis is isomorphic with the *Mahābhārata*'s modeling of conventional morality in the game of dice.

Nietzsche's modeling of conventional morality is rich with observations that participants self-police by problematizing their masters as evil while taking pride in their subservience. The slave's morality is resentful, as it is unable to formulate an account of the good without linking it with the evil it seeks to avoid. This models the Pāṇḍavas' inclination to restrict themselves to conventional moral expectations while criticizing the Kauravas for their departure from it.

Nietzsche's analysis is filled with many Westcentric views about religion, the Judeo-Christian view of God, and its relationship to morality as a system based on concepts of debt and sin. Where it differs from the de-colonial analysis of the *Mahābhārata* is that Nietzsche normalizes oppression not as a moral fact of our interaction but rather as a natural fact of the weakness of those who are oppressed. This renders being the oppressor preferable to being the oppressed on Nietzsche's account—he doesn't contemplate a third option. He also paints a picture of conventional morality as fully egalitarian, when the reality of conventional morality, as displayed in the game of dice, is that it is patriarchal, misogynistic, but also agnostic about moral philosophy. Nietzsche's idea of slave morality is an abstraction that doesn't track our actual slave morality. Our actual slave morality—the moral order that keeps us in states of oppression—is the conventional morality that treats good character, ends, and rules as mutually enforcing reasons for compliance—with misogyny and patriarchy as system properties. The more we are distracted by being good, the more the parasite can take advantage of us.

4.3. Exploitative Colonization Is the Rigged Game of Dice

We have already observed how though South Asia was originally a space of Secularism, moral theorizing, it comes to reflect the colonial interpretation of South Asia as deeply religious, with a native religion, Hinduism. That is in and of itself remarkable, and all concerned usually do not take enough time to let that sink in. In this case, foreigners showed up, told South Asians they were Hindus, and now one billion people the world over believe themselves to be Hindus. This is the power of colonization—or imposing a perspective on the colonized that they may choose to adopt. But why would they? Because they view it as a way to play the game of conventional morality with hope of further gain, or in time as a way to recover what was lost.

If we attend to the very origins of Indian normative theory, caste and hierarchy were not basic moral principles, and the egalitarian, anti-ableist thrust of this theorizing that was trying to solve the cosmic problem of freedom in a determined universe didn't provide any normative foundation for caste hierarchy. Caste was not denied. It was rather affirmed as a natural fact about our context that required either abandonment (this was the Jain and Buddhist approach insofar as they recommended a *śramaṇa* life style of asceticism outside of conventional social relations), appropriation and subversion for our personal ends (as we see in Karma Yoga) or a complete disruption via a personal devotion to Sovereignty (as we find in Yoga).

There were Brahman (priestly) caste theorists who constituted the Pūrva Mīmāṃsā tradition, who wrote copious texts on ritual purity and caste hierarchy called, often, *dharmaśāstra* (*treatise on dharma*)—the most famous being the treatise by Manu (often translated as "the Laws of Manu" or even "Hindu Law"). This tradition positions itself as creating a secondary literature that is either consistent with or based on the Vedas, which it presents as the foundations of moral guidance. Central to this tradition is the articulation of a four-part caste system. So whereas the sociological facts about caste were plural and diverse and there was no single hierarchical system in place in South Asia, the Mīmāṃsā tradition theorized that there were three upper castes eligible to study the Vedas—*brāhmaṇa*-s (priestly, intelligentsia), *kṣatriya* (military and government), *vaiśya* (commerce class). And there was a fourth caste: *śūdra*-s (laborers). Moreover, Brahmins were at the top of this list. One can read this list in the Vedas, in one creation myth of the Cosmic Person (*Ṛg* 10.90), which is part of the earlier, Consequentialist, sacrifice portion of the text. This four-part list does show up in the *Bhagavad Gītā* and other Brahminical literature, but as noted, Karma Yoga and Bhakti Yoga have the effect of deflating or gutting these systems.

Philosophically, the Pūrva Mīmāṃsā tradition has some interesting arguments to make. In it we find, for instance, an argument critical of natural moral semantics (prefiguring later criticisms by G.E. Moore for instance). Specifically, the Mīmāṃsā philosopher Kumārila Bhatta (seventh century CE) argues that:

(1) *Either* we can define morality in terms of natural properties of happiness or pleasure, *or* in terms of the injunctions of the Vedas.
(2) We have to reject the natural definition of moral terms as it leads to absurd results and it consists of vacuous circularity (where the idea of morality and some natural property mutually define each other).

(*Therefore*) We ought to treat morality as set out by Vedic injunctions. (*Ślokavārttika* II.242–7)

It's not the greatest argument as we can certainly concede the point of the problems with naturalism without thinking that Vedic Deontology is the only other option: indeed, any alternative that does not engage in the problem of the interdefinability of natural traits and moral terms would do just as well for the purpose of this criticism. But what is noteworthy is that it is a serious argument of moral philosophy that engages in a sustained criticism of naturalistic approaches to ethics. Kumārila argues that if we were really interested in happiness and pleasure then young strapping students should have affairs with their teacher's (young) wives as that would increase net pleasure, which is his *reductio ad absurdum*. But the idea that we could simply define moral terms by way of happiness or pleasure leaves unexplained why happiness or pleasure is ethical, leading to a vacuous circularity where the moral term and the natural property are supposed to justify each other but neither does.

Yet, this particular Deontological tradition quite clearly had a conflict of interest. Brahmins comprised a small minority, with no military or commercial power. Their only talent was that they were literate and scholarly. Propagating views about the indispensability and superiority of the Brahman by situating themselves as defenders of the Vedas, and it as the foundation of all moral guidance, was a self-serving political agenda. If anyone listened, and further if anyone bought this story, we would have to look to their motives, which would likely also be quite self-serving. While these Pūrva Mīmāṃsā theorists articulated visions of caste hierarchy, which placed the *brāhmaṇa* at the top and the *śūdra*, or laborer at the bottom, the actual political reality on the ground was often very different. South Indian emperors were often technically of the *śūdra* caste according to these Brahminical codes but wielded actual political and military power. The Mīmāṃsā story of four castes, arranged hierarchically, was a pure sociological fantasy—though no doubt it reflected the normative aspirations of this group. And yet, academics today treat the Laws of Manu as "Hindu Law"—as though Manu's scribblings about caste were actually ever law, and as though there was such a thing as Hinduism prior to the British.

The geographer Sanjoy Chakravorty puts it well in his *The Truth About Us: The Politics of Information From Manu to Modi*, that timing is the key historical factor that sheds light on whose idea Hinduism or even caste hierarchy as the basis of South Asian society was. This narrative is constructed under British colonialism. And while Chakravorty notes that it would have been impossible for the British to construct such as story without the help of natives who knew Sanskrit and were willing to collaborate, "research assistants or informants do not get to define or set the project agendas, and, more to the point, their names are not on the patents" (Chakravorty 2019, 81). The South Asian informants were hence fitting into a political project set by the moral parasites—British Colonizers—who wanted colonized people to adopt a certain conventionalized interaction so they could be robbed of ideas and material wealth.

Chakravorty reports that the British guided this construction of Hindu, caste-based, South Asian identity via census politics, which continues today. The basic idea of this politics is social identity and numbers: "which group has how many people." The British initiation of the census provided the first Indian picture of the various groups that supposedly made up Indian society: but it was the British who defined the categories, and it was Indians who self-identified. This created a feedback loop where the population that was being studied became agents who would influence the outcomes of those studies by their voluntary affiliation with group identities. One outcome Chakravorty notes is that it is now possible to generate a Hindu nationalism based on the perceived numerological threat posed by non-Hindu groups to Hindu supremacy. It is important to remember that "Hindu" as a religious group was a creation of the census. Similarly Muslims could now quantify the threat posed by Hindus—"Hindu" being a term originally used to identify Indigenous people of South Asia by earlier Muslim Colonizers, but now a religion thanks to the British. Peoples identifying with disadvantaged groups could now take advantage of affirmative action programs (Chakravorty 2019, 146–8). All agents were in this case acting on beliefs about how they ought to represent themselves in this new order.

A certain outcome of all of this is the actual structuring of South Asian society along the lines of categories of the census. So whereas caste would have been mercurial before, and hierarchies were not determined by a unitary system, the census creates conventionalized schemas of oppression with conventional moral expectations. Everyone responding to the census does so to recover what is lost in a world of colonial oppression. And as a result of this entirely parasitic, managerial, and bureaucratic exercise of foreign interpreters, the British created an ahistorical picture of India as Hindu, which is based on the caste hierarchies of the *Laws of Manu*. The remarkably egalitarian, anti-oppressive Indigenous moral-philosophical tradition that situates all agents in the same moral predicament in a world of natural oppression is represented as deeply committed to anthropocentric and communitarian social hierarchy. What is usually not noted is that the resulting Orientalist narrative of Hinduism *sounds a lot like Plato*: caste hierarchy, deeply communal, run and orchestrated by the (Brahmin) intellectuals (*Republic*), a belief in reincarnation (*Timaeus* and the *Laws*), along with a disregard for all things bodily in pursuit of spiritual matters (the body as the prison of the soul, *Phaedo* 82a). It was Westerners who, using their tradition to interpret South Asia as part of their colonial rollout, created this myth of Hinduism that comes to have social dimensions in a colonized world. In the face of the radically anti-anthropocentric and anti-communitarian tradition that was South Asia, the British would retreat to their safe space—the very start of their tradition of anthropocentrism and communitarianism in Plato—to make sense of this world of people engaging in moral experimentation while choosing their own values—which Mill and his followers would claim as their own idea. It also allows *Westerners* to define Hindus in terms of the *West's* past of hierarchy, and to define the *Westerner* in terms of appropriated concerns (from South Asians) for egalitarianism, moral experimentation, and self-determination of values. The British, the *Westerner*, then depict themselves as the benevolent dictators freeing BIPOC from their backward, oppressive, religion-based ways, with their newly developed Liberal political orientation. In this *colonial-exchange*, the Westerners can treat Indology as a way to study their own past, and to never learn from South Asians. Hence, it's saturated with Western people who are attracted to the Indo-European basis of ancient Indian culture but with absolutely no interest in the moral-philosophical insights of South Asians.

This generalizes.

- Colonizers project their past (of not being in charge) on to the colonized, and appropriate the colonized's past (of relative freedom) as their future.

Here we see the mechanism by which interpreters, especially when they are being critical, are just talking about themselves. This *colonial-exchange* is a pervasive theme of colonization as it is a direct result of interpretation that at once projects and appropriates. The beliefs we have are based on our past, including the past we culturally inherit, especially insofar as we endorse LAT, which freezes beliefs of formative generations as though the content of thought. When this is used as an injury to colonized people, as the perspective imposed on them, the interpreter by way of epistemic mimicry appropriates the explicatory activity of the colonized. Hence Zionists, for instance, project their past of oppression that they are trying to flee on to the Palestinians, and then appropriate the free life of Palestinian past in Palestine as the Zionist's future. The same can be said of other settler colonial projects on Turtle Island and elsewhere. As Graeber and Wengrow note, the French Colonizers literally lifted the explicated ethos of Indigenous people as though their novel moral theoretical ideas, and this was in the context of colonization. In the case of *exploitative colonialism*, the difference is that colonized people *willingly* adopt the projection of the Colonizer's past on to the colonized as they participate in the rigged game of dice.

This picture makes possible the Dalit criticism in the works of Dr. Ambedkar of the caste injustice of Hinduism ("*dalita*" is the Sanskrit meaning "broken," a term of choice for people treated as outcastes). Dalits, outcastes, are then people not even allowed into the Plato-as-Hindu community. This is, of course, the absurdity of the entire polemic. If it actually tracked something precolonial, we could see the political importance of blaming Hinduism and its commitment to caste hierarchy as the cause of oppression. But given that this was not the input but the output of the colonial version of the rigged game of dice, where the Colonizers were the Kauravas—the moral parasites rigging the game—and citizens less susceptible to colonial manipulation were the innocent victims—the Draupadīs of colonization—this diagnosis of the problem confuses effect for cause. Sure, there was injustice prior to colonization, but we would have to look for historical explanations for this, not to a story curated by foreign Colonizers. And if we did look to the history of South Asian moral philosophy, what we find is not a unanimous consensus on the propriety of the caste system and its marginalizing implications. What we find is a history of moral theorizing that entails criticisms of oppression. The marginalization of people on the basis of caste identity was hence something that was readily criticized on the basis of the major moral-philosophical theories of classical South Asia. None of the four major South Asian versions of basic moral theories that we reviewed, for instance, could justify such discrimination, and all would provide grounds for criticizing it. An Indigenous world is not a perfect world. But it is a world where we can criticize oppression. Indeed, it is a world where the burden of proof, philosophically, is placed on anyone in favour of oppression. In a colonial world, oppression is the moral order and it is up to anyone who would object to any form of oppression to make their case. Hence, we find ourselves here having to make the case for what should be obvious: oppression is irrational.

It is entirely possible to get distracted by interpreted facts. Yes, Dalits did and *do* suffer, and yes there was and *is* a constructed preference for the South Asians who could play a managerial part in colonial administration. But none of this happened in a vacuum. As Shashi Tharoor notes in his *Inglorious Empire: What the British Did to India*, the British reduced India's share of the world economy from that of Europe to a sixth of that, while unleashing horrendous violence on its inhabitants. But to look at how South Asians suffered in this case as though a result of the Indigenous idea of Hinduism is ahistorical. What we know of today as Hinduism and South Asia is a result of colonization.

But the point I am making is that this process of oppression was made possible by South Asians playing along. To paint South Asians as mere victims is to ignore their agency and their part in colonization. They were also perpetrators insofar as they bought identities prefabricated for them by the Colonizer. Just as in the game of dice participants and observers, who were formerly principled, adopt agnostic views about moral theory, while moral criticism is discarded, eventually, South Asia's Indigenous history of moral philosophy is forgotten by its colonized inhabitants as they transition to a colonized mode of existence, structured by the census. South Asians, like the Pāṇḍavas, are then people exiled everywhere, including in their own homeland by Secularism$_2$. To de-colonize, they would have to learn to explicate and rekindle their ancestral practice of Secularism$_1$. And this is as easy as returning to their precolonial traditions.

5. Conclusion

Conventional morality is an unphilosophical exercise where agents' beliefs in being good, aiming for the good, and doing good mutually enforce their compliance with conventional expectations. What is excluded is a moral-philosophical exploration of options. Conventional morality is the morality of colonization, where participants slow-walk their subjugation to an oppressive order because they buy the beliefs that are being imposed on them as the condition of their participation. Rejecting interpretation and engaging in moral philosophy is the prophylaxis to this voluntary participation in one's own oppression. It is our rational obligation to de-colonize.

6

Devotion to the Ideal of the Right

Three Levels of De-Colonization

1. Introduction

In the past chapters, I have focused on the problems of colonization and oppression as something we can come to appreciate if we explicate the options. Explicating the options reveals that colonization and oppression are a result of the irrationality of interpretation, which is incompatible with the explicatory activity of moral philosophy. In this chapter, I turn to the historical origins of the ethical theory that sets the table for the arguments we reviewed in Chapter 1, which I explore in this book: Yoga.

If we explicate the options of moral philosophy, normative ethical theories are *discovered* to be accounts of the basic topic of THE RIGHT OR THE GOOD. And moreover, if we explicate the options from the *Western* tradition, we see that there are three basic Normative Ethical options:

- *Virtue Ethics*: The good (character, person) conditions or brings about the right (choice, action).
- *Consequentialism*: The good end justifies the right (action, choice, omission).
- *Deontology*: The right (choice, procedure) justifies the good (action, choice, omission).

As we have seen, all three of these options are present in the South Asian tradition and they contribute to conventional morality insofar as they provide ways to think about choice in terms of good character, good ends, and good rules. The Indian tradition contains a fourth basic variety of ethical theory:

- *Yoga/Bhakti*: the right (devotion to the procedural Ideal of the Right) conditions or brings about the good outcome (our autonomy)

Yoga/Bhakti and Virtue Ethics mirror each other as do Deontology and Consequentialism. Yoga is radically procedural for it does not define the Right by way of an independent Good. Rather, Goodness is defined by way of the Right, and the right thing to do is to perfect a practice of devotion to the procedural Ideal of the Right, which is Īśvara, or Sovereignty. This perfection is the recovery of our procedural health, our autonomy: *kaivalya*. The good outcome of a Yoga practice is just ourselves, but without the oppression of a nonautonomous life. What this means is that as a matter of practice there is no independent outcome to aim for or to guide moral considerations: moral practice is procedural all the way down. It should come as no surprise that Yoga is absent in the other two ancient LAT-based traditions of philosophy (the Western and the Chinese traditions). Yoga is a practice of devotion to the normative essence of what it is to be a person: to be free to choose and do as one determines, without external interference. LAT in contrast institutionalizes interpretation, which consists in a subordination of the agent to propositional attitudes. With this subordination, the behavior of agents is scripted by the propositions they have attitudes to.

As extended things, agents are easily manipulated, coerced, and injured as they are vulnerable to various causal forces. And yet, agents are a special kind of thing: agents are best understood in terms of their normative dimensions, namely their own choices and actions. The more an agent is explainable by way of their own choices, the less their life is explainable by way of external causation. Likewise, the more an agent is caused to do something, the less they have a choice in the matter, and the less their life is a reflection of who they are. Being devoted to Īśvara allows agents, by way of their own choice, to introduce into their lives ethical dimensions that are contrary to external manipulation. Autonomy, *kaivalya*, is brought about by the realization of Sovereignty in our own life. This is a radical ethical cleansing (*dharmameghasamādhi*) that consists of eschewing interpretation in all contexts (YS IV.29–34). To get rid of interpretation is to get rid of a methodology of epistemic parasitism and mimicry that leads to the political regularities of the external world coming to influence our own agency. Not only does this prevent us from colonially appropriating other people's epistemic labor. It also prevents us from appropriating the pathologies of the world we experience as though they were our idea, belief, and desire.

In the next section, I review the *Yoga Sūtra*'s approach to de-colonization at the three levels of Metaethics, Normative Ethics, and Applied Ethics. In the third section, I will explore what Yoga teaches us about Moral Injury, Moral Trauma, and Moral Recovery. In the fourth section, I will explore how the West's politics of colonization interferes with our understanding of Yoga by way of its ubiquitous colonial activity—activities that are rendered explicit by Yoga. In the fifth section, I conclude.

2. Metaethics to Non-Ideal Political Theory

Yoga, the basic contribution to moral philosophy, is found in three classical sources. The earliest is in the *Kaṭha Upaniṣad* where Death teaches the boy, Naciketa, about how we have a choice to integrate the functioning of our senses, mind, body, under the guidance of the intellect into a coherent whole that serves the interest of the self. When we do this, we end up in the realm of Viṣṇu—preservation but also unconservatism. If we fail at this, we are led by our outlook to our ruin. This is a very early distinction between explication and interpretation. In the case of interpretation we are led by our outlook. Explication in contrast requires logic or reason—intellect. The other source is the *Bhagavad Gītā*, where Kṛṣṇa (Viṣṇu) makes a case for devotion to Īśvara, or Sovereignty. The *Yoga Sūtra* deserves special attention as it is the academic, and systematic, articulation of Yoga. Here, we find it accounted for at three levels: the Metaethical, Normative Ethical, and the Applied Ethical or political level.

The opening lines of the *Yoga Sūtra* are dense. Actually, the entire text is dense. It is written in the *sūtra* format, where every word is chosen for its polysemy. The resulting concatenations are each like a zip file: compressing lots of ideas that make up rich arguments. Interpreters usually try to cherry-pick the meanings they believe are relevant to the text, discarding the rest. Though the *Yoga* Sūtra is likely the most widely read philosophical text the world over, closely connected with postural yoga training, it is generally misunderstood as naive readers try to interpret the text. As an explicator, one is committed to taking seriously all the meanings of a *sūtra* as setting out arguments. The key concept in the opening distinction between interpretation and explication is that of influence—*vṛtti*—which also means ethical behavior (normativity) and waves. In its opening lines, we find what I listed (in Chapter 1) as *Argument 1* (which made the case for explication) and *Argument 2* (which identifies interpretation as the error theory). Either we engage in influencing mental content (explicating) or we are influenced by mental content (interpreting). Either we arrange and rationally influence what we contemplate to conclusions so that our autonomy is ethically respected, or we allow mental content to influence us as though it were our emotions. If we choose the latter, we collapse the distinction between what we are contemplating and ourselves, and the result is error. We ought to, in contrast, choose the responsible, explicatory approach for the sake of our epistemic autonomy (YS I.2-4).

In the *Yoga Sūtra*, where this distinction is articulated, we also find the definition of Īśvara, or Sovereignty: it is unconstrained by its past, and also free to move forward. It is both unconservative and self-governing (YS I.24). This ideal is abstract, atemporal, and gender neutral. To practice devotion to Sovereignty is to take on the practice of unconservatism and self-governance. But we get to devotion to the ideal of Sovereignty by engaging in explication. When we are explicating, we are practicing being unconservative (unconstrained by past thoughts and experiences) while allowing ourselves the freedom to determine our own values and make our own choices, which is to self-govern. This three-part activity—devotion to Sovereignty (*Īśvara Praṇidhāna*), unconservatism (*tapas*), and self-governance (*svādhyāya*)— sets out the Normative Ethics of Yoga (YS II.1). It is a public practice of moral philosophy insofar as this involves unconservatively explicating options while self-determining our own values. So from the very metaethical distinction between explication and interpretation, we can derive explication's Normative Ethics: accordingly, devotion to the Ideal of the Right (and practicing its component procedures of unconservatism and self-governance) brings about the good: our autonomy. The Normative Ethics is hence something that helps us rise over waves of external influences, as depicted in that famous tableau of devotion to Sovereignty (Ādi Śeṣa), unconservatism (Viṣṇu), and self-governance (Lakṣmī) floating over that sea of external influence.

Devotion to Īśvara as a central normative practice serves to bring to light what people have in common—an interest in Sovereignty—and hence one's own devotional practice to Īśvara constitutes a politics of solidarity with people. Persons so understood are not reducible to their natural attributes: they are definable by their normative interest in being free. A person is something that thrives given their own unconservatism and self-governance. To create a space that makes this devotional exercise possible, we need to create a public space safe for individuals. And hence, what is entailed by this basic ethical commitment of Yoga is a non-ideal politics, that is, a remedy (*upāya*) to failing practice (YS I.26).

Often "ideal theory" is invoked with prejudice and as a term of criticism: ideal moral theories are out of touch with what is possible. But in this case at least the idealism of the theory shows us what we ought to expect as a baseline of practice, and if we cannot engage in that because of oppression, we need to create the space for the ideal practice. The non-ideal practice is the remedy that consists in the political disruption of interpretation and the creation of public spaces for explication. It is hence, as an area of applied ethical interest, and non-ideal political practice, that is, a practical implementation of explication.

The non-ideal practice has eight implementations (Eight Limbs of Yoga).

The first limb, called *yama* (YS II. 30–6)—also the name of the god Death—is a universal obligation to disrupt systemic harm (*ahiṃsā*), that reveals the fact (*satya*) of people not deprived of their requirements (*asteya*), their personal boundaries respected (*brahmacarya*), resulting in no appropriation (*aparigraha*). This is a political commitment. But it is also the political corollary of explicating, for when we explicate, we do not engage in hepeating or the parasitic mimicry of interpretation. We do not deprive other people of what is theirs and we respect personal boundaries for we are not enforcing our opinion on others. Yama, this first limb—also the name of Death who teaches Naciketa about Yoga as a process of devotion to our autonomy by the analogy of the chariot—is the public practice of explication. And this is the inverse, or the opposite, to the public practice of oppression, namely, interpretation.

This first limb and the emphasis on *ahiṃsā* have been extremely influential on public awareness of the possibilities of direct action, as an exercise of nonviolence, that undermines oppression. M.K. Gandhi's *Collected Works* contains numerous references to Patañjali, whom Gandhi credits for his ideas of nonviolence, and his program of direct action—*satyagraha*—is a straightforward application of the entire first limb, which begins with nonharm. Gandhi's practices and writings were of course extremely influential on M.L. King Jr., who cites Gandhi as an example of how oppression can be successfully countered (M.L. King, Jr., September 1, 1958). And of course, this model becomes replicated by progressive activism the world over. It is entirely possible to confuse the role of *ahiṃsā*, in Yoga, as this is usually read as a teleological value. According to the teleological reading, nonviolence is about not breaking things. Hence, to engage in *ahiṃsā* is to never do anything destructive or violent. This is the Jain idea of *ahiṃsā*. But as Yoga is a radically procedural ethical theory, *ahiṃsā* here is procedural, which means it is about destroying barriers to public participation—or it is about harming harm. And as the *Gītā* and other sources note, this can be violent in conventional ways. The main point in the *Yoga Sūtra*, however, is that the activity of the Yogic activist is pedagogical: it sets the tone for public interaction. So while it does disrupt the status quo, it is disruptive in ways that we must normalize. As Gandhi puts this: "They say, 'means are, after all, means.' I would say, 'means are, after all, everything.' As the means so the end" (Gandhi and Prabhu 1959). This procedural constraint on ethical practice, where the ends are understood as no different from the means, does not preclude violence. But acceptable violence has to be what we can live with in contexts free of oppression. Self-defense, for instance, is an obvious example of this variety of violence that is acceptable both in terms of means and ends. Genocide would not be.

We engage in this act of political activism to create a space to practice Yoga. And so, the second limb, *niyama*, consists in engaging in devotion to Sovereignty, unconservatism, and self-governance, with contentment and purely without watering down the practice with something else (YS II.32). In other words, once we have created this oppression-free space, people are then in a position to challenge their prior propositional attitudes by engaging in the metaethical organizing of options, and they can then transparently acknowledge the values they empower. This is the space of moral-philosophical work. It is the de-colonial space where, in practicing self-governance, one determines bonds with one's own chosen values (YS II.44).

At this point, it is worth clarifying for whom this activism is making space. If we assumed LAT, and followed the usual trajectory, we would confuse persons with humans (language users) and then more specifically people in one's own community. In Yoga, however, a person is anything that has an interest in its own Sovereignty as constitutive of its own thriving. So persons are not constrained by species. Animals, including us, are typically persons as limiting their independence typically compromises their health. The Earth is a person: it too is something that thrives when it can be unconservative and self-governing. Plants, in contrast, while living things, have a different kind of interest. Whereas persons thrive given their own unconservatism and self-governance, plants are the opposite. They thrive when they are conservative with respect to their past (rooted in it) and when they are governed benignly by their environment. This is not to say that plants do not have interests: they are just a different kind of interest from persons. And given that the Earth is a person on whom plants depend so much, it is appropriate for us to appreciate the ways in which not only are their interests different from persons, but they (plants) are also dependent on a person (the Earth). The case of a fetus and a plant in this respect is very similar.

Fetuses do not thrive given their own Sovereignty and independence. They thrive given a lucky environment, dependent on a person. When babies are born, though somewhat still plantlike, their interests become personal: their interest in challenging themselves (unconservatism) and owning their own choices (self-governance) cannot be denied without introducing harm into their life. In engaging in unconservatism and self-governance, children grow and learn. These distinctions are of course relevant to considering questions of a person's control over their own body, and pregnancy. It also entails that eating plants is very different from eating persons: the former activity can play into the interests of plants over time, while the latter undermines the interests of persons. In general, these considerations help paint a picture of what Yogic activism that creates a safe public space looks like: it is one safe for people, regardless of species, who share this interest in unconservatism and self-governance.

The third limb is *āsana*, which is literally described as the comfortable steady state of continuous practice (YS II.46–8). This is the limb of occupying the space one has created by one's activism. The fourth Limb is *prāṇāyāma*, which superficially relates to practices of breath, but is also described as the process of deconstructing natural barriers between oneself and the external world (YS II.51). This is to appreciate that our interests are continuous with public space: there is no way to be personally well while the air and the environment is poisoned. But having created a public space of de-colonization we have to learn to appreciate the ways in which we are coextensive with this space. Moral autonomy is not about living in a bubble. It is an autonomy of choice and behavior, not social isolation. The fifth limb of *pratyāhāra* is the withdrawal of the senses from objects, which is the Yoga tradition's way of directing us to engage in a personal, explicatory practice that is content neutral (*YS* II.54–5).

The last three limbs are bundled together as what one practices "with-yama" (*saṃyama*). They constitute three procedures essential for research and problem-solving: *dhāraṇā* (concentration, focus, enumerating options), *dhyāna* (following implications, second order generalizations), and *samādhi* (drawing conclusions, best explanations given the sorted data) (YS III.1–4). They gesture to the three levels of explicatory research. While this practice enables prediction and control, and the generation of powers that enable practitioners to live safe and protected lives, it is only complete when we make room for the conclusions of moral philosophy (*dharmameghasamādhi*) that lead to our own autonomy (IV 29–34). In laying bare choices and options we are free to choose, as opposed to being compelled into behavior.

Yoga in sum provides us three levels of de-colonization. At the metaethical level, in making a case for explication it both reveals oppression as a function of interpretation and provides an alternative. In grounding practice in an explicatory elucidation of options, Yoga is de-colonizing as it will not permit just one option as the frame of understanding. Secondly at the normative ethical level Yoga elucidates a normative practice as an unconservative departure from states of oppression while also affirming the importance of self-governance, and the self-determination of values. It is the public practice of moral philosophy. Finally at the non-ideal or political level it concerns the existential conditions of our own explicatory practice, which is a public space where people are free to engage in such explicatory practices. Such a space is not compatible with oppression and hence creating this space is de-colonial.

3. Moral Trauma, Moral Recovery

In contrasting explication and interpretation as contrary metaethical choices, Yoga provides us with an error theory it simply calls *avidya* (ignorance): interpretation. Interpreters are irrational, and that's bad enough. Knowledge is not going to be possible by interpreting. But interpreters, as noted, appropriate content they experience as the content of thoughts they then have attitudes toward, creating a firewall that prevents them from appreciating the historical origins of their thoughts. This accounts for the appropriative mimicry of the interpreter. But the interpreter also thereby ends up treating the content of the world, as it is, as the contents of their thoughts that they then relate to via their attitudes. And in this process, they appropriate their experiences and treat them as the contents of their beliefs and desires about themselves. They hence form a false sense of self—an ego (*asmitā*)—in terms of those beliefs and desires.

Once an individual defines themselves by way of propositional attitudes, they create a sense of fragility—what Patañjali calls a fear of death, which is a fear of change: *abhiniveśa*. The agent thus irrationally confuses the contingencies of their propositional attitudes with a safe space for themselves, and hence directs their own agency to protecting that egotism. Hence, they become agents of these propositional attitudes which haunt them. This state of haunting is an affliction, or trauma (*kleśa*, YS II.3). Instead of autonomy, the interpreter creates an existence that is a function of the experiences and politics of their world. Instead of a life that is self-directed, the interpreter lives a life of oppression.

3.1. Trauma

In contemporary talk, "trauma" is usually reserved for bad or unpleasant experiences—and a result of a subconscious that one has no control over. But Yoga teaches us that the nature of trauma is not about the content of the experience. Rather, trauma, or affliction, is the result of interpretation, a ritualization of the application of propositional attitudes called a *saṃskāra* (rite, ritual). In trauma, the interpreter spooks themselves out by strong propositional attitudes (like a fear that, anger that, or desire that *p*) that they cannot control or seem to shake. And while someone experiencing trauma cannot overcome or blot out the strong emotional experience of such propositional attitudes, the trauma is supervenient on their own interpretive practices, which is a metaethical choice. It creates a fake subconscious, which is only subconscious insofar as one chooses not to render it explicit via explication. They could shut that interpretive predilection (*saṃskāra*) off, but they choose not to. Indeed, their agency is so sequestered by interpretation that instead of switching off the methodological cause of trauma, they leave it on and attempt to battle their own emotions. They are like people yelling at a wall (their mind) to get it to be quiet, only to have their scream echoed back to them. The more they yell at the wall, the more it screams back at them. (Explication will not allow this as it will not allow us to treat mental content as something static that informs our sense of self that we could yell at but as something that requires organizing.) Ignorance creates a false sense of an inescapable self—*asmitā*, egotism—devoted not to Sovereignty but defined by a set of experiences limited by the initial trauma-inducing content. And this self-spooking can occur even when the experiences that constitute the haunting propositional attitudes are positive.

For instance, if one experiences racial privilege, for being White in a country with a history of White Supremacy, in identifying with that experience as one's egotism, constructed out of an interpretive practice that uses a desire for White Supremacy as a key content, one is thereby motivated to defend that political order. The White Supremacist thereby feels alarm at the existence of Brown or Black people—even though their experience of White Supremacy is favorable to them. They are alarmed by the existence of Brown or Black people as their existence poses a threat to White Supremacy.

Likewise, if an agent has bad experiences of illness, or even assault, if an agent manages to explicate the injurious context, the agent has rendered themselves autonomous relative to those experiences and events. And that allows them to move on without trauma. The experience no longer haunts the explicator for they do not relate to those events emotionally, via propositional attitudes.

Just to be clear, while we often have no control over the content of experience—furnished to us by others in many cases—and once we adopt interpretation, we have no control over the wild emotions we feel as we relate to propositions emotionally, we do have control over the choice to interpret. And hence a proper Yoga cure for trauma is to get us to abandon interpretation via all three levels of de-colonial practice. Our own trauma is a self-colonization—a self-imposition of a perspective—and hence our own cure is our own de-colonization.

Let us consider the difference between explication and interpretation with respect to the same event to illustrate how trauma is a form of self-colonization.

During the Second World War, the Nazis engaged in a massive campaign of genocide, with Jews being the principal targeted population. Explicated, the explanation of the Holocaust was the ideology and actions of the Nazis. Jews (the people, not the racist Nazi tropes) are not part of the explanation of why the Holocaust occurred. Jews are blameless and irrelevant to the real cause of the event. It was not their idea or their doing. Rather it was the racial theories of the Nazis, coupled with their own moral perspective essentialism, which depicted people outside of the Nazi ethnolinguistic identity as the problem. If one explicated every event where Jews were persecuted, the explanation would track the ideas and actions of the perpetrators of these persecutions. Jews as the victims would be blameless.

Explication is an account of the logic that gets us to a conclusion: it isn't tracking truth. But when we turn to interpretation we are concerned with propositional attitudes like beliefs, and the most believable propositions (or the attitudes that are most strong) are the ones that track what seem obviously true to us. The most believable proposition that unfolded in the Holocaust is that Jews were persecuted because of their ethnolinguistic identity. This was certainly observable in the unfolding of the Holocaust. On this interpretive approach, that employs beliefs generated by the Holocaust in the explanation of the event, this event is primarily about Jews, not Nazis, as Jews are *prima facie* people persecuted for their ethnolinguistic identity in the Holocaust. If one were to repeat this interpretive approach for every event where Jews were persecuted for their Jewishness, then one could develop a grand narrative of Jews being particularly vulnerable to persecution because of their ethnolinguistic identity. Zionism, Jewish Nationalism, is based on and motivated by this narrative of Jews as needing their own nation state because they are otherwise particularly vulnerable to ethnolinguistic persecution. And, as noted in Chapter 2, this interpretive self-identity, emboldened and stitched into place by LAT, creates the conditions for Zionists engaging in genocide. And so the Zionist sense of persecution that arises from interpreting and their genocidal action toward others that also arises from interpretation are two sides of the same problem.

The Yogic analysis here, on this point of an interpretive approach to life, is that it *replicates* the harm that one suffers via a process of self-colonization. Abused people go on to be abusers *if they* interpret. Accordingly, there is a causal relationship between the Nazi treatment of Jews, and the Zionist actions of Israel in Palestine, where the latter replicates the abuse suffered by Jewish people, but visited on the Palestinians. This causality is facilitated by Zionists interpreting. In this exercise of *colonial-exchange*, Zionists project the past they want to escape on Palestinians, and take the Palestinian's past in

Palestine as theirs. This project of *colonial-exchange* is a function of the fear of death the interpreter is haunted by: it is the fear of the vulnerability of the agent as defined by their propositional attitudes, not their interests as agents. And in this irrational projection, the victim of colonization (the Palestinian in this case) is depicted as integral to the traumatic past the Colonizer (the Zionist in this case) wants to avoid. This supports the irrational notion that advocating for Palestine is anti-Semitic.

Interpretation renders us functionally non-autonomous agents who simply repeat what we experience. For in allowing ourselves to treat our experiences as the content of propositional attitudes that then informs our sense of self, we replicate what we experience in defense of this sense of self. The parasitic, epistemic mimicry of the interpreter is not an agentless crime: it is enabled by the irrational choice of interpretation. But in this case of parasitism, the interpreter replicates the abuse they experience because they have confused that experience with their sense of self. An utterly bizarre aspect of this dynamic is that the very racism that explains the crime, which we should reject (the racist idea that Jewishness explains the abuse Jews experience), becomes internalized by Zionist advocacy for Jews. The problem is that there is *no way to understand a reason without endorsing it if we interpret*. So if the Nazi reason for persecuting the Jews is that there is something problematic about Jews that renders them fitting recipients of this abuse, we take that on as our reason if we interpret. In this way, interpreter victims take on the most disparaging beliefs of their oppressor as their own motivation. One outcome is Jewish nationalism, as though Jews can only be at home if they have their own ethno-linguistic homeland: unlike others they cannot be at home wherever they happen to live. Anti-Zionist Jews are often described as "self-hating Jews." But on this analysis, it is the Zionist Jew who is actually the self-deprecating Jew.

The interpretive approach to understanding one's own oppression can lead to a story about oneself as the exceptional victim: no one else, or no other group, will appear to be persecuted as one's self or one's own group because one will discount other people's suffering if it does not fit with one's interpretation. In the case of the genocide in Gaza, Zionists will ironically feel that they are the primary victims in this case. And it will also be the same interpretive orientation that creates moral perspective essentialism and marks out the Palestinians as threats to a Zionist identity. Jews who are not Zionists, in contrast, do not interpret their history.

As the *Yoga Sūtra* notes (YS II.34), there is no end to this cycle of violence without appreciating its root cause, and by adopting a posture that is contrary to this violence.

These considerations shed light on a phenomenon called "moral injury." The Syracuse University Moral Injury Project defines it as a damage to one's moral compass when one "perpetrates, witnesses, or fails to prevent acts that transgress one's own moral beliefs, values, or ethical codes of conduct" (Syracuse University 2024). This way of framing the problem depicts it as a violation of one's propositional attitudes, and hence is an entirely colonial approach to the topic. And to depict this as a moral injury is to confuse oneself with one's beliefs. Actual moral injury, injury to the function of the moral agent, is what colonization does: it prevents agents from explicating options.

When we are devoted to the ideal of music, for instance, we engage in the practice of music, and in proportion to our devotion, so too is the time we devote to practicing it. But, such a practice is motivated by *procedural* considerations, and involves many teleological failures (such as bad-sounding music). All devoted students of music when they begin or even as they progress will make mistakes, and perform in ways that are contrary to their normative expectations. And yet, *no serious* music student would call this a *musical injury*. The reason this is not a musical injury is that their practice of music has not been injured as a result of these errors. In contrast, the musical errors are produced within and as a part of an aspirationally driven project of learning and practicing music. This is consistent with an arc of musical improvement. While the dedicated student of music does not excuse their musical errors, they also do not view it as counter-evidence to their practice. In ethics, we tell the same story but the procedural ideal is Sovereignty, and the practice we are working on is being a free person.

The actual work lies in the self-correction and the self-analysis that leads to identifying repetitive failures as a result of *some* choice that sets up such *saṃskāra*-s, and then the practitioner, in doing this personal history, chooses to make a different kind of choice, thus ridding themselves of that *saṃskāra*.

Assessing one's musical practice teleologically, in terms of the quality of one's performance, creates an unwinnable standard against which the success of one's practice is to be judged. The same goes for moral practice. Of course, there are people who don't know this, and they will suffer needless emotional crises over their entirely predictable outcome failures. Being devoted to Sovereignty is not the same as assuming that one is Sovereign. But certainly, those who do assume their own sovereignty will be very surprised when they fail at living up to their beliefs about themselves. That's not a moral injury. That's catching up to reality.

3.2. Self-Care

Framing ethical action in terms of ends, whether the goodness of the virtuous agent, the consequences of ethical actions, or the good actions that we ought to endorse for special reason, problematizes moral action in cases of oppression. For in this case, goodness is hunted. And this is part of the diabolical tax levied on good people whose very goodness is marked out for oppression. This is an important part of the manipulation that the conventionally moral experience: as they are concerned with goodness, oppressors target them with wrongness. And as the conventionally moral are generally not paying attention to procedural questions of justice, they become easy targets, as they are distracted by beliefs about their own goodness, the goodness of their stated ends, and the goodness about their activities—which may even be true.

Self-care (personal care) and moral action amount to the same thing. For in this case, departing from the ignorance of interpretation by explication creates the context for an agent to attend to their procedural needs, without being distracted by goodness and beliefs about goodness. And those needs are understood not teleologically but procedurally. The more an agent is devoted to Sovereignty, the more they explore this procedural space by their unconservatism and self-governance, the more they create a life that suits them as an agent. Teleological thinking constitutes an epistemic constraint on our action. For if we have to constrain ethical action to outcomes, we are really restricted by the outcomes we can imagine, and those we believe we can accomplish. The feasible outcomes, the expected utility, and the ones we have evidence for—the ones we can imagine—are constrained by the oppression that we experience. Great and unusual outcomes have a low expected utility and hence thinking teleologically about their feasibility downgrades their role as ends for action, and up-favors whatever is favored by oppression which has a higher expected utility. But when we can simply stop acting with concern for outcomes, and instead in devotion to Īśvara, we allow ourselves to create opportunities we didn't imagine were possible. The grace of devotion to Īśvara, a procedural ideal, is real. Part of that grace is the permission we give ourselves to move on from self-limiting propositional attitudes. Part of that grace is what we experience by our own exploration of its essential traits of unconservatism and self-governance.

Activism is nearly impossible if measured by teleological considerations. If the motivation for activism is the end of some injustice, then we will burn out as activists for anything we do individually is unlikely to bring the injustice to an end. However, if we can live our lives on our own terms, and if that is the same as our activism, then we never burn out and we actually stand a chance of changing things for the better. And living life on our own terms is always activistic for it confronts and interrupts oppression.

The full gamut of the Eight Limbs plays a role in self-care for every implementation creates opportunities for personal thriving.

What is striking about the South Asian tradition is how this original insight and wisdom about the grounds of oppression and what liberation amounts to, as a matter of practical action, is itself occluded by centuries of colonization. Already by the 1400s, about 500 years after the beginning of Islamic colonization in South Asia, we find in the *Haṭha Yoga Pradīpikā* the rebranding of Yoga as an agoraphobic activity, that one does in a gentrified part of town, under the tutelage of a human teacher. And the activities, all of them trainings of mind and body, avoid disrupting oppression and rather constitute the very descent into a space of a fear of one's own mortality that classical Yoga shows to be the grounds of our self-oppression. In this case, practitioners engage in disciplines of mind and body to open energy centers in the body, ensuring liberating experiences. And whereas classical Yoga is Vaiṣṇava—procedural—this newfangled agoraphobic "yoga" is Śaiva— teleological.

3.3. Relativism: The Other Kind

In ethics, we are accustomed to moral relativism as the prescriptive idea that what counts as one's obligations is relative either to oneself or one's community. But there is another variety of relativism (encoded in Yoga) that those interested in ethics tend to ignore. That is the kind of "relativism" that we find in physics. Accordingly, the laws of physics are the same for everyone in whatever frame of reference they are in. But what they experience will be different depending upon what they are doing. In ethics this translates into the idea that moral interests are *agent-relative*: for everyone. And the experiences we have, including our propositional attitudes, are not data but the output of choice and activity in a public world. Living life according to universal agent relativity is a life where agents allow each other the space they need to explore this agent relativity. And it is also possible in such a world that some agents will prevent others from having this space. In the case of trauma, and more generally in the case of interpretation, individuals act as though they are stationary in a world conveyed to them by their experiences. Trauma is hence this sense of not being able to transcend the experiences that constrain one's sense of self.

Yoga, an activity (*kriyā*), aims to realign the procedural basis for life by affirming the universality of agent relativism. Appreciating that there are basic interests all agents share—an interest in Sovereignty—allows life to be an exercise of what we all have an interest in: our agency.

4. Don't Make Me Think—Tell Me What to Do: "Yoga" in a Colonized World

To understand history, one has to explicate for interpretation just projects backwards onto the past our current beliefs. There's no way to understand the history of Yoga this way. If one explicates, it becomes obvious there is only one option that contributes to the disagreements of philosophy, that is called Yoga. And, moreover, if we understand this moral-philosophical practice of what I call capital "Y" Yoga, then one can understand how lower case "y" yoga—like postural or breathing exercises—can be ways to practice capital "Y" Yoga—ways to implement one's own unconservatism and self-governance. If one interprets one will use one's beliefs about yoga, whatever that is, to explain whatever one calls yoga. In this way, stories about what yoga is proliferate. But as the dominant interpretive paradigm of the world is White Irrationality, it is the *saṃskāra*, interpretive tendencies, of the Western tradition that come to animate stories about what Yoga is.

Especially in geographically western countries, there is an obvious racial component to what transpires as yoga. It's like a giant *hepeating* event but the appropriators are largely White women (*shepeating*), and the people who generated the appropriated content and are treated as though they didn't say anything are dark, Brown, South Asian philosophers of Yoga. I have personal experience with this too, which I disclose in my book for Yoga practitioners. (Ranganathan 2024, 113–18). Specifically in my case, I went through a period when White women who saturate Yoga teaching and professional organizations in North America tried to erase me. In all cases, I would be invited as a contributor given my expertise, but then erased. In an emblematic case, my name and image in an advertisement for a course I was teaching on Yoga and activism (at a large and famous center for yoga education in the United States) was replaced with that of a nameless stock-image White woman because the organizers thought it would have a broader appeal to their followers. The White men and all the women in the same announcement were not erased. The need to make spaces devoted to yoga education philosophy-free is tantamount to erasing dark males—my ancestors and myself—who had a hand in exploring and articulating Yoga. The dark males that are allowed or celebrated in those spaces in contrast are exactly who exemplify the colonizing tradition. The de-colonial Brown philosopher—including Patañjali—is not allowed without erasure. While White Irrationality treats Black men and Brown men differently, it was difficult to not view this mild form of erasure that involved no bodily injury as connected with a wider project of removing dark (Black) men (violently) from public space, often because White people feel threatened. White Irrationality would lead to both outcomes.

To understand what unfolds in this and all cases of oppression, we have to understand what a *saṃskāra* is. The word "*saṃskāra*" means "ritual" or "rite." In Yoga, these are patterns of interpretation, where we impose a perspective on ourselves. We might do so on purpose. If I have a couch potato *saṃskāra* that keeps me planted on my couch, then developing a daily jogging *saṃskāra* can counter the former *saṃskāra*. However, the new *saṃskāra* can take on a life of its own, needing itself to be canceled by a moderating *saṃskāra*. In most cases, we absorb *saṃskāra*-s passively by interpretation: the political order we experience becomes the content of our propositional attitudes and then animates our actions. And in this way, we become agents of continuing intergenerational trauma and various intergenerational pathologies insofar as we passively take on the automated errors of the past as our rites and rituals. An important part of an actual Yoga practice is understanding the history of our *saṃskāra*-s and abandoning them in favor of a fully intentional life free from automation.

I call the resulting interpretations of Yoga according to Western *saṃskāra*-s Western Appropriated Culture (WAC). In the case of WAC-ky Yoga, South Asian ideas and practices are appropriated to recreate Western political institutions and thereby normalize White Supremacy and colonization.

Westerners with the Plato's *Republic saṃskāra* recreate pyramid schemes in Yogaland with an enlightened guru at the top whose choices and preferences are treated as curriculum that climbers of the pyramid have to master. Westerners with the Aristotle Ethics *saṃskāra* treat learning as cultural performance and enculturation—being raised properly. This results in cringey cosplay where "yoga" practitioners say "namaste" (it just means "hello") especially at the end of class (?), and display the idea that knowledge of Yoga is a performance of some South Asian cultural competence. The Stoicism *saṃskāra* treats Yoga as an opportunity to realign one's emotional responses to the natural world. On this approach, yoga is no more than a technique one employs for emotional regulation, for calming oneself down, breathing, being present, and recharging. All of these are expressions of Western colonization as they impose a Western ethical theory on spaces nominally devoted to the study and practice of Yoga. That is the point of this colonial exercise: to use "Yoga," which is an anti-colonial project of devotion to Sovereignty, to name (in Orwellian fashion) the opposite of de-colonial activity—namely, techniques of wellness that help one cope and acclimatize to oppression. Ubiquitous in this space is an intentional confusion of Yoga with Buddhism and derivative techniques of mindfulness, where the point is the reduction of suffering. Buddhism is committed to denying our autonomy for on its account there's no such thing: we're all dependently originating, not autonomous. Hence, the most we should aim for is the reduction of suffering. This is a very different moral and political project from Yoga and confusing it with Yoga is intentional: it is about getting rid of the space that ought to be devoted to de-colonization and autonomy to the management of symptoms. It is also colonial as it denies the contemplation of alternatives, like the distinction between Yoga and Buddhism.

According to Yoga, suffering is just a symptom, not the problem. We suffer because our autonomy is compromised. And hence, the motivation for practicing Yoga is not suffering reduction: it is to recover our autonomy. That radically de-colonial project is so incompatible with White Irrationality that one will rarely hear about it in "yoga" spaces.

None of this entails that we cannot take back postural practices or breathing practices as part of a genuine practice of Yoga. As I explore in my *Yoga—Anticolonial Philosophy: An Action-Focused Guide to Practice* (2024), when we are engaged in a genuine practice of Yoga, all of our activities are part of our exploration of Īśvara, including postural and breath work. But to really engage in this de-colonial learning of Yoga, we have to center philosophy and explication in Yoga pedagogy. The idea that philosophy is a waste of time is as colonial and *Western* as it gets. The idea that you can learn Yoga but not philosophy is as *Western* as it gets.

5. Moral Philosophy as Public Practice

The argument of this book contrasts colonialism and its irrationality with moral-philosophical practice and its rationality. Yoga, the fourth basic ethical theory unique to South Asia, and not part of the global colonizing tradition, the *West*, contrasts interpretation and its oppressive outcomes with explication, which entails a Normative Ethics of moral philosophy. These are incompatible. Colonization, or the imposition of a perspective, is what we do to ourselves when we live suboptimal and irrational lives, by adopting interpretation as our method of explanation. To explicate is to adopt the opposite and mutually exclusive approach to understanding, which involves a commitment to unconservatively exploring options while self-determining one's own values. This is a public and active engagement in moral theorizing and moral philosophy. We cannot do both oppression and practice moral philosophy publicly. Insofar as we each have an interest in our own independence, we each have an interest in a public practice of moral philosophy. And at any rate, of the two, only the latter is rational.

Part Four

Applied Ethics

7

Applied Ethics and the De-Colonial Politics of Moral Philosophy

1. Introduction

In moving from Metaethics to Normative Ethics we are moving from the most abstract level of moral-philosophical investigation, to the substance of moral philosophy, namely theories of THE RIGHT OR THE GOOD. To move to Applied Ethics is to move to the topics that theories of THE RIGHT OR THE GOOD should have something to say about, but are frequently ignored. Given the anthropocentrism and communitarianism of LAT-based ethical theory, almost everything morally relevant that does not play an essential role in the bureaucratic concerns of an anthropocentric and communitarian outlook is orphaned as an Applied Ethical topic, including animal ethics (as though humans are not animals) and the environment. When we examine the general trends of *Western* Normative Ethics in the next section, we shall see that its preoccupation is with legitimizing oppression as the cost of moral behavior: this narrow scope ensures that almost every moral topic is orphaned as an Applied Ethical topic. In the third section we will switch the focus from the *West* to a de-colonial Indigenous approach. And we see that the singular concrete topic of Applied Ethics that is not addressed by an indigenous, LE-based Normative Ethical Theory is the political challenge of de-colonization. This is the politics of Yama (the first limb of Yoga), which we examined in the previous chapter. Here, I will address matters that are of particular concern for our rollout of this de-colonial politics in a world of LAT. In the fourth section I consider objections and then I conclude.

2. *Western* Normative Ethics Is the Rationalization of Colonization

LAT in identifying thought with linguistic meaning encourages us, in the realm of ethics, to believe that ethical questions are anthropocentric, as language is this human capacity, or communitarian, insofar as language itself is a marker of communities. Typically we find both together with rare exceptions, which is why I have shortened the characterization of LAT as "anthropocentric and communitarian."

There are two versions of LAT-based ethical thinking in the *Western* tradition, which are two different approaches to the same topic. The first is the social engineering version—the Plato-Hobbes version—and the second is the social investigation version—Aristotle-Kant version.

The Plato-Hobbes (Confucius too) version does not assume that we have a functioning society to study as the topic of moral philosophy. It rather imagines constructing one. In this case, Normative Ethics is a solution to a coordination problem of how humans are supposed to get along. Humans are conceived as naturally clueless, in need of being included within a larger community. Moreover, morality is conceived in explicitly oppressive terms as a solution to a natural inclination to not be virtuous or cooperative. For Plato this involves the Noble Lie that tricks people into cooperating. Hobbes rather tries to mount an argument that given our prospects in nature we are best advised to choose a third-party dictator—Sovereign—who will impose minimal standards on us, so that our basic interests in life and limb are preserved. In this case, our interests and that of the Sovereign—the Leviathan—unite. Plato's version is actually not that different.

Hobbes motivates his argument in the *Leviathan* by thinking about a State of Nature that can be captured in the idea of a *Prisoner's Dilemma*. According to this story, outside of society, in a State of Nature, when we both want an apple, and we see one apple on the tree, we will both rush toward it and end up fighting. Life is hence "nasty, brutish and short." Why is this the natural outcome? We are really "rational" maximizers of our preferences who act independently of others. Both of our top choice is to have the apple for ourselves. Next, we would prefer half an apple, to share. And what we want least is no apple. If I decide to be cooperative but you take the apple for yourself, I lose. If I try to take the apple for myself and you cooperate, you lose. Only one outcome promises some apple for both of us, the outcome that comes from both of us sharing. But since I don't know what you are going to do, and since I don't want to try to cooperate and have you take the apple, it seems I should take the chance and go for it all for myself. As we will both reason this way, we'll end up fighting and not enjoying an apple. This is the *Prisoner's Dilemma*, named after prisoners jointly accused of a crime. Each is given the option to confess and accuse the other or remain silent. For the same reasoning, both prisoners accuse each other and get a bad deal.

Now, this argument is strange in some ways but so part of the *Western* tradition that it's not that strange, in the sense of being unusual. In Plato's

Republic, after Socrates dismisses Thrasymachus' argument that justice is whatever is in the interest of the stronger, Glaucon rehabilitates the intuition that might makes right by articulating the same Prisoner's Dilemma decision matrix resulting in bad outcomes for all who pursue what they prefer. And so social contract to institute justice and law come into place not because people would prefer that but because it's the way to avoid the worst case outcome (*Republic* 358c-359a). Plato's solution begins with Socrates bringing up the wonderful thought experiment of Gyges Ring that allows anyone who wears it to be invisible: would the just person constrain themselves under these circumstances if they could get away with crime with impunity? Socrates thinks yes. But in the end the solution that Socrates (Plato) argues for is not so different from Hobbes for what he suggests is that we need an unequal, top-down society, to move us away from these kinds of problems where people act on the basis of selfishness and then live suboptimal lives. Only the philosopher king would have the appropriately ordered soul for justice on this account: everyone else must be put in their place.

Hobbes is directly relevant to our topic of colonization for his discussions of the State of Nature are ways that Europeans would have viewed Indigenous people, outside of the Leviathan of their colonial order. All the arguments that Hobbes provides for why joining the Leviathan is a good idea are Eurocentric arguments for why Indigenous people should accept colonization. To European Colonizers, it would appear that without someone forcing Indigenous people to cooperate, they would live lives that are nasty, brutish, and short. Of course, this is not true. For Indigenous people who are better understood by LE, would not be inclined to confuse their propositional attitudes, like desires, as the content of reason. And hence they would not be given to framing rational action in the way that leads to prisoner dilemma type problems, as these require that we are confusing reason with our desires.

The Aristotle-Kant version assumes that we have a functioning moral practice as the foundation of moral theorizing. And the job of moral philosophy is to make clear the values and principles that make this arrangement possible. Aristotle gives voice to this idea in the *Nicomachean Ethics* where he stipulates that someone who speaks on ethics has to be raised properly as the enculturation serves as the data for the topic (I.30). This is of course consistent with (and likely reveals) the supposed natural inferiority of slaves and women (*Politics*, 1254b16–21). Today, Aristotelians will have a different culture to draw from, but it will continue to be anthropocentric.

Kant in the *Groundwork* frequently assumes ordinary interactions in the society of his day, with customs such as shopkeepers giving the correct change and promise keeping. This is the ethnographic data of his moral theorizing. Moral theory, in Aristotelian fashion, is supposed to elucidate these customs.

Kant is often lauded for an emancipatory moral philosophy. However, his actual track record on the topic of colonialism and the treatment of nonhuman animals is not great. Nonhuman animals are on Kant's account lacking moral standing in any direct way, for the only beings that count as having such standing are capable of a self-legislation, and he believes nonhuman animals lack this. They are lesser because, he believes, they do not self-represent themselves as an "I" (*Anthropology from a Pragmatic Point of View* 7: 127). Lower beings have a nature that marks themselves out as a means, but higher beings (humans) have a nature that marks them as an end in themselves, dependent on their own will (*Groundwork* 4: 428).

A volume devoted to Kant's thought on colonialism begins with acknowledging his ambivalence on the topic (Flikschuh and Ypi 2014). As his thought matures, he develops arguments against colonialism (Ripstein 2014) and imperialism (Stilz 2014). What seems to have been missed in all discussions of Kantian ethics is how central colonization is to the way Kant formalizes his ethics. Central to Kantian ethics is the Categorical Imperative, which is supposed to specify the procedural considerations for endorsing candidate norms as moral obligations—obligations that scope over the category of agents who can engage in this kind of legislation. Famously, Kant shares four competing formulations, which are different ways on Kant's account of cashing out the same idea.

- *Universal Law of Nature (Groundwork 4:421)* "Act only on that maxim whereby thou canst at the same time will that it should become a universal law."
- *Principle of Humanity (Groundwork 4:429; cf. 4:436)* "Act in such a way that you treat humanity, whether in your own person or in the person of another, always at the same time as an end, never merely as a means."
- *Autonomy Formula (Groundwork 4:431; cf. 4:432)* "Act only so that your will can regard itself at the same time as making universal law through its maxims."
- *Kingdom of Ends (Groundwork 4:439)* "Act according to maxims of a universally legislating member of a merely possible kingdom of ends." (Patton translation, see Kant 1948)

What is remarkable about this way of conceiving the project of moral theory is that it treats us as legislators for others, which is colonial. Most problematic is the conflation between the Kingdom of Ends formulation, where we are tasked with considering the rules of an ideal community, with the Universal Law of Nature formulation, where we are tasked on deciding what should be imposed on everyone. *Ironically*, the Autonomy Formulation explicitly defines obligations in terms of legislation for others. Kantians don't see these problems as they are impressed with Kant's regard for the subject of this Categorical Imperative as a self-legislator. That does not erase all the ways in which this project is just how we would think about moral issues if we were Colonizers. Kant's ethics is hence emblematic of the irony of the Western tradition. In this most Western formulation, individual autonomy and the colonization of others (the imposition of a perspective of what to do on others) amount to the same thing. The "liberal" aspect of Kant's project is that we all get to be Colonizers, of each other.

A figure worth noting who is certainly very influential in this tradition is Hegel, who finds a way to introduce a nuanced distinction between the Aristotle and Kant approaches. In the Philosophy of Right, he distinguishes between *Sittlichkeit*—the ethical life—which has an Aristotelian flavor, and *Moralität*, morality, which has an abstract Kantian aspect. Both Aristotle and Kant treat actual moral practice as the focus of Normative Ethics, but Aristotle prioritizes the lived, shared aspect of our communal existence, while Kant allows us to engage in a more abstract reconstruction of such conditions. And indeed, the possibilities of viewing the Kantian project as reconstructive has not been lost on philosophers like David Gauthier, who argued that by using Hobbesian considerations we can reconstruct Kantian aspects of moral philosophy. But whichever Hegel prefers (and he seems to prefer the Aristotelian flavor) his thinking on these issues is firmly within this tradition.

Mill and Bentham, the famous Utilitarians, would fall somewhat more naturally in the Plato-Hobbes camp as they consider moral theorizing as revising ordinary custom as opposed to explaining it.

Mill shares Kant's disregard for the moral standing of nonhuman animals. Like Kant, this disregard is based on an interpretation of nonhuman animal lives and our own. Mill in *Utilitarianism* (Chapter 1) provides an inductive generalization of the most basic moral principle, the Principle of Utility (that we ought to strive for the greatest happiness), based on various other acknowledged goods. But then there is a hierarchy of goods, which has to do with the hierarchy of agents. Nonhuman animals are capable of experiencing pleasure. Humans or more advanced beings can experience pleasure and an intellectual variety, which is a better good, which he calls "happiness" as opposed to mere "pleasure." Evidence of this? Those who can experience both the lower and the higher variety of pleasure prefer the intellectual variety. And this is evidence of the superiority of the latter because of any candidate pleasures, the one preferred in general by those who can experience both is the superior pleasure: "better to be a human being dissatisfied than a pig satisfied; better to be Socrates dissatisfied than a fool satisfied." Mill proceeds to express great sympathy for those of higher intellectual capacities: it's harder to make them happier, and they can feel greater suffering (Chapter 2). Mill is so confident of his interpretation that he doesn't contemplate an alternative explanation that is consistent with the data: it is not that "lower" animals are incapable of experiencing intellectual pleasures—perhaps they have some awareness of it and simply prefer other things. This would throw a wrench in the idea that his "intellectual" pleasures are the better. As someone who has taught Mill to an auditorium with hundreds of students, many times, I'm quite sure that they too would have preferred a back rub or a tasty snack to the intellectual pleasure of a lecture on Mill. The upshot of Mill's case is that ethics should really be geared toward maximizing the greatest happiness, which involves preferring the happiness of higher beings—like his lot, and not South Asians who, in *On Liberty*, he describes as lacking the maturity to appreciate these pleasures. Like Kant, we see in Mill a colonizing ethical theory designed around prioritizing the Colonizer's preferences, and one that is hierarchical and set out to oppress nonhuman animals.

Mill was building on and altering a more basic egalitarian form of Utilitarianism from Bentham, who was unusual in his criticism of speciesism. On Bentham's account, we ought to be maximizing pleasure, and if that's the criterion, there is no just ground to maximize the happiness of one animal over another. In *The Principles of Morals and Legislation* 1781, he asks: "The question is not, Can they reason? nor, Can they talk? but, Can they suffer?" (Chapter XVII, Section 1).

There are colonizing metaphors in Bentham's moral theory, such as the idea that moral standing has to do with membership in a "moral community." The idea that moral standing requires being included in a community is a colonial model of standing: an Indigenous approach can recognize the moral standing of agents in no community.

A bigger problem with classical Utilitarianism as we find in Bentham, as noted by John Rawls, is that it is indifferent to the distribution of utility (Rawls 1971, 22–7). There's nothing in the theory that prevents us from choosing an oppressive order if it maximizes happiness on some measure. Oppression on this approach would be seen as an acceptable cost of maximizing happiness given a certain spread of expected utility. Or, oppression is nothing we can complain about if an oppressive order's total utility is equivalent to a less oppressive distribution with the same total utility.

Yet, Bentham's thinking remains influential and is reborn in a movement called *Effective Altruism*. Taking a page from Peter Singer's Benthamite work (with earlier classics like "Famine, Affluence and Morality," where he argued that if we can offset harm without bringing ourselves into a state of marginal utility, we ought to do so), it recommends that we ought to do what we can to reduce harm. But as observed, this does not alter the fundamental political structure of the world: it is rather against the backdrop of this structure that we as agents are supposed to assess how we can make a positive impact, given our surplus resources. "For Singer and his brand of moral philosophy," Kent and Lazurus (2022) write, "nothing fundamental can be changed . . . Moral reflection, and philosophy more broadly, is reduced to an administrative role: do the most good you can do within a world that is broken." What they do not appreciate is that this is an apt description of the entire *Western* tradition's canon. In this canon we can't understand ourselves to be responsible for the oppressive infrastructure of the world because we need that to make sense of permissible options.

Surely, one might think that there are exceptions to this generalization. There are *Western* moral and normative theories that are concerned to change things. We might think of Marxism, for instance, and Marx's famous eleventh thesis on Feuerbach: "Philosophers have only interpreted the world, in various ways; the point, however, is to change it." How would one apply Marxism, however, without it being an interpretation? A communist society on the basis of Marx's analysis is structured around beliefs about the central importance of work and the communal role of owning the means of production, contributing what one can, and making use of what one needs. For if we abandon the interpretive, LAT-based focus on the human in communities, and if we went Indigenous, we couldn't reconstruct a requirement for communism: agency would not be limited to human communities and Indigenous agents would not understand their activities in terms of this human community but in terms of a cosmic continuity of agents, including the Earth. Viewed within the project of *Western* LAT-based ethical theory, Marxism is not a departure from the *West's* trend of oppression that prioritizes humans in communities. It is an example of the trend. It couldn't change anything because it's in some ways a very conservative example of *Western*, LAT-based thinking. We already noted in Section 2.2, The *Religification* of South Asia, of Chapter 3, that Marx's diagnosis of religion, the institutionalization of White Supremacy, is that it is a result of humans not centering themselves, and that the opposite is actually true. This is a remarkable exercise of victim blaming but one that also shows how Marx's project is indebted to *Western* colonization. It doesn't stop there. He faults Colonizers for being "Hindooized," which is to say, rendered participants in Secularism,—and praises the British for not allowing that to happen. If we want to be rid of oppression we need to look to Indigenous moral philosophy.

3. Applied Ethics by De-Colonization

LAT-Based thinking creates an anthropocentric and communitarian-focused ethics, which functions as a rationalization for colonization: the imposition of a perspective that everyone has to conform to, resist, or perish under. The outcome is that most all questions of *THE RIGHT OR THE GOOD* are orphaned as applied ethical matters given this very narrow concern.

In relocating moral philosophy to its proper home within LE, that permits a wide range of moral-philosophical debate, Normative Ethical Theory scopes over most of what gets orphaned by LAT-based ethical theory. Normative Ethical Theory in this Indigenous space addresses questions of the treatment of animals, the Earth, as well as various personal matters (such as, for instance, diet, or substance use) because it is not an exercise of normalizing oppression. To learn about what this wide range of moral philosophy looks like, we need only explicate the history of South Asian moral philosophy. To normalize oppression is to redefine the scope of the ethical in such a narrow way that only the paradigm agents are acknowledged and everything else suffers in proportion to their deviation. Applied Ethics has to deal with all the matters left unaddressed by this narrow focus. What, in contrast, is left out of an Indigenous, LE approach to Normative Ethics? Contending with oppression and colonization. That is a topic that would fall out of an idealized exercise of moral philosophy. That is the First Limb of Yoga, which we examined in the last chapter. Though indeed the topic of de-colonization is orphaned by an idealized discussion of moral philosophy, South Asian moral philosophers nevertheless gave attention to the topic as the basic Applied Ethical question.

In our case, the colonization we have to contend with is colored by LAT and the *West*. Much of what preceded in this book addresses what this exercise of de-colonization has to contend with. It has to contend not only with Secularism$_2$ and White Irrationality, it has to do the work that *Western* theorists never bothered to do: to identify LAT as just an option in modeling thought. The exercise of de-colonization hence operates at all three levels: in accounting for a wider Metaethical understanding that renders colonization explicit as an entailment of just one approach to understanding (interpretation), in accounting for an explicated range of moral theorizing that goes beyond what *Westerners* will permit discussion on, and now we have to address the miscellany. Our version of the Applied Ethical discussion that addresses what is not addressed in an idealized review of Normative Ethical Theory concern peculiar confusions that arise from attempting to understand the possibilities of de-colonization without eschewing the *West*. I will identify some of these topics in this section.

Violence. I dealt with violence in explicating Yoga. There, I noted that the First Limb of Yoga's prioritization of *ahiṃsā* is often taken to imply a prohibition against harming anything. But if we adopt a procedural approach to the idea, constitutive of Yoga, *ahiṃsā*, is better understood as disrupting procedural harm, the harm that keeps individuals from exercising their own exploration of moral philosophy. As we must engage in the radical procedural metaethics of explication to engage in de-colonization we have to take the procedural approach to nonviolence seriously. We can note that there are at least two ways to exercise violence. Colonizers irrationally engage in violence to impose a perspective. But Indigenous people can rationally engage in violence to protect a world of agential diversity: this is to engage in a procedural nonviolence, or the procedural disruption of harmful regularities. In this manner, Indigenous people may engage in hunting practices that protect a balance of ecosystems (an act so radically different from raising nonhuman animals on farms for slaughter), or they may engage in violence as a measure of self-defense that protects their possibilities of engaging in this public exercise of reasoning. And Indigenous violence against colonization will always thereby be rational as it protects the possibilities of a public exercise of explication against the imposition of a perspective that is the interpretive project of colonization. This is the opposite of a colonial model of violence, where the only legitimate aggressor is the colonial state, and the victims' efforts at resisting are ever depicted as illegitimate. That is nothing different than colonialism.

Acknowledging Indigenous violence as a de-colonial response to oppression (and as an example of procedural nonviolence) is not the same as green lighting every kind of violence that oppressed people engage in. Oppressed people may themselves be Colonizers. They may resort to tactics that do not create a public space for explication, but which have the sole objective of revenge. However, to acknowledge Indigenous violence as a de-colonial response is to explicate an option open to resisting oppression that is usually erased. The idea that oppressed people must always be nonviolent in their response is a story told by oppression, and one that is generated by assuming that *ahiṃsā* is always a teleological matter, and never a procedural matter.

Speech. Another topic that public de-colonization in a Westernized world must confront is free speech. Given LAT, free thinking is conflated with free speaking, and then any value there is to free thought is taken to cover the importance of free speech. Given our criticism of LAT, and its irrationality, de-colonization has to reject that there is any independent value in free speech, and instead we ought to value free thinking. This entails that thinking, like research, may involve very little or no speech, and some speech is irrational violence, such as hate speech. It also shows that the most vocal proponents for free speech, who are LAT-based interpreters, will also be, if given any power, the least tolerant of speech they disagree with. This is a trend on the far-right, where figures will initially claim that their speech is infringed upon. When given any power, they move to ban books and the articulation of opposition. In confusing the thinkable with what they are inclined to say, LAT-based interpreters are not able to tolerate anything that does not fit with their perspective. So while they will feel aggrieved if they are not allowed to spew hate speech and while they will avail themselves of any and all legal protections for speaking, they will destroy those when in power.

In this space of LAT-based confusion about thought, speech takes on a political function of propaganda. As thought is conflated with speech in LAT-based context, repeating claims to normalize its sayability leads people to believe it. Moreover, as interpreters appropriate content as their belief, if one gives interpreters a repetition of a claim, at some point they appropriate it as their belief as what is permissible to say. They are hence easy to hypnotize into complacency or complicity in mass violence. One central piece of propaganda in the current US administration's efforts to take control of universities is the idea that anti-Semitism is rampant, and the only correlate to this supposed problem is student-led protests against Israel. Not only is this not a problem but a large portion of students protesting against Israel and for Palestinians are Jewish themselves (Lober, Meyerhoff, and Schneider 2025). The point of this repeated claim is to shut down explicatory criticism of genocide and occupation. This would have no hypnotic effect if people rejected LAT, but its conflation of speech, belief, and thought leads to people coming to believe something if they hear it said enough times. Just as in the case of hepeating, at some point, the articulated content becomes appropriated content of the hearer's propositional attitudes. LE confers immunity to propaganda as we view claims, in LE, as having content only insofar as it shares a disciplinary use with other such claims. For LAT, a claim has content insofar as it is what we would say, and believe.

Similarly, *disinformation* is a problem for interpreters who confuse their endorsement of a thought as epistemic relevance. That they believe something is treated by the interpreter as evidence. The explicator is immune to disinformation as they do not see the role of information to be the content of belief, but rather a contribution to dissent.

And in this context, where everyone is trying to cast a hypnotic spell on everyone else by the repetition of their commitments, we find *polarization*. Accordingly, there are two sides with intractable perspectives who are not able to engage with each other. In colonized spaces, often, one finds a far-right, "conservative" group, and a contrary "liberal" group. Liberalism, and any other left of center anthropocentric and communitarian political posture, is not an exception to colonization but a result of the epistemic appropriation of Indigenous freedom, for the purposes of articulating the legitimacy of colonizing traditions. This is evidenced in Liberal (or leftist) states and groups being for their own freedom but quite tolerant of the oppression of other groups, such as other humans, the Earth or nonhuman animals. The reason that Conservatives and Liberals will create a polarizing public space is that both sides are interpreting. What will not work to defeat this is for Liberals (or the left) to move to the center. The only way to get rid of polarization is to introduce the public practice of explication: de-colonization. But that is *radical* relative to the anthropocentrism and communitarianism of LAT. It involves realizing that soft appeals to shared humanity as a foundation of progress is itself a function of the LAT-based interpretive practices that give us colonization and genocide. It is to move to an Indigenous mode of existence. For if we can introduce explication, at least one side is not interpreting, which means at least one side can engage in an open conversation of options and possibilities. When we explicate, and engage in its three levels, *no one* is defined by their side. We can explore the options together. But when we interpret, we confuse a logical debate with a rhetorical debate, and each side becomes entrenched.

The main difference, however, has to do with the nature of the propositional attitudes of the two groups. Liberals tend to have appropriated Indigenous values of freedom and individuality and they hence attempt to systematize this as either a shared view or an overlapping consensus (to use John Rawls' famous formulation), but for their group only and at the expense of other groups (like other humans, the Earth and nonhuman animals). Conservatives tend to lean on the propositional attitudes of formative generations. But this means that they tend to appropriate the fear and reactions of the formerly colonized (a fear of outsiders coming to take their space) as their own too, as though they (Conservatives) are under threat of colonization. This drives them to genocide. Within this spectrum, there is room for various forms of political arrangements, including authoritarianism and fascism. But these are different forms of anthropocentrism and communitarianism. And in this realm of competing interpretive exercises, we find a polarized political space. Here no one can actually disagree: everyone insists on their own way. To make room for disagreement would require abandoning LAT and adopting LE and its practices of explication.

This analysis shows how Liberal societies so easily fall into authoritarianism. One way of explaining this is the so-called "paradox of tolerance," identified by Karl Popper. Accordingly free and tolerant societies run the risk of becoming overrun by intolerance because their tolerance allows it. The de-colonial analysis is that Liberal societies were already oppressive—the only reason individuals don't notice that is because they aren't paying attention. Travel through any grocery store with a meat section and one will see the fruits of oppression in packages with bar codes. Look at the products that one can purchase in a Liberal society and one will find consumer items from areas with ongoing genocide or produced in oppressive conditions.

Both groups will have some account of an acceptable range of propositional attitudes that can be expressed and discussed, sometimes called the Overton Window. To de-colonize is to *get rid of any and all Overton Windows* because every proposition can be explored, and no propositional attitude should be treated as the means or medium of inquiry. On a de-colonial approach, all propositions, even the bad proposals (like colonialism and interpretation), would get a thorough airing. No proposition would be banned. But this would also mean that certain forms of oppression that can be articulated via some media (say hate speech, or gratuitous depictions of sexual violence) would be out of the realm of the public exercise of moral philosophy as they are nothing but expressions of oppressive propositional attitudes. And yet, for the same explicatory considerations, these same tokens contextualized within art, scholarly work or perhaps legal documents would not be ruled out of explicatory public space if they are part of an exploration of an error theory or the explication of evidence.

Conservatives will try to claim that the media, or public discourse, or educational systems, are biased against them. But what is that except an admission that those organizations are against adopting the Conservatives' outlook as the default interpretive frame. That is not biased. That's an effort to push back against the Conservatives' overreach. But because we operate within a realm of White Irrationality that normalizes interpretation, it is very difficult for Liberals and others to articulate a criticism of Conservative tactics as they too are committed to the same tactics, only with a wider Overton Window. Within this space of White Irrationality, Conservatives will claim that there is more than one side to a disagreement, and theirs should not be dismissed. That is like one of the Conservative blind men with the elephant (who insists he is feeling a tree) complaining that the others, who pooled their data and concluded that they were feeling an elephant, marginalized or canceled his side of the discussion. Inquiry is not about sides. The idea that we have an obligation to hear all sides of a controversy (sometimes called "both sideism") is confused. It changes the focus from what we can disagree about, to people posturing to be heard as though their propositional attitudes have any probative value. Inquiry is about the objective: what we can disagree about. Indigenous people know that. Colonizers do not. At some point the data is in, and the Conservative is shown to be mistaken about the object of inquiry. For them to continue identifying with their side is evidence of their interpretive posture.

Identity. Another matter that is obscured by Western colonization is identity. In this context, it seems that religious identity, ability identity, racial identity, sex, gender, and orientation are of the same sort as all of these are markers that track discrimination. The earlier analysis of White Irrationality showed that racial identity, ability identity, and religious identity are created by interpretation, so in a de-colonial space, they would not survive. We would see them as straightforward creations of oppression. Gender identity in contrast is a personal choice and that would certainly survive de-colonization. And so it should not be a surprise that the most blatantly colonial among Western participants are anti-trans. Sex is harder to choose, but it is not impossible with medical intervention to make adjustments on that matter. Species too may be something that one day we tweak. As these markers are not created by the oppression of interpretation, but discovered through explicating, there will be ways for people to explore flexibility and fluidity in these markers in a de-colonial space. And that implies that de-colonization ought to protect such freedoms of personal determination.

This shows that a proposal by Rebecca Tuvel in her "In Defense of Transracialism"—a famously controversial paper published in *Hypatia* in 2017—is confused. She proposes that just as people ought to be allowed to change their gender, they should be allowed to change their race. These are disanalogous: race is created by interpretation. Gender is explicated as a category that people can choose for themselves. Yes, this also entails that we ought not to treat religion as something we should choose for ourselves. That is because we should be getting rid of that idea, just as we get rid of race, via de-colonization.

Reparations. How do we make up for the disproportional costs borne by those who were oppressed? I think that this is a difficult question to answer if we leave oppression and colonization in place, for then the disadvantage and oppression is ongoing. But if we can actually de-colonize by jettisoning the mechanism of oppression, interpretation, we allow people to use life as an opportunity to self-determine (*svādhyāya*) and unconservatively self-liberate (*tapas*). And if no one else imposes limitations on what such transformations are allowed to look like, people will have an opportunity to live a life of their own choosing. Ableism would disappear for we would no longer impose on people arbitrary external expectations of the propositional attitudes of the oppressor, but we would also in disrupting procedural harm create an environment where people formerly dubbed as disabled have the wherewithal to transform their life as part of their own practice of moral philosophy in their own way, via their own unconservatism and self-governance.

Much of this would involve moving away from colonial modes of identity. We wouldn't hence acknowledge the wrong of human slavery as a failure to acknowledge the full humanity of slaves (Zack 2003). If we Indigenize and de-colonize, we understand the moral outrage of slavery in terms of a denial of personhood, not a denial of humanity. Persons come in all sorts of shapes and forms. We would similarly not expect to treat victims of oppression as epistemic authorities on what they went through (Lackey 2022). We would have to acknowledge that colonial oppression is actually an epistemic injury, and hence people who are harmed by oppression are not well placed to speak about what happened to them. Rather, it would be incumbent on us to seek out and undermine oppression without having to wait for victims to inform us about what has transpired. And we ought to allow them to move on and not be defined by the injury that they were subjected to.

Guilt and innocence. The greatest change that we would have to work through in de-colonization is about how guilt and innocence are framed. Within a colonial context, the main currency of explanation is some type of propositional attitude, like belief, and then, the determination of guilt and innocence is cast as a question of whose narrative we believe. Framing the question thus leads to guilty parties engaging in a smear campaign of Deny, Attack, and Reverse Victim and Offender (DARVO) (Harsey and Freyd 2020), in which the offender casts themselves as victim. If we shift to the public practice of moral philosophy, innocence is consistent with what we can disagree about, and the guilty party is the interpreter, needing to fall back on their propositional attitudes to account for their choices and agency. So our challenge isn't to believe victims. Our challenge is to determine who needs their beliefs to justify their activity: they are the guilty party. The innocent in contrast is the agent whose activity is consistent with a multiplicity of perspectives converging on objectivity. The oft-repeated justification for violence, that one *believed* oneself to be under threat, for instance, would be evidence of guilt. The agent who chose to engage in violence to protect space for controversy is always innocent.

Human Societies. Humans are social animals, but they do not need to only associate with humans. The reality is, without a healthy, respectful relationship with a diversity of agents in our biosphere, humans are destined to extinction after they have gotten rid of pollinators and poisoned the Earth. Given LAT's anthropocentrism and communitarianism, LAT-based societies act like ever-expanding bubbles in a finite outside that is always perceived as a threat to be swallowed. Given LE, and a switch to an Indigenous world, humans do not live in bubbles: they live in, and as part of, a wider universe of agency. The public practice of moral philosophy provides us each a way of mediating our relationship with others. That is the essence of responsible behavior. One main difference is that in a LAT-based world, as J.P. Sartre puts it in his *Existentialism Is a Humanism*, following Kant's liberalization of colonialism, when we choose, we're choosing for everyone else. But when we switch to LE and Secularism₁, when we engage in moral philosophy, choice is clarified as something that we self-impose via our self-governance. We are each selecting our own life values and plans. Imposing our choices on others is rather an exercise of propositional attitudes, which consists in a belief in what others must do. The second difference in this move to the public practice of moral philosophy is to Indigenize our lives. One entailment of this is that we cannot engage in LAT-based nationalism or oppression of nonhumans (like livestock agriculture). As we Indigenize, we can create human societies that are ecologically responsive. Borders would be understood in terms of the space humans need to responsibly interact with their wider social world beyond the human. Borders would not be designed to keep other people out but to demarcate limits of direct agential interaction between humans and other organisms. To choose to live in such a space is to choose to live in a way that respects that diversity.

4. Objections

The *sympathy for the devil* objection is that it is wrong to be particularly critical of colonizing people because they were not exposed to explicatory or Indigenous options, and so they do not know any better. The reason this objection is perverse is that if people interpret, it would make no difference whether they were exposed to explicatory (Indigenous) options: for they would simply colonize the latter. The interpreter deserves no sympathy as theirs is a completely contingent choice. That they do not know any better is a direct consequence of a bad choice. We ought to rather ridicule this choice. Understanding the wisdom of explication requires choosing it.

The *Indigenization/De-colonization will do nothing* objection claims that merely switching to LE will do nothing to right the wrongs of the past. One response to this is to note that merely departing from the wrongs of the past is to right the past. So transitioning from interpretation (the wrong of the past), based on LAT, to explication, based on LE, is to right the past. Another way to formulate the objection is to claim that the problems left over to us from the past will not be solved by merely giving up on the methods of colonization, namely, interpretation. The response to this is to ask the question of how problems of the past linger. They linger because people treat the entirely believable facts of these wrongs as the content of their explanations, and they thereby reify and perpetuate these wrongs into the future. That requires interpretation. If we abandon interpretation, we no longer reify oppression as part of our method of understanding. And with it no longer being reified, it will come to an end. These problems of oppression and colonization only linger because we reify and regenerate them as part of our interpretive practices. If we get rid of the methodology that maintains this *saṃsāra* it's done. We will be free hence in every context, and with respect to every institution, to de-colonize them.

Overgeneralization. One objection that I often hear is that the wholesale indictment of anyone whose intellectual pedigree is part of the tradition going back to Greek philosophy is incorrect as many of the intellectuals in this tradition do not support the outcomes or commitments of the *West*.

This defense of the honor of the *West* is a lot like refutations of the claim that we are undergoing global warming, a refutation that relies upon treating each locale in isolation in order to discern whether temperatures are steadily increasing in each case. And what this would show is something far more mixed: some places the temperature may be increasing but many places will also be observed to have uncharacteristically cold weather. The amateur climate scientist thinks they have all that they need to show that the scientists are speaking nonsense.

But this response of individualizing bits of data is mistaken for the argument for global warming and climate crisis are about the large-scale trends. And that requires a historical approach—a historical appreciation of the differential effect of greenhouse gases on the atmosphere's retention of heat, and how changes in human activity not only produced more of those gases but were correlated with long-term trends in the increase of global temperatures.

To ask the question about the *Western* tradition is hence to ask the historical question about a global trend. Individual *Western* philosophers who seem nice are not counterevidence, any more than a cold winter in Toronto proves that global warming is not happening. To examine this trend and to determine its cause is to identify the assumptions that would give rise to it. That is to ask what assumption would entail this kind of tradition, focused on the anthropocentric and communitarian, that assumes and never questions LAT, when pressed to talk about reason or knowledge typically talks about propositional attitudes, grows into a global colonizing tradition that defines the world in terms of Secularism$_2$ and erases BIPOC moral philosophy, and, is a tradition where intellectuals buy and reify its inventions, like religion. How do we make sense of this tradition where the burden of proof is placed on those who object to oppression, whereas the status quo is treated as *prima facie* correct. The failure of thinkers in this tradition to appreciate their active participation in colonization by greenlighting interpretation is not exculpatory: it speaks to a cluelessness that is part and parcel of the irrationality of oppression.

De-colonization is like claiming to be "color-blind." It is not uncommon for folks to claim that they do not see the race or color of others. Racialized people often find this offensive. De-colonization that encourages us to get rid of race and religion would be equally problematic. The response to this is to explain why it is hurtful to pretend not to see someone's race or religion: the claim of blindness is a belief, an interpretation. So far from addressing the original colonial harm of racialization or religification, it adds a further layer of interpretive erasure. An actual move to de-colonize would require acknowledging how the original harm of racialization or religification happened as a result of interpretation, how people have color or religious designations as a result, it would require acknowledging that it was a harm, and to choose another way to go about life that does not result in this harm. The claim of color-blindness, in contrast, fails to acknowledge the harm.

Choosing our own values will result in conflict and oppression. If everyone is allowed to engage in moral philosophy and choose their own values, then it would seem that everyone is in a position to impose their values on others. This will simply recreate colonization. The error of this objection is that it confuses *choosing* a value with imposing a perspective. The former is an action. The latter is a propositional attitude. Colonizers engage in oppression because they are not choosing anything except to interpret: this results in their imposition of their perspective on others. To choose a value in contrast is to identify what oneself takes to be important. It is not a matter of colonization but self-governance. In a de-colonial space, everyone is invited to do this philosophical work. To engage in this de-colonial work is not to impose the value of de-colonization on others. It is to prevent people from imposing their perspective, so that the space for people to choose values is restored. People who think that there is a tension between creating a space for justice and intruding on personal freedom are engaging in a category confusion that confounds the propositional-attitude imposition of bullies with the self-determining choice of De-Colonizers.

If we de-colonize, we will lose the advances of colonization. Not true. All the epistemic advantages of colonization are really the appropriated fruits of explication. Getting rid of the colonial frame is a net advantage: all the explicatory gems of the Indigenous would remain without the stupidity of the Colonizer.

5. Conclusion

The main argument of this book concludes that moral philosophy and colonialism are incompatible exercises. Assuming LAT that generates a particularly anthropocentric and communitarian history of moral theorizing, Applied Ethics balloons into a miscellany of all topics not essential to the managerial goals of colonization. If we adopt LE, Applied Ethics is primarily concerned with the political exercise of de-colonization that attempts to institutionalize the public practice of moral philosophy—explication. Again, we cannot both engage in colonization and the public practice of moral philosophy. Only the latter is rational.

Part Five

Conclusion

8

Research and Activism

1. Summary and Implications

In the first chapter, I set out the main argument:

(1) *If* one is engaged in moral philosophy (M), *then* one is explicating a diversity of perspectives on THE RIGHT OR THE GOOD (L).

(2) *If* one is engaged in colonialism (C), *then* one is interpreting—imposing a perspective as explanation—which violates basic considerations of logic (*not* L).

(*Therefore*) Colonialism and moral philosophy are incompatible, inimical, endeavors: *not* (C *and* M), and one has to reject either colonialism or moral philosophy (*not* C or *not* M).

This argument relied upon more basic arguments that contrasted explication and interpretation, and altogether, these arguments provided resources for constructing a further coda argument, that we have a rational obligation to de-colonize. Since interpretation that supports colonialism is irrational, and rejecting it requires adopting explication that supports the public practice of moral philosophy, we have only one rational choice before us: to reject colonialism by getting rid of irrationality. Put another way, we have a rational obligation to engage in moral philosophy. Engaging in moral philosophy supports the public practice of explication. And this in turn is de-colonial as it is incompatible with irrationality that supports colonization and oppression.

Chapters 2 to 4 explored the main argument at a Metaethical level. Chapters 5 and 6 explored this argument at the Normative Ethical level. Chapter 7 addressed the issue with respect to Applied Ethics. In each case, the chapter concluded with a summary of how, indeed, moral philosophy and colonialism are incompatible endeavors. All the considerations that got us to this conclusion provide grounds for the argument that we have a rational obligation to de-colonize. When we abandon an interpretive approach to truth, we see that these arguments are sound.

In this concluding chapter, I will draw attention to important implications of the core arguments of this book.

First, when we compare LAT and LE as the interpretive and explicatory models of thought, we see the ways in which colonization is a LAT-based exercise and LE is an Indigenous exercise. As the latter is rational while the former is not, no epistemic innovation or advance can be attributed to colonization. LAT is to blame as it confuses a perspective encoded in language with the thinkable. I suppose there could be other such models of thought that rely upon other forms of representable perspectives but in our world, LAT has done all the damage. And, of course, the *West* as the tradition that uniquely acclaims LAT is the face of this irrationality.

Second, Indigeneity is not the same as a particular language or culture. It is a rational approach to linguistic and cultural resources as an exercise of thinking in a universe teeming with thinking agents, based on LE. Thinking according to LE is an exercise of dissent: every thought crystallizes a debate, and the meaningfulness of the entire proposition is its role in inquiry.

Third, the colonizing tradition only seems like it is the champion of human rights and the tradition of research and progress because of its appropriative function as a rollout of interpretation. And, importantly, the epistemic progress it shows is mediocre: whatever explicatory gems it appropriates are stifled by its interpretive stupidity. We ought to be solving world hunger and climate crisis. Instead, we are perpetually leaning back on the modes of existence that got us into this trouble in a *Western* world.

Fourth, colonialism makes it seem as though we cannot choose to be Indigenous. This is nothing different from colonization. De-colonization means choosing to be Indigenous, which is not the same as the cosplay offense of what we call a Pretendian (a "pretend Indian") on Turtle Island. No matter what our cultural context, we could choose to be Indigenous by explicating and adopting LE.

Fifth, categories of oppression are not an artifact of explication but a cost of interpreting, and LAT as an anthropocentric and communitarian model of thought creates tiers of oppression in terms of those priorities, with the colonial culture filling in the details. But as the *West* is the dominant colonizing tradition, its cultural priorities become the tiers of oppression that structure the world. We are all hence living under White Irrationality—an interpretive practice that advantages what is prized in the *West*. For those who choose to conform, this creates the sense that freedom is a zero-sum game: being anti-oppressive seems to risk one's relative place in a privilege hierarchy. But when we see that oppression is just a function of the interpretive exercise, it is clear that solving the problem of anyone's oppression is about solving it all.

Being an explicator is hence to not support the infrastructure of oppression: interpretation. Single issue activism or voting is a symptom of the problem.

Sixth, moral philosophy is as objective as any other avenue of research: objectivity is what we discover when we allow ourselves to pursue a theoretical disagreement in a field of research to the end. And the best account of the debate in moral philosophy is Yoga, for it alone begins at the metaethical level with the choice to explicate. The Normative Ethics is simply the exercise of that rational freedom to engage in moral philosophy. Its Applied Ethics is the politics to create that freedom as a social reality. Without explication we couldn't account for moral philosophy's objectivity. Western packages can't account for the objectivity of ethics as they assume LAT.

Seventh, as irrationality and oppression come to the same thing—interpretation—and this constitutes an impediment to explicatory research, engaging in actual explicatory research is activism. Academics can and should take a leading role in de-colonization by actually engaging in research made possible by explication, instead of propping up White Irrationality. That would involve overhauling peer review to outlaw interpretation.

Eighth, the difference between interpretation and explication has a temporal characteristic. Insofar as interpretation treats the content of the world as the content of propositions that are then appropriated via attitudes of interpreters, interpretation is always backward-looking. We see this also by appreciating how LAT, in treating linguistic meaning as thought, confuses a political fossil (linguistic meaning) with the thinkable. Explication is disruptive: it isn't constrained by a perspective, and it thus makes room for diversity, reason, and new possibilities. Whereas colonization is always conservative, and always backward-looking, Indigeneity is the future.

2. The Rational Obligation to Overcome the Algorithm

The rollout and maintenance of oppression and colonization in our world is only explainable by interpreting on the basis of the *Western* tradition, including the world as we know it, structured by *Western* colonization. We do not get to here by explicating moral philosophy from South Asia. I called this White Irrationality as it was irrational and it favored White bodied people. It's not something that is unique to White people: anyone can participate and most humans do insofar as they buy artifacts of White Supremacy, like "religion," "race," or "ability," and its anthropocentrism and communitarianism, as though real things and not a construct of oppression. But this also explains how peer review and gatekeeping operates in the absence of prohibitions against interpretation: it operates by appropriating the epistemic labor of thinkers by interpreting everything, and then building on this edifice of interpretation, by more interpretation. Interpretation is appropriative as it treats the epistemic artifacts of agents as the content of what is believed by the interpreter. I noticed that this is no different from how AI is trained. This is problematic in two ways. First it is an exercise of appropriation and colonization. But secondly much of what is appropriated is second-order, already interpreted content online. And hence, the actual oppressive structures of the world become the content of the artificially "intelligent" explanation. This is not different in practice from what is allowed to occur in peer review and gatekeeping, but it is faster, more user friendly but unfortunately like peer review (without prohibitions against interpretation), stupid. Actual epistemic progress is stymied by this normalization of mediocracy that combines the appropriative idiocy of interpretation with the appropriated gems of explication. And the reason all of this matters, moral-philosophically, is that the methodologies of data processing—interpretation versus explication, irrationality versus reason, colonization versus moral philosophy—are simply the possibilities of how agents can relate to each other. The oppressive option is irrational.

De-colonization is not just an external project. It means moving away from being devoted to propositional attitudes to being devoted to Sovereignty. It is entirely doable. The only obstruction is a bad choice to interpret. Once we make that bad choice, it is as though we do not choose: all of our behavior is scripted by the propositions we have attitudes to. Rejecting this lack of freedom is as easy as learning to think and reason. Given that the artificial problems we have to deal with are created by interpretation (irrationality) and a failure to respond rationally to challenges (whatever their source) is also a function of interpretation, we have every reason to be optimistic if we adopt explication. This is the rational optimism of Indigenous people. Learning how to live that way means learning from Indigenous people. Since we have a rational obligation to de-colonize, we are obliged to learn how to be Indigenous. But even if we are irrational, and governed by propositional attitudes like desires, we will have to learn this, if we want a future.

Bibliography

Adamson, Peter. 2017. "Rules for History of Philosophy." In *History of Philosophy Without Any Gaps*. https://web.archive.org/web/20190425204102/https://historyofphilosophy.net/rules-history-philosophy.

Adluri, Vishwa, and Joydeep Bagchee. 2014. *The Nay Science: A History of German Indology*. New York: Oxford University Press.

Ainslie, M. J. 2021. "Chinese Philosemitism and Historical Statecraft: Incorporating Jews and Israel into Contemporary Chinese Civilizationism." *The China Quarterly* 245: 208–26.

Alfred, Taiaiake, and Jeff Corntassel. 2005. "Being Indigenous: Resurgences against Contemporary Colonialism." *Government and Opposition* 40: 597–614.

American Sociological Association. 2019. "Statement on Student Evaluations of Teaching." https://www.asanet.org/wp-content/uploads/asa_statement_on_student_evaluations_of_teaching_feb132020.pdf.

Appiah, Kwame Anthony. 2006. "How to Decide if Races Exist." *Proceedings of the Aristotelian Society* 106 (3): 363–80.

Arneil, Barbara. 2024. "Colonialism versus Imperialism." *Political Theory* 52 (1): 146–76.

Ayer, A. J. 1946. *Language Truth and Logic*. New York: Dover Publications.

Beard, Mary, John A. North, and S. R. F. Price. 1998. *Religions of Rome*. 2 vols. Cambridge; New York: Cambridge University Press.

Bilimoria, P., and A. Rayner, eds. 2025. *The Routledge Companion to Indian Ethics: Women, Justice, Bioethics and Ecology*. London: Routledge.

Boyd, Richard N. 1988. "How to be a Moral Realist." In *Essays on Moral Realism*, edited by G. Sayre-McCord, 181–228. Ithaca, New York: Cornell University Press.

Buolamwini, Joy. 2023. *Unmasking AI: My Mission to Protect What is Human in a World of Machines*. New York: Random House Publishing Group.

Bytwerk, Randall L. 2005. "The Argument for Genocide in Nazi Propaganda." *Quarterly Journal of Speech* 91 (1): 37–62.

Carnap, Rudolph. 1950. *Logical Foundations of Probability*. Chicago: University of Chicago Press.

Césaire, Aimé. 2000. *Discourse on Colonialism*. New York: Monthly Review.

Chakravorty, Sanjoy. 2019. *The Truth about Us: The Politics of Information from Manu to Modi*. Gurugram, India: Hachette India.

Charny, Israel W. 2003. "A Classification of Denials of the Holocaust and other Genocides." *Journal of Genocide Research* 5 (1): 11–34.

Code, Lorraine. 2013. "Reason and Women." In *Reason and Rationality*, edited by Cristina Amoretti Maria and Nicla Vassallo, 71–92. Berlin, Boston: De Gruyter.

Cook, D. 2015. *Understanding Jihad*. California: University of California Press.

Crane, Tim. 2018. "The Philosopher's Tone." In *The Times Literary Supplement*. https://www.the-tls.co.uk/articles/public/philosophy-journals-review/.

Dalrymple, W. 2024. *The Golden Road: How Ancient India Transformed the World*. London: Bloomsbury Publishing.

Davidson, Donald. 1986. "A Coherence Theory of Truth and Knowledge." In *Truth and Interpretation: Perspectives on the Philosophy of Donald Davidson*, edited by Ernest Le Pore, 307–19. Cambridge: Blackwell. Original edition, Read at a colloquium organized by Richard Rorty as part of the 1981 Stuttgart Hegel Congress.

Davidson, Donald. 1996a. "The Objectivity of Values." In *El Trabajo Filosofico de Hoy en el Continente*, 45–60. edited by C. Gutieirez. Bogata: Editorial ABC.

Davidson, Donald. 1996b. "What Metaphors Mean." In *The Philosophy of Language*, edited by Aloysius Martinich, 415–26. New York: Oxford University Press. Original edition, Chicago.

Davidson, Donald. 2000. "Objectivity and Practical Reason." In *Reasoning Practically*, edited by Edna Ullmann-Margalit, 17–26. New York: Oxford University Press.

Davidson, Donald. 2001. "On Saying That." In *Inquiries into Truth and Interpretation*, 93–108. Oxford: Claredon Press.

Derrida, Jacques. 1981. "Plato's Pharmacy." In *Dissemination*, 61–172. Chicago: University of Chicago Press.

Derrida, Jacques. 1998. *Of Grammatology*. Corrected ed. Baltimore: Johns Hopkins University Press.

Doak, Brian R. 2020. *Ancient Israel's Neighbors*. Oxford: Oxford University Press.

Donner, F. M. 2014. *The Early Islamic Conquests*. Princeton: Princeton University Press.

Donohue, William A. 2019. "There's a Dark Political History to Language that Strips People of their Dignity." *The Conversation*.

Dreier, James. 1990. "Internalism and Speaker Relativism." *Ethics* 101: 6–26.

Duff, R. A. 1997. *Criminal Attempts*. Oxford: Oxford University Press.

Edwards, Tai S., and Paul Kelton. 2020. "Germs, Genocides, and America's Indigenous Peoples." *Journal of American History* 107 (1): 52–76.

Epley, Kelly. 2018. "Emotions, Attitudes, and Reasons." *Pacific Philosophical Quarterly* 100 (1): 256–82.

Erichsen, C., and D. Olusoga. 2010. *The Kaiser's Holocaust: Germany's Forgotten Genocide and the Colonial Roots of Nazism*. London: Faber & Faber.

Evans, Gareth. 1996. "Causal Theory of Names." In *The Philosophy of Language*, edited by Aloysius Martinich, 271–83. New York: Oxford University Press.

Fabian, Emanuel. 2023 (October 9). "Defense Minister Announces 'Complete Siege' of Gaza: No Power, Food or Fuel." *Times of Israel*.

Fenech, Louis E. 1997. "Martyrdom and the Sikh Tradition." *Journal of the American Oriental Society* 117 (4): 623–42.

Feng, Emily. 2022. "Uyghur Kids Recall Physical and Mental Torment at Chinese Boarding Schools in Xinjiang." *National Public Radio.*

Flikschuh, Katrin, and Lea Ypi. 2014. "Introduction: Kant on Colonialism—Apologist or Critic?" In *Kant and Colonialism: Historical and Critical Perspectives*, edited by Katrin Flikschuh and Lea Ypi. Oxford: Oxford University Press.

Frege, Gottlob. 1988. "Thoughts." In *Propositions and Attitudes*, edited by Nathan U. Salmon and Scott Soames, 33–55. Oxford; New York: Oxford University Press.

Fricker, M. 2007. *Epistemic Injustice: Power and the Ethics of Knowing.* Oxford: Clarendon Press.

Gadamer, Hans-Georg. 1990. "Culture and the Word." In *Hermeneutics and the Poetic Motion Translation Perspectives V*, edited by Dennis J. Schmidt, 11–24. Binghamton: SUNY.

Gadamer, Hans-Georg. 1996. *Truth and Method.* Translated by Joel Weinsheimer and Donald G. Marshall. 2nd Revised English Language ed. New York: Continuum.

Gandhi, M. K., and M. K. Prabhu. 1959. "Sarvodaya." In *India of My Dreams*, 65–8. Ahmedabad: Navajivan Pub. House.

Glanzberg, Michael. 2023. *Truth.* Edited by Edward Zalta. *Stanford Encyclopedia of Philosophy.* http://plato.stanford.edu/archives/fall2014/entries/truth/.

Goodman, Nelson. 1954. *Fact, Fiction & Forecast.* London: University of London Athlone Press.

Government of India. 1950. *Glossary of Technical Terms. Constitution of India.* New Delhi.

Gordon, R. 2008. "Superstitio, Superstition and Religious Repression in the Late Roman Republic and Principate (100 BCE-300 CE)." In *The Religion of Fools?: Superstition Past and Present*, edited by S.A. Smith and A. Knight. Oxford: Oxford Journals.

Graeber, D., and D. Wengrow. 2021. *The Dawn of Everything: A New History of Humanity.* New York: Farrar, Straus and Giroux.

Greenawalt, Alexander K. A. 1999. "Rethinking Genocidal Intent: The Case for a Knowledge-Based Interpretation." *Columbia Law Review* 99 (8): 2259–94.

Gugliucci, Nicole. 2017. "hepeated." *Twitter.*

Harman, Gilbert. 1977. *The Nature of Morality: An Introduction to Ethics.* New York: Oxford University Press.

Harrison, Victoria S. 2006. "The Pragmatics of Defining Religion in a Multi-Cultural World." *International Journal for Philosophy of Religion* 59 (3): 133–52.

Harsey, Sarah, and Jennifer J. Freyd. 2020. "Deny, Attack, and Reverse Victim and Offender (DARVO): What Is the Influence on Perceived Perpetrator and

Victim Credibility?" *Journal of Aggression, Maltreatment & Trauma* 29 (8): 897–916.

Heidegger, Martin. 2010. *Logic: The Question of Truth*. Translated by Thomas Sheehan. English ed. *Studies in Continental Thought*. Bloomington: Indiana University Press.

Hochschild, A. 2019. *King Leopold's Ghost: A Story of Greed, Terror and Heroism in Colonial Africa*. London: Pan Macmillan UK.

Holyoake, G. J. 1896. *The Origin and Nature of Secularism*. London: Watts and Co.

Horgan, Terence, and Mark Timmons. 1991. "New Wave Moral Realism Meets Moral Twin Earth." *Journal of Philosophical Research* 16: 447–65.

Indigenous Foundations, University of British Columbia. Accessed Spring 2015. "The Residential School System." *Indigenous Foundations*. http://indigenousf oundations.arts.ubc.ca/the_residential_school_system/.

Jaini, Padmanabh S. 1998. *The Jaina Path of Purification*. Delhi: Motilal Banarsidass Publisher.

James, Michael. 2016. "Race." In *Stanford Encyclopedia of Philosophy*, edited by Edward N. Zalta. http://plato.stanford.edu/archives/spr2016/entries/race/.

Jinping, Xi. 2022. "Regarding the Construction of Socialism with Chinese Characteristics (2013)." In *Redsails.org*. Original edition, Qiushi.

Kagan, Shelly. 2007. "Thinking about Cases." In *Ethical Theory: An Anthology*, edited by Russ Shafer-Landau, In Blackwell Philosophy Anthologies, 82–93. Malden, MA: Blackwell Pub. Original edition, Cambridge.

Kant, Immanuel. 1948. *The Moral Law: Kant's Groundwork of the Metaphysic of Morals*. Translated by H. J. Paton. 1st ed. London: Hutchinson's University Library.

Kaplan, David. 1968. "Quantifying In." *Synthese* 19 (1/2): 178–214.

Kent, James, and Michael Lazarus. 2022. "Peter Singer Is the Philosopher of the Status Quo." *Jacobin*.

Khalidi, Muhammad Ali. 2005. *Medieval Islamic Philosophical Writings*. *Cambridge Texts in the History of Philosophy*. Cambridge, UK; New York: Cambridge University Press.

Khalidi, Rashid. 2022. *The Hundred Years' War on Palestine: A History of Settler Colonialism and Resistance, 1917–2017*. First Metropolitan paperback edition. New York: Metropolitan Books, Henry Holt and Company.

King, C. R. 1994. *One Language, Two Scripts: The Hindi Movement in Nineteenth Century North India*. Oxford: Oxford University Press.

King, Martin Luther, Jr. September 1, 1958. "My Pilgrimage to Nonviolence." In *The Martin Luther King, Jr. Research and Education Institute*. https:// kinginstitute.stanford.edu/king-papers/documents/my-pilgrimage -nonviolence.

Kohn, Margaret, and Kavita Reddy. Fall 2017 Edition. "Colonialism." In *The Stanford Encyclopedia of Philosophy*, edited by Edward N. Zalta. https://plato .stanford.edu/archives/fall2017/entries/colonialism/.

Kripke, Saul A. 1980. *Naming and Necessity*. Cambridge, Mass.: Harvard University Press.

Kripke, Saul A. 1988. "A Puzzle about Beliefs." In *Propositions and Attitudes*, edited by Nathan U. Salmon and Scott Soames, 102–48. Oxford; New York: Oxford University Press. Original edition, Dordrecht.

Kuhn, Thomas S. 1970. *The Structure of Scientific Revolutions*. 2nd ed. Chicago: University of Chicago Press.

Kuikman, Jacoba. 2014. "The Bene Israel of India and the Politics of Jewish Identity." *Studies in Religion/Sciences Religieuses* 43 (1): 102–15.

Lackey, Jennifer. 2022. "Epistemic Reparations and the Right to Be Known." *Proceedings and Addresses of the American Philosophical Association* 96: 54–89.

LaMonica, Christopher. Accessed 2021. "Colonialism." In *Oxford Bibliographies Online*. https://www.oxfordbibliographies.com/view/document/obo -9780199743292/obo-9780199743292-0008.xml.

Larson, Gerald James. 1972. "The Trimurti of Dharma in Indian Thought: Paradox or Contradiction?" *Philosophy East and West* 22: 145–53.

Lenski, Noel. 2014. *Constantine (Classics).Oxford Bibliographies Online*. https:// www.oxfordbibliographies.com/view/document/obo-9780195389661/obo -9780195389661-0127.xml.

Leslie, Donald Daniel. 2000. "Integration, Assimilation, and Survival of Minorities in China: The Case of the Kaifeng Jews." In *From Kaifeng to Shanghai: Jews in China*, edited by Roman Malek, 45–78. London: Routledge.

Lingat, Robert. 1973. *The Classical Law of India*. Translated by J. Duncan M. Derrett. Berkeley: University of California Press.

Lober, Brooke, Eli Meyerhoff, and Emily Schneider. 2025. "It's Not Too Late to Tell the Truth About Antisemitism on Campus." *Academe Blog (Blog of the Academe Magazine)*. https://academeblog.org/2025/04/25/its-not-too-late-to -tell-the-truth-about-antisemitism-on-campus/.

Mackie, J. L. 1977. *Ethics: Inventing Right and Wrong*. Harmondsworth; New York: Penguin.

Mallon, Ron. 2004. "Passing, Traveling and Reality: Social Constructionism and the Metaphysics of Race." *Noûs* 38 (4): 644–73.

Mallon, Ron. 2006. "Race: Normative, Not Metaphysical or Semantic." *Ethics* 116 (3): 525–51.

Mallon, Ron. 2007. "A Field Guide to Social Construction." *Philosophy Compass* 2 (1): 93–108.

Mallon, Ron. 2016. *The Construction of Human Kinds*. 1st ed. Oxford: Oxford University Press.

Marx, Karl. 1965. "The Future Results of the British Rule in India." In *On Colonialism*, 66–8. Moscow: Progress Publishers.

Marx, Karl. 2009. *A Contribution to the Critique of Hegel's Philosophy of Right*: *Marxist Internet Archive*. https://www.marxists.org/archive/marx/works /1843/critique-hpr/intro.htm#05.

Matilal, Bimal Krishna. 1989. "Moral Dilemmas: Insights from the Indian Epics."
     In *Moral Dilemmas in the Mahābhārata*, edited by Bimal Krishna Matilal,
     1–19. Shimla; Delhi: Indian Institute of Advanced Study in association with
     Motilal Banarsidass, Delhi.
McDaniel, June. 2013. "A Modern Hindu Monotheism: Indonesian Hindus as
     'People of the Book.'" *The Journal of Hindu Studies* 6 (3): 333–62.
McDowell, John. 1998a. "Aesthetic Value, Objectivity, and the Fabric of the
     World." In *Mind, Value, and Reality*, 112–30. Cambridge: Harvard University
     Press.
McDowell, John. 1998b. "Virtue and Reason." In *Mind, Value, and Reality*,
     50–73. Cambridge: Harvard University Press.
Myers, R. H., and C. Verheggen. 2016. *Donald Davidson's Triangulation
     Argument: A Philosophical Inquiry*. Abingdon: Taylor & Francis.
Nielsen, Cynthia R. 2022. "Putin's Dehumanizing Discourses and the Power
     of Ukrainian Resistance and Resilience." In *Forum for Ukrainian Studies*.
     Canadian Institute of Ukrainian Studies, University of Alberta.
Pappe, I. 2007. *The Ethnic Cleansing of Palestine*. Oxford: Oneworld
     Publications.
Parshin Shojaee, I. M., Keivan Alizadeh, Maxwell Horton, Samy Bengio, and
     Mehrdad Farajtabar. 2025. "The Illusion of Thinking: Understanding the
     Strengths and Limitations of Reasoning Models via the Lens of Problem
     Complexity." *Apple*. https://machinelearning.apple.com/research/illusion-of
     -thinking.
Patañjali. 2008. *Patañjali's Yoga Sūtra: Translation, Commentary and
     Introduction by Shyam Ranganathan. Black Classics*. Delhi: Penguin Black
     Classics.
Patnaik, Utsa. 2017. "Revisiting the 'Drain', or Transfer from India to Britain
     in the Context of Global Diffusion of Capitalism." In *Agrarian and Other
     Histories: Essays for Binay Bhushan Chaudhuri*, 277–317. New Delhi: Tulika
     Books.
Picard, Michel. 2005. "What's in a Name? Agama Hindu Bali in the Making." In
     Hinduism in Modern Indonesia, edited by M. Ramstedt, 56–75. Abingdon:
     Taylor & Francis.
Putnam, Hilary. 1975. "The Meaning of Meaning." *Minnesota Studies in the
     Philosophy of Science* VII: 131–93.
Quine, Willard van Orman. 1956. "Quantifiers and Propositional Attitudes." *The
     Journal of Philosophy* 53 (5): 177–87.
Quine, Willard van Orman. 1960. *Word and Object*. Cambridge: MIT Press.
Ramstedt, M. 2005. "Introduction: Negotiating identities – Indonesian 'Hindus'
     Between Local, National, and Global Interests." In *Hinduism in Modern
     Indonesiae*, edited by M. Ramstedt, 1–15. Abingdon: Taylor & Francis.
Ranganathan, Shyam. 2007. *Translating Evaluative Discourse: The Semantics of
     Thick and Thin Concepts*. Dissertation. Vol. PhD. *Philosophy*. York University,
     Department of Philosophy (Dissertation).

Ranganathan, Shyam. 2011. "An Archimedean Point for Philosophy."
  Metaphilosophy 42 (4): 479–519.
Ranganathan, Shyam, ed. 2016. *Ethics 1*. Edited by A. Raghuramaraju,
  Philosophy, E-PG Pathshala, University Grants Commission, Government of
  India. https://epgp.inflibnet.ac.in/Home/ViewSubject?catid=oYPhnOmK5lh
  Y4GGCoKqF5Q==.
Ranganathan, Shyam. 2017. "Western Imperialism, Indology and Ethics."
  In *The Bloomsbury Research Handbook of Indian Ethics*, edited by Shyam
  Ranganathan, In Bloomsbury Research Handbooks in Asian Philosophy,
  1–122. London: Bloomsbury Academic.
Ranganathan, Shyam. 2018a. "Context and Pragmatics." In *The Routledge
  Handbook of Translation and Philosophy*, edited by Philip Wilson and J Piers
  Rawling, In Routledge Handbooks in Translation and Interpreting Studies,
  195–208. New York: Routledge.
Ranganathan, Shyam. 2018b. "Jñāna, Pramāṇa, Satya and Citta (not: justified,
  true, belief)." In *Hinduism: A Contemporary Philosophical Investigation*,
  138–53. London: Routledge.
Ranganathan, Shyam. 2018c. "Vedas and Upaniṣads." In *The History of Evil in
  Antiquity 2000 B.C.E. - 450 C.E.*, edited by Tom Angier, In History of Evil,
  239–55. London: Routledge.
Ranganathan, Shyam. 2022. "Hinduism, Belief and the Colonial Invention of
  Religion: A Before and After Comparison." *Religions* 13 (10). https://www
  .mdpi.com/2077-1444/13/10/891.
Ranganathan, Shyam. 2024. *Yoga—Anticolonial Philosophy; An Action Focused
  Guide to Practice*. London: Jessica Kingsley.
Rangaswami Aiyangar, Kumbakonam Viraraghava. 1952. *Some Aspects of the
  Hindu View of Life According to Dharmaśāstra Sayaji Row Memorial Lectures,
  1947–48*. Baroda: Director Oriental Institute.
Rawls, John. 1971. *A Theory of Justice*. Cambridge, Mass.: Harvard University
  Press.
Ripstein, Arthur. 2014. "Kant's Juridical Theory of Colonialism." In *Kant and
  Colonialism: Historical and Critical Perspectives*, edited by Katrin Flikschuh
  and Lea Ypi, 0. Oxford: Oxford University Press.
Śabara. 1933. *Śabara Bhāṣya*. Translated by Ganganatha Jha. Vol. 66, 70, 73.
  Gaekwad's Oriental Series. Baroda: Oriental Institute.
Salmon, Nathan U. 2005. "Two Conceptions of Semantics." In *Semantics vs.
  Pragmatics*, edited by Zoltán Gendler Szabó, 317–28. Oxford; New York:
  Clarendon Press; Oxford University Press.
Sayre-McCord, Geoff. Spring 2023 Edition. "Metaethics." *The Stanford
  Encyclopedia of Philosophy*, edited by Edward N. Zalta & Uri Nodelman.
  https://plato.stanford.edu/archives/spr2023/entries/metaethics/.
Schabas, William A. 2009. *Genocide in International Law: The Crime of Crimes*. 2
  ed. Cambridge: Cambridge University Press.

Setiya, Kieran. 2022 (Winter). "Intention." *The Stanford Encyclopedia of Philosophy (Winter 2022 Edition)*, edited by Edward N. Zalta & Uri Nodelman. https://plato.stanford.edu/archives/win2022/entries/intention/.

Sharma, Jyotirmaya. 2007. *Terrifying vision: M. S. Golwalkar, the RSS, and India*. New York: Viking.

Sharma, Jyotirmaya. 2011. *Hindutva: Exploring the Idea of Hindu Nationalism*. Delhi: Penguin.

Shoemaker, Nancy. 2015. "A Typology of Colonialism." *Perspectives on History; News Magazine of the American Historical Association*. https://www.historians.org/research-and-publications/perspectives-on-history/october-2015/a-typology-of-colonialism.

Siderits, Mark. 1991. *Indian Philosophy of Language: Studies in Selected Issues*. Vol. 46. Dordrecht; Boston: Kluwer Academic Publishers.

Smith, Andrea. Accessed 2021. Indigenous Peoples and Boarding Schools: A Comparative Study. *Secretariat of the United Nations Perminant Forum on Indigenous Issues*.

Smith, David. 2004. "Nietzsche's Hinduism, Nietzsche's India: Another Look." *Journal of Nietzsche Studies* 28: 37–56.

Soni, Jayandra. 2017. "Jaina Virtue Ethics: Action and Non-Action." In *The Bloomsbury Research Handbook of Indian Ethics*, edited by Shyam Ranganathan, 155–76. London: Bloomsbury Academic.

Steeves, Paulette F. 2018. "Indigeneity." *Oxford Bibliographies*. https://www.oxfordbibliographies.com/display/document/obo-9780199766567/obo-9780199766567-0199.xml.

Stilz, Anna. 2014. "197Provisional Right and Non-State Peoples." In *Kant and Colonialism: Historical and Critical Perspectives*, edited by Katrin Flikschuh and Lea Ypi, 0. Oxford: Oxford University Press.

Švorcová, J. 2023. "Transgenerational Epigenetic Inheritance of Traumatic Experience in Mammals." *Genes* 14 (1). https://doi.org/10.3390/genes14010120.

Syracuse University. 2024. "Moral Injury Project." https://moralinjuryproject.syr.edu/about-moral-injury/.

Tirrell, Lynne. 2012. "Genocidal Language Games." In *Speech and Harm: Controversies Over Free Speech*, edited by Ishani Maitra and Mary Kate McGowan, 174–221. Oxford University Press.

Travis, Charles. 2010. *Objectivity and the Parochial*. Oxford: Oxford University Press.

UN. 2022. "China Responsible for 'Serious Human Rights Violations' in Xinjiang Province: UN Human Rights Report." In *UN News*. United Nations.

UN. 2023. "China: UN Experts Alarmed by Separation of 1 Million Tibetan Children from Families and Forced Assimilation at Residential Schools." In *Press Releases Special Procedures*. United Nations.

UN, General Assembly. 1948. "Convention on the Prevention and Punishment of the Crime of Genocide." *Resolution 260 A (III)*. https://www.un.org/en/

genocideprevention/documents/atrocity-crimes/Doc.1_Convention%20on
%20the%20Prevention%20and%20Punishment%20of%20the%20Crime
%20of%20Genocide.pdf.

United Nations. 2017. *Belligerent Occupation: Duties and Obligations of Occupying Powers.* United Nation.

Urzedo, Danilo, and Catherine J. Robinson. 2023. "Decolonizing Ecosystem Valuation to Sustain Indigenous Worldviews." *Environmental Science and Policy* 150: 100–115.

Weil, Shalva. 2023. "Indian Jews." *Oxford Bibliographies.* https://www.oxfordbibli ographies.com/view/document/obo-9780199840731/obo-9780199840731 -0046.xml.

Whitehead, Alfred North. 1978. *Process and Reality: An Essay in Cosmology.* Edited by David Ray Griffin and Donald W. Sherburne. Corrected ed. *Gifford Lectures; 1927–28.* New York: Free Press. Reprint, Macmillan. New York.

Williams, Bernard. 1985. *Ethics and the Limits of Philosophy.* Cambridge: Harvard University Press.

Williamson, Timothy. 2002. *Knowledge and its Limits.* Oxford: Oxford University Press.

Wittgenstein, Ludwig. 1958. *Philosophical Investigations.* Translated by G. E. M. Anscombe. 2nd ed. New York: Macmillan.

Wolfe, Patrick. 2006. "Settler Colonialism and the Elimination of the Native." *Journal of Genocide Research* 8 (4): 387–409.

Xiang, S. 2023. *Chinese Cosmopolitanism: The History and Philosophy of an Idea.* Princeton: Princeton University Press.

Zack, Naomi. 2003. "Reparations and the Rectification of Race." *The Journal of Ethics* 7 (1): 139–51.

Zack, Naomi. 2018. *Philosophy of Race: An Introduction.* London: Palgrave.

Zastoupil, Lynn. 1994. *John Stuart Mill and India.* Stanford: Stanford University Press.

Zilli, Ishtiaq Ahmed. 1971. "FATHNAMA—I CHITOR, March 1568: An Annotated Translation." *Proceedings of the Indian History Congress* 33: 350–61.

Index